STRATEGIC STAFFING

STRATEGIC STAFFING

A Practical Toolkit for Workforce Planning

Thomas P. Bechet

AMACOM

American Management Association

New York • Atlanta • Brussels • Buenos Aires • Chicago • London • Mexico City • San Francisco
Shanghai • Tokyo • Toronto • Washington, D.C.

Special discounts on bulk quantities of AMACOM books are available to corporations, professional associations, and other organizations. For details, contact Special Sales Department, AMACOM, a division of American Management Association, 1601 Broadway, New York, NY 10019.
Tel.: 212-903-8316 Fax: 212-903-8083
Web site: www.amacombooks.org

Library of Congress Cataloging-in-Publication Data

Bechet, Thomas P.
Strategic staffing: a practical toolkit for workforce planning / Thomas P. Bechet.
p. cm.
ISBN 0-8144-0728-5 (hard : alk. paper)
1. Manpower planning. 2. Strategic planning. I. Title.
HF5549.5.M3 B43 2002
2002004851

Printing number

10 9 8 7 6 5 4 3 2

To Ann and Leigh:
Thank you for your love and support—
and for putting up with all those nights away from home.

Contents

Preface

Most organizations understand the benefits that a longer-term approach to staff planning can bring. Many actually attempt to develop staffing strategies (or strategic workforce plans, as they are also known). Unfortunately, these companies often find that the traditional approaches to strategic staffing and workforce planning that they are trying to implement are ineffective, and that the expected benefits are not realized. To me, the solution to this problem lies not in trying to improve the effectiveness of the traditional approach, but in implementing a completely different kind of process for strategic staffing.

This book describes that process. It is a practical resource for those who are just starting to implement strategic staffing as well as for those who are searching for ways to make their current practices more effective. It can be followed step by step to initiate a strategic staffing process or used as a sourcebook that is referred to periodically to maintain or improve the effectiveness of a process that is already in place. It contains process descriptions, hints, tools, examples, and other practical advice. I've included only those approaches and techniques that have proved to be the most valued by clients and other practitioners.

Many of the ideas here are new (at least, I hope they are!); others are simply improvements on the tried and true. Some of my suggestions may seem unorthodox at first, but based on my more than twenty years of consulting in this area, I know that they really work. Some of what I propose may challenge your understanding of what strategic staffing is and how it should be implemented. In some cases, I may seem to push the bounds of conventional thinking and challenge those more traditional approaches.

Needless to say, the strategic staffing processes described here are not the only ones that can be beneficial. Your organization may have been successful in implementing some of the very practices that I suggest should be avoided. In these cases, use my suggestions as a mirror in which you can reflect your practices and identify opportunities for improving the effectiveness of what you are doing. You may end up confirming that those approaches are right on target for your organization.

All the pieces are described here: setting the context, defining staffing requirements, identifying and forecasting staffing availability, calculating staffing gaps and surpluses, and developing staffing strategies and plans that eliminate staffing gaps and surpluses effectively and efficiently. Remember, though, that the successful implementation of a strategic staffing process does not only depend on how these basic components are defined. The ''devil is in the details''—or (perhaps more appropriately in this case) the devil is in the implementation. It is not just the steps themselves that are important, it is how well they are developed, integrated, and implemented that count. In addition to describing the components themselves, this book provides important tips to ensure an effective implementation of the processes I suggest.

One final note: Some HR professionals that I have met do not consider staffing to be strategic in nature, especially when it defines specific plans and actions. I could not disagree more. To me, a business strategy that does not identify and address staffing implications is a strategy that cannot be implemented!

Good luck on your journey!

Tom Bechet

SECTION

1

Setting the Context

CHAPTER 1

An Overview of This Book

This book describes pragmatic approaches for developing and implementing practical, effective, targeted staffing strategies. It includes process descriptions, actual examples and case studies, advice and hints, a series of spreadsheet templates that can actually be used to develop strategic staffing models, and slide presentations that can be used to communicate (and train others on) the strategic staffing process. Specifically, the book is divided into five sections:

1. **Setting the Context.** Part 1 sets the stage for effective strategic staffing. It provides an overview of the strategic staffing process and its objectives and describes the context in which strategic staffing works best. The section focuses on descriptions of specific nontraditional approaches to strategic staffing that have proved effective in a wide variety of organizations and industries.

2. **Developing the Strategic Staffing Process.** There are many approaches that can be used to organize and structure your strategic staffing efforts. Part 2 describes *in detail* an effective, practical approach that can be (and has been) implemented successfully in a wide variety of situations. This approach includes:

- A detailed description of the strategic staffing process itself (both long-term staffing strategies and short-term staffing plans)
- Specific examples of how required staffing levels can be determined (including actual, numeric examples with solutions)
- A discussion of various techniques that can be used to define useful staffing plans even when specific business plans are not complete or available
- A complete numerical example of a staffing strategy (and the staffing plans that result)
- Two detailed, "real-world" case studies, each of which describes the issues that an organization was facing and the staffing strategies and plans that the organization developed to address those issues
- A series of less detailed summaries of projects in which strategic staffing was implemented successfully

3. **Implementing and Supporting Your Strategic Staffing Process.** Developing the right strategic staffing process won't help if that process is implemented incorrectly. Part 3 describes the context within which strategic staffing is best implemented. It includes:

   - A framework that ensures effective implementation of the process
   - A diagnostic that you can use to define the strategic context in which the process will be implemented in your particular situation
   - A form that you can use to evaluate your company's current strategic staffing process and identify opportunities to improve its effectiveness
   - A discussion of how you might involve line managers in the process, including an interview guide that can be used to

help identify staffing issues and define staffing requirements

- A description of what might be included on a strategic staffing Web site that could reside on your company's intranet

4. **Beyond Staffing Plans: Analyzing and Applying the Results.** One of the key deliverables of the strategic staffing process is a set of very specific staffing plans that should be implemented to address critical staffing needs. There are times, though, that a broader analysis of your results will be needed if you are to select the appropriate course of action. The fourth section of the book describes what those analyses might look like, including:

   - A description of how to measure the effectiveness and efficiency of your staffing practices
   - A discussion of how an analysis of staffing costs can be integrated into your strategic staffing process
   - A discussion of the overall, "big picture" analyses (over and beyond specific staffing plans) that can be supported by the output of a well-designed strategic staffing process

5. **Appendices.** The appendices include a number of supporting materials that will help you implement an effective strategic staffing process. Specifically, the appendices include:

   - Frequently asked questions (with answers, of course!)
   - Specific instructions for modifying the generic spreadsheet staffing model templates (provided with this book) so that they can be used to support the development of your own staffing strategies and plans
   - Two sets of overheads (both handouts and PowerPoint files)—one that can be used to convince management to im-

plement strategic staffing, and a second that can equip a team to develop and implement staffing plans

- A glossary of key terms

Summary

While no approach is foolproof, this book is designed to help you get an effective strategic staffing process up and running (even if on a limited basis) quickly and easily. If your organization is not yet creating staffing strategies, these tools will ensure that you will get off on the right foot and avoid many of the pitfalls that other companies have encountered. These tools can also be used to jump-start or improve the effectiveness of an existing strategic staffing process. If you are already developing staffing strategies, the approaches and tools provided in this book will help you improve the quality and effectiveness of your results. In either case, be forewarned: Many of the ideas in this book may differ from what you think strategic staffing is and what you think the process entails. Just read it with an open mind and be ready to consider alternative approaches.

CHAPTER 2

What Is Strategic Staffing, Anyway?

Definition

Strategic staffing is the process of identifying and addressing the staffing implications of business strategies and plans. Better still, strategic staffing can be defined as the process of identifying and addressing the staffing implications of *change*. To me, putting the emphasis on change indicates that staffing implications should be identified and addressed (or at least discussed) on a continuing basis (whenever changes to business plans are being considered), not just once a year as part of a set planning process. The strategic staffing process has two major outputs:

- **Staffing strategy.** A staffing strategy is a long-term, directional plan that describes what an organization is going to do over the course of its planning horizon (e.g., the coming three to five years) to ensure that its supply of staff (both staffing levels and required capabilities) matches its demand for staff (i.e., the number and types of staff needed to implement business strategies and plans).
- **Staffing plans.** Staffing plans are short-term, tactical plans that describe what an organization will do in the short term (e.g., the current year or quarter) to address immediate staffing gaps and surpluses.

Some companies may call this process *strategic workforce planning*. However, the phrase *strategic staffing* better communicates both the idea that the process has a longer-term business orientation (i.e., the *strategic* part of the phrase) and the idea that the results of the process are staffing *actions*, not just plans (i.e., the word *staffing* implies action, not simply planning). Don't worry too much about what you call it—just be sure that you do it!

Other Key Definitions

As you read through this book and begin to consider implementing some of the processes it describes, you will need to keep in mind some very specific definitions of some very common terms. I am not suggesting that *you* need to use these terms this way, but you do need to understand how *I* am using these words. In some cases, my definitions are quite normal; in other cases, they may deviate significantly from your own definitions.

Issue

In staffing terms, an *issue* is simply a difference between the staff that will be required to support strategy implementation at some point in the future and the staff that will be available at that same point in the future. This difference can be expressed in terms of staffing levels, required capabilities (type), or both. In some cases, an organization may have the wrong number of people and the people that they do have may not possess the skills that are required. In these situations, the company is sometimes said to be facing a staffing *mix* issue. Issues/differences can take the form of either gaps (where requirements exceed availability) or surpluses (where availability exceeds requirements).

In order to calculate a difference (and thus determine whether or not there is a staffing issue), an organization needs to define *in specific terms* both its staffing requirements *and* staff availability. Unless both supply and demand are calculated, it is impossible to determine whether there is a critical staffing need. Supply and demand must also be defined in consistent terms (and at the same level of detail) so that they can be compared directly. It is very difficult to measure impact or progress unless these specific gaps are calculated.

Here is an example: Suppose an organization perceives that it has a "lack of management depth." Will the management pool become sufficiently deep if the organization develops and deploys five more qualified candidates? Ten more? Given the vague definition of the issue, it is just not possible to determine what the proper solution will be. In order to determine whether or not this really is an issue, the organization should:

- Define its needs for management talent at a particular point in the future.
- Project the availability of qualified staff at that same point in time.
- Compare the two to see if there is indeed a critical gap.

Clearly, a definition of an issue that is based on a "gut feel" alone is inadequate.

Strategy

Typically, a strategy is defined as a long-term, directional plan of action. I add one more element to that definition: A strategy (whether it is a staffing strategy or a business strategy) should define *how* an organization is going to achieve its objectives; it should not simply restate those objectives. Some organizations define a strategy that includes such items as becoming the low-cost producer of their product, achieving specific growth or revenue targets (e.g., becoming a top five player in their market), or achieving a certain product mix. To me, these are objectives, not strategies. While they are more detailed and specific than broad objectives, they still just describe *what* is to be accomplished, not *how* those things will be done.

Here is why I think this distinction is important in the area of strategic staffing: It is simply impossible to identify and address the staffing implications of business objectives. To define its staffing requirements, an organization needs to define what it plans to do throughout the planning period in order to achieve its objectives (e.g., become the low-cost producer). Once a plan of action has been proposed or defined, it is possible to determine the numbers and types of staff that will be needed to fully implement that plan.

Here is an example: Suppose two manufacturing companies state that they intend to become the low-cost producer of their respective products. To do this, both companies need to reduce their operating costs. One company chooses to do this by relocating its manufacturing facilities to low-cost countries in Southeast Asia. The second decides to implement a more efficient production method in its existing domestic facilities that takes advantage of new production technology. Obviously, the staffing issues and implications of these two approaches are quite different. It is impossible to determine staffing implications by looking at objectives alone.

Two additional clarifications are necessary:

- **Strategic** does not mean "organization-wide" or "integrated." True, many strategies are broad and comprehensive in nature, and most effective strategies directly support the integration of functions and actions. However, just because a plan covers many organization units or provides overall solutions to common problems does not mean that it is strategic. It is quite possible to have broad, common approaches that are defined strictly for the short term (and thus lack the longer-term context of strategy).

- **Strategic** does not mean "innovative." There are many standard staffing practices that can be implemented in a very strategic manner. Conversely, many innovative staffing practices are implemented only in the short term (and thus are not strategic at all).

Staffing

I have a very broad definition of *staffing*. To me, staffing includes any action or movement that relates to getting people into, around, and/or out of an organization in a planned way—including retention. Staffing is not simply a process that is triggered by an opening, nor is it the internal equivalent of external recruiting (although both of these would be included in my definition of staffing). Staffing includes (but is not limited to) recruiting, hiring, transfers, promotions, redeployment, "decruiting" (i.e., the active management/movement of staff out of an organization), retirements, terminations, and retention. Some organizations also include the development that supports planned staff movement as part of their staffing plan.

What Is the Objective of Strategic Staffing?

Let's start thinking differently by defining a new, nontraditional objective for the strategic staffing process itself. In many cases, firms think that the objective of strategic staffing is to predict future staffing needs (usually with some degree of certainty) and then define the staffing actions that should be taken in the near term to eliminate problems that may (or may not) occur in the future.

At best, this is difficult to do well (and accurately); at worst, it proves to be an academic exercise that has little impact on the organization. Some companies give up on the process right away because managers lack the skills and understanding to predict their long-term staffing needs reliably. In other companies, predictions are made and staffing plans based on those predictions are produced, but the plans are not implemented because the predictions they are based on are not perceived as accurate. Consequently, managers often view these long-term staff planning efforts as something that may be nice to have, not as a required, valued component of the overall business planning process.

Instead of thinking of strategic staffing as a way of predicting future needs and acting in the near term to avoid future problems, think of it as a way of creating a longer-term staffing strategy that can be used as a context within which the most effective near-term staffing plans can be made and staffing actions implemented. This relationship is depicted in Figure 2-1.

Not only is defining this long-term context a more realistic objective for the process, but this approach might engage line managers more than traditional long-range staff forecasting does. The idea of

Figure 2-1. Integrating Your Long-Term and Short-Term Staffing Processes

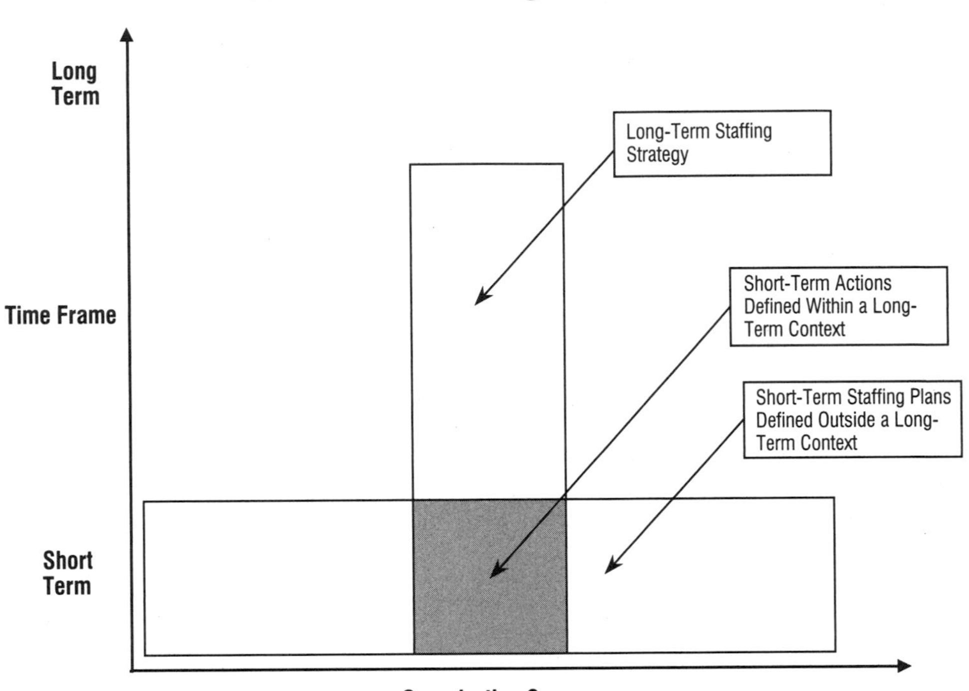

creating a context that allows better decisions to be made immediately might just capture the attention of those line managers, who are being measured by and rewarded for achieving near-term objectives. This approach to strategic staffing allows them to manage their own, current staff resources most effectively right now. Unlike what happens with the traditional approach, you are not asking them to manage differently in order to help their successors avoid problems and achieve improved results in the future. Placing the focus on defining effective short-term staffing actions makes it more likely that the line managers making the staffing decisions will still be in place to reap the benefits of that decision later on.

An Overview of the Process

This book describes all aspects of the strategic staffing process in detail. From an overall perspective, the process usually includes the following steps:

- Identify and prioritize longer-term staffing issues and implications—those that arise from your business strategies and plans. A staffing issue usually involves a significant difference between the staff that will be available and the staff that will be needed to implement business strategies effectively.

- Create a staffing model that specifically defines shortages and surpluses of talent, including:

  —Defining the number (staffing levels) and types (capabilities) of employees that will be needed at a particular point in the future to implement business plans effectively (often including how that staff should be organized and deployed)
  —Identifying the staffing resources that are currently available
  —Projecting the supply of talent that will be available at that point in the future for which requirements have been defined (e.g., factoring in the effects of turnover, retirements, planned movement, etc.)
  —Calculating specific differences between anticipated demand and forecasted supply

- Develop specific staffing strategies that most effectively address the most critical staffing issues in the long run. Staffing strategies are usually long-term, directional plans of action that describe what will be done to address critical staffing issues.

- Finally, define and evaluate near-term staffing alternatives within this strategic context, selecting and implementing those short-term staffing actions (such as recruiting and internal placement) that best support the implementation of the staffing strategies.

By implementing this process, you can be sure that all staffing actions taken in the short term will fully support the implementation of your organization's longer-term strategies.

Here is a simple example of how a longer-term staffing strategy might create a context for making an effective short-term staffing decision. Suppose an organization has determined that it will need twenty-five additional project managers by the end of its fiscal year. How should a need like this be met? What staffing actions might be taken? These positions could be filled through hiring, redeployment, promotion, work reassignment, or use of contract/contingency staff, or in many other ways. Which of these options is most effective? Which would be the best choice?

To select the most appropriate option in the near term, the organization must have a sense of its future staffing requirements. If those project managers will still be needed beyond this fiscal year, a more permanent solution (e.g., hiring or promotion) is probably most effective. If the need is really just a "blip" in the curve, and those managers will not be needed in the future, a more temporary solution (e.g., hiring contractors to fill these slots) may be better. If the need is a result of some project scheduling irregularities, it may be possible to reschedule new projects or delay them to the first quarter of the next year so that the existing project managers can fill those slots (thus avoiding any additions to staff). In any case, the company does not want to build an unneeded surplus of talent in a subsequent period, which hiring additional project managers might do. In situations like this one (and most others), the most effective near-term solution can be determined only after the longer-term context has been defined.

Staffing Strategy

As stated previously, staffing strategies are long-term, directional plans that describe what will be done over the course of the organization's planning horizon to address critical staffing issues. Therefore, staffing strategies usually span several planning periods (e.g., all three years of a three-year business strategy); they are not developed for each planning period individually. Staffing strategies should be specific enough to describe how staffing needs are to be met, but not so specific that they describe individual staffing needs or actions. "Promote from within" is an example of a simple staffing strategy. It describes, in directional terms, the approach that an organization will take to meet certain staffing needs, yet it does not specifically identify who should be promoted when. Those specific descriptions are part of the organization's short-term staffing plans. Other examples of staffing strategies include:

- Meeting needs for management talent by blending hires and promotions from within
- Developing and retaining critical technical capabilities within the organization while contracting out noncritical skills
- Using accelerated development and redeployment to eliminate a major talent surplus in one area while meeting a critical need in another
- Building a full-time staffing base for minimum workloads and using part-time employees to meet workloads that exceed those minimum levels

In almost every case, staffing strategies are (or at least should be) an integral part of the organization's business strategy. Business strategies might even include the specific staffing implications of those strategies and what will be done to address those implications.

Staffing Plans

Staffing plans describe the specific, near-term staffing actions that an organization is going to take so that it can best implement the staffing strategies that most effectively address critical staffing issues. Unlike staffing strategies, which span planning periods, these plans are usually fully implemented within a planning period. They are detailed enough to define and guide individual staffing actions. These plans specifically address:

- Recruiting
- Internal movement, including promotions, transfers, and redeployment

- Retention
- Planned losses

Summary

Strategic staffing is the process of identifying and addressing the staffing implications of business strategies and plans (or perhaps even of change). The objective of the process is to create a long-term context (i.e., a staffing strategy) within which short-term decisions (i.e., staffing plans and actions) can be made. The strategic staffing process consists of four steps: identifying staffing issues, calculating differences (gaps and surpluses) between staffing requirements and availability, developing staffing strategies, and defining staffing plans.

As you read on, all of the ideas and concepts included in this overview will be described in detail. Most descriptions are supported with concrete examples designed to cement your understanding of those ideas and concepts. All are designed to allow you to implement the strategic staffing process and see real benefits quickly.

CHAPTER 3

Developing Staffing Strategies That Really Work

Traditional Approaches Just Aren't Effective

Most organizations that attempt to implement a strategic staffing process follow a fairly traditional approach. Usually, these companies make staff planning a component of their annual business planning process. Often, they request that managers identify their future staffing needs for each year of the planning period (usually in terms of headcount, not required capabilities), using a common template or form. The templates are at a common level of detail and are based on common planning parameters (e.g., all units define requirements at a job-specific level for each of the coming three years). Once these templates are completed, they are often combined or compiled at various levels to create overall pictures of needs (e.g., unit plans are "rolled up" to a divisional level, and divisional plans are compiled to create a firm-wide view). The organizations then attempt to create meaningful staffing plans to address these overall staffing needs. Some organizations supplement these plans with a series of staffing-related reports and listings (e.g., a list of openings and how they were filled or a summary of turnover rates over time for various types of employees).

Unfortunately, these efforts rarely result in specific staffing and development plans that are actually implemented. Managers tend to see the process as being of limited value and complain loudly about the work involved. In addition, managers are often measured and rewarded for achieving short-term objectives, and this may be inconsistent with the longer-term view that strategic staffing entails. Forecasts of needs are often "hockey stick" projections that are inaccurate, unrealistic, and not grounded in business plans. Some managers (especially those in more volatile areas where business is changing rapidly) question the validity and value of processes that ask them to provide estimates of staffing needs for points in time that are well beyond their ability (or need) to forecast. Staff planning is also often incomplete—required staffing levels may be forecast, but required capabilities are not.

The staffing plans that result from traditional processes such as these often provide little valuable information and are rarely used to drive staffing decisions. Estimates of needs are imprecise and inaccurate. In many cases, the output from the process is too high-level and generic to drive recruiting plans, especially once the output has been rolled up to create that firm-wide view. Since required capabilities usually are not defined specifically, it is difficult (if not impossible) to create action-oriented development plans for individuals that address anticipated capability shortages. Some organizations do not even create staffing plans, opting instead to focus their "workforce planning" efforts almost entirely on compiling and reporting staffing information from the past (e.g., conducting detailed turnover studies and descriptions of recent staffing actions) rather than planning to meet future needs. In the end, much work has been completed, but few results are seen. The strategic staffing process then becomes solely staff-driven—or, worse yet, disappears completely.

More Effective Approaches to Strategic Staffing

Often, implementing a different, more pragmatic approach to strategic staffing can yield the high-quality results that organizations need and expect. Any approach to strategic staffing (or workforce planning) will include estimating staffing requirements, projecting staff availability, and calculating the difference between demand and supply. In more effective strategic staffing processes, this basic approach will not change, but the context within which it is applied will differ greatly from that of more traditional methods.

When searching for ways to improve (or initiate) the strategic staffing process, there are several options that should be considered.

Address Staffing from a Proactive, Planning Perspective, Not Just as an Implementation Concern

It is no longer appropriate to consider staffing solely from an implementation perspective, or to create business plans that simply assume that qualified staff will be available whenever and wherever they are needed. It is no longer realistic for businesses to assume that the staff needed to implement their plans will be readily available and can be recruited, developed, and deployed quickly. In many cases, staffing constraints (e.g., an inability to recruit a sufficient number of individuals with critical skills) may actually restrict the company's ability to implement its business strategies and plans.

Staffing cannot be a process that begins when an opening is identified. Staffing needs and actions must be defined on a proactive basis. Staffing issues and constraints should be identified and addressed as part of the planning process, not left as surprises to be uncovered when implementation begins. From a more positive, proactive perspective, a company may even choose to implement some part of its business strategy (e.g., try to capitalize on a market opportunity) specifically because of the staffing levels and capabilities it has at its disposal.

Here is an example of a situation in which a staffing issue can influence business strategy. In order to take advantage of population growth and migration, an HMO planned to expand into a geographic region of the state that it was not serving currently. The marketing and medical economics functions determined that four new medical centers would have to be built to meet the member needs and potential of this new market effectively and efficiently. It was decided that the new centers should be constructed simultaneously so that the HMO could enter this market quickly. As the buildings neared completion, staffing began in earnest. Unfortunately, the HMO found it extremely difficult to recruit physicians to the inner-city locations of the new medical centers. Consequently, the company did not have enough physicians and medical technicians to staff the four new centers all at once, at least not without having a catastrophic impact on its existing facilities. As a result, the newly constructed medical centers could be staffed (and opened) only one at a time, as a sufficient number of physicians were sourced and placed. This meant that the newly built medical facilities remained shuttered (some for many months). Obviously, maintaining the unused facilities was quite costly. A review of available staffing *before* the construction decision was made would have shown that a sequential (not simultaneous) opening of the medical centers would be more cost-effective.

Focus on Issues, Not Organizations

Many organizations feel that because a particular staffing strategy is beneficial in one area, strategies should be created and implemented by the organization as a whole—that plans should be created for every unit, regardless of its situation. This type of process usually proves to be both ineffective and inefficient, because not every unit merits the detailed analysis that is typically needed to create and implement an effective staffing strategy.

Instead of creating models or analyses for every unit, focus on those areas or job categories in which staffing strategies are really needed. Then develop a series of separate staffing strategies that address these particular areas and jobs. Here are some examples of strategy development that addresses particular critical staffing issues:

- Build a staffing strategy that focuses solely on positions that are absolutely critical to business success.
- Create a strategy for a series of positions that are hard to fill or for which external competition for talent is great.
- Focus a strategy on a business unit that will experience significant change.
- Create a strategy that is concentrated on jobs for which the organization needs to tap new, nontraditional sources of key talent.

Identifying and addressing specific issues will allow you to concentrate your planning resources where they will have the most advantageous effect. You will not waste time and resources creating long-term plans where they really aren't needed.

Here is an example of this focus. To increase its staffing flexibility, the Department of Transportation of a state government was considering combining several separate job classifications (each of which required a particular set of skills) into a single category, "transportation worker," that included individuals with multiple skills. A staffing strategy was developed to define the impact that this change would have on classification, scheduling/deployment, and training. The staffing plan that was developed included transportation workers in all districts (because of bargaining unit considerations, the change had to be implemented on a statewide basis), but it focused only on the positions that were affected. The strategy did not attempt to address any other staffing issues that surfaced in the department (i.e., in positions other than transportation workers). Where necessary, separate staffing strategies were developed for such issues.

This focus on staffing issues does not mean that staffing strategies cannot span organizational units. In some cases, staffing strategies that cross organizational boundaries are needed. These cross-unit staffing strategies should be developed whenever an organization intends to manage key talent across organization lines (e.g., managing information technology [IT] staff, a pool of project managers, or entry-level engineering talent from a corporate perspective). However, an issue orientation can still be maintained in these cases. When creating cross-unit staffing strategies, include in the analysis only those positions that are to be managed from a broader, cross-unit perspective (e.g., the project managers). Don't look at *all* jobs across all units just because you need to look at *some* jobs that way.

Here is an example of a focused staffing strategy that spanned organizational units. A company was implementing a new nationwide data collection and analysis system that would support all of its regions (some of which had their own such systems already). However, the company needed to maintain its legacy systems while implementing the new system. This raised numerous staffing issues. New talent (with new IT skills) had to be acquired to support the development of the new system, yet critical talent had to be retained in order to keep the old systems functioning in the meantime. The organization could not simply hire or contract for the new talent, since the skills of its existing talent would then become obsolete (i.e., these people would understand and be able to employ only the "old" technology needed to maintain the legacy systems). The only sensible course was to address these critical issues from a nationwide, cross-region perspective. The company developed a staffing strategy that focused on the critical IT skills needed to support the transition—but only for the positions that required these specific skills. Additional plans (some strategic, some tactical) were developed for other positions.

The identification of issues (or the selection of specific job categories to focus on) is perhaps the most critical step in the strategic staffing process. Before going any further, let's make sure that you have a good understanding of the concept. Here are three mini-cases. In each of them, an organization is trying to implement a particular change. Read each case and:

- Identify what is changing (and perhaps what is not).
- Define the job categories on which your strategic staffing efforts should focus.

A suggested solution is provided for each case.

Mini-Case 1. ABC, a commercial lines insurance provider in the United States, wants to become a "top ten" company (in terms of domestic revenue) within the next five years. ABC has determined that in order to do this, it must grow its revenues by 30 percent over that five-year period. The company does not expect to change its business focus or expand into new geographical areas. In what functions or units will staffing requirements change most? On what job categories would you focus your staffing strategies and plans?

Suggested Solution. In this case, it is important to define what is changing and what is not. It appears that ABC will attempt to meet its growth targets by doing more of the same in the areas it already serves. Given this, I'd start by looking at those functions that would be most directly affected by the change—probably the sales and marketing functions—and create specific staffing models for each of these functions. Once those were completed, I would then analyze the functions whose workloads would increase significantly if the sales efforts proved successful (e.g., underwriting, claims, and customer service), building staffing models where appropriate.

Mini-Case 2. XYZ Pharmaceuticals has just gained FDA approval to market a product for monitoring patients' blood sugar levels. Up until now, the company has primarily marketed its products directly to physicians, hospitals, and testing labs, but this new product could be sold directly to patients over the counter. What might the staffing implications be if XYZ continues to market the product only to physicians, hospitals, and labs? If it markets the product directly to patients?

Suggested Solution 1. If XYZ markets the new product to physicians, hospitals, and labs, what is changing? If the company is already selling its products to the same group that would buy the new product, this product may have a minimal impact on staffing requirements. It is likely that the current sales force will simply add the new product to its sample case; there might be a small increase in the required number of salespeople. In this case, an in-depth staffing analysis may not even be required.

On the other hand, if XYZ is going to market the new product to a new group of customers that does not currently buy its existing products (say a new set of specialists), then there will probably be a significant increase in the number of sales staff required. In addition, it is likely that both the number of marketing staff and the capabilities that they will need will also change. I'd build a staffing model that focuses on these two functions.

Suggested Solution 2. If the company moves from selling to physicians, hospitals, and labs to selling directly to patients over the counter (e.g., through pharmacies), this will be a major change that is likely to affect many job categories in XYZ. Clearly, the sales staff requirements will be different. Instead of a large sales force selling to a large number of relatively small customers (as is the case currently), XYZ will need to develop a wholesale sales force that will sell its products to a relatively small number of very large customers. Similar changes will also need to be made in marketing; it will have to move from a point of sale to a more broad-based approach. It may even be necessary for XYZ to create an entire distribution and logistics function from scratch, since it will no longer be able to distribute its products solely through its current network of sales staff. Again, I'd build models for the sales and marketing functions, but in this case I'd build separate staffing models for each of the other areas that will be affected (e.g., distribution).

Mini-Case 3. TPB Corporation has developed a new technology that will allow the manufacturing of personal computer printers to be 25 percent more efficient. This new technique, which involves more automation and the use of some preassembled components, will be implemented on a line-by-line basis over the next four quarters. How will the required skills change? In what areas might required staffing levels go up? In what areas might they go down?

Suggested Solution. Again, let's look at what is changing—and what isn't. Clearly, production methods and roles will be changing, and this will probably affect the number and type of production workers that will be needed. In many cases, increases in production efficiency as a result of improvements in technology allow a company to use fewer production staff, but the staff that it does use will require a higher order of skills.

I'd focus the analysis on production staff. First, I would define the skills and staffing levels that will be needed to implement the change. Next, I would identify current staff that can be deployed to the new jobs (including defining any specific training and development gaps that would need to be addressed in order to make the redeployment successful). Finally, I'd determine the number of current production staff that may become surplus, identify opportunities to redeploy some of this surplus, and develop options for reducing the surplus that still remains (e.g., early retirement and layoffs).

It is important to note that in this case, nothing other than production technology is changing. There is nothing in the case that implies increased sales, different markets, or any other strategic shift that might affect staffing requirements. Consequently, there may be no need to build and run staffing models for any other area or function.

Finally, don't attempt to resolve a second issue or problem until you have created (or at least are well on your way to creating) staffing strategies that fully address the first!

Tailor the Process for Each Issue

In a traditional system, each unit is typically asked to provide the same information regarding staffing, using a common template, at the same time each year, for the same planning period/time frame. While this approach may bring consistency, it also forces every unit to adopt a process and a set of planning parameters that may not be appropriate. Rather than creating a one-size-fits-all process that is applied everywhere, you should vary the planning parameters (e.g., the population to be included, the planning horizon, and the structure of the model itself) so that they are appropriate for each issue being addressed.

Here is an example of this kind of tailoring: An engineering/construction firm created a long-term staffing plan that addressed critical staffing needs in its IT unit. Given the rapid pace of technological change (and the fact that so little was known about the future of the technology), it was difficult to define staffing needs (whether in terms of capabilities or of staffing levels) beyond a twelve-month period. Consequently, the staffing strategy for IT incorporated a one-year planning horizon. Even though the organization had a five-year business plan, it was perfectly appropriate for IT to develop staffing plans for the one-year horizon because so little was known about year 2 and beyond. Past that first year, managers would simply have been guessing at what the staffing requirements might be. A staffing strategy based on those guesses would have been of little value.

That same organization also found it necessary to increase the depth and breadth of its project management pool. Given the rate of change for the business as a whole (and the time needed to implement, observe, and measure any significant changes in project management capabilities), a three- to five-year staffing and development plan was developed. This, too, was an appropriate planning horizon for the issue being analyzed.

What would have happened if the two groups had had to use a single planning horizon? The use of a common horizon would probably have forced the IT function and the project management teams to use the same time frame, and this most probably would have resulted in ineffective plans for both groups. Would it have been appropriate to ask IT to create staffing plans for years 2 and 3, even though the managers knew that information beyond year 1 would not be useful (and therefore probably would not be applied)? Alternatively, would it have been appropriate to ask the project management unit to plan its talent needs for just a one-year time frame, given that it would take several years to address the depth and breadth issues that were identified? Clearly, the answer to both questions must be no. Would it have been possible to compromise and have each group prepare a two-year plan? I don't think so—that would probably result in a process that was ineffective for both groups.

Similarly, the level of detail of these two analyses also needed to vary. When defining IT capabilities, the organization needed to focus on very specific technical skills (e.g., specific languages and/or platforms) that varied widely from job to job. In contrast, the analysis of project management would focus on broad core skills that were common among jobs. It certainly would have made no sense to force the IT analysis to include generic management skills, but neither would it have been appropriate to ask those involved in the project management analysis to define specific technical skills for project managers.

In these cases (and many others like them), it is only sensible to vary planning horizons, populations, and levels of detail, allowing each group to define a staffing plan that is appropriate for its particular needs. Obviously, this tailoring of parameters is viable only when separate staffing strategies are defined for each critical issue. The typical one-size-fits-all approach simply doesn't allow for this needed variation.

Focus on Particular Positions, Not All Positions

Some organizations attempt to develop staffing strategies that include all jobs. This is simply not required. It isn't necessary to address every job from a strategic perspective. For example, it is rarely necessary to develop a long-term staffing strategy for a job that can be filled relatively quickly from known internal sources or relatively abundant external pools. Because the development of effective staffing strategies requires a great deal of work and significant resources, it is usually unrealistic to include each and every position in the analysis. Including all jobs in the strategic staffing process (including those for which a strategic perspective is not required) simply bogs down the process and spreads limited resources even thinner, making thc process even more inefficient.

It is usually most effective to focus your strategic staffing efforts on two types of positions or situations: those where the organization needs to be proactive and those where the organization needs time to respond.

The Organization Needs to Be Proactive. A longer-term perspective is usually required where an organization is trying to be proactive in meeting staffing needs. Suppose, for example, that the organization is staffing and training a customer service unit so that it is fully functional before a new product is launched. Which jobs will be staffed just before launch? Which will be filled a month or two before launch in order to build continuity and teamwork? Which senior management/leadership positions should be filled a year in advance in order to set direction and strategy? A proactive staffing plan that addresses these questions will ensure a smooth implementation.

Here is an example of a situation in which a more proactive response is necessary. After conducting a demographic analysis of the external workforce, an oil company discovered that, from a recruiting and staffing perspective, it was particularly vulnerable in the area of geoscience. Competition for graduate geologists and geophysicists was intensifying, and the company anticipated that attracting the number of recruits it thought it needed would be difficult. Given the criticality of this need, the company wanted to be proactive in its staffing efforts. It created a model and staffing strategy that focused solely on these hard-to-fill categories. Because of the needs that it defined, the company decided to develop contacts and relationships with graduate students well before they entered the job market (e.g., through presentations and internships), to develop "ties" with these individuals and increase the possibility that they would work for the company upon graduation.

The Organization Needs Time to Respond. Strategic perspective is needed when an organization determines that its staffing needs can be best met in ways that require some advance preparation. This would include cases in which new sources of talent must be identified because the current channels have become less productive and cases in which talent needs will be met through longer-term development and promotion from within, not through short-term hiring. If a future need is to be filled from within, what development must take place before such moves can be made? What plans for development should be created and implemented so that planned promotions or redeployments will be realistic and successful? If you are to develop new relationships with alternative sources of talent (e.g., new schools or search firms), it will take time to identify such sources and develop possible partnerships with them.

Here is an example of a situation in which the company needed time to respond. In an insurance company, the traditional career path to branch manager passed through the underwriting function. Most branch managers began as trainees, became underwriters, were then designated "managers in training," and subsequently were named branch managers, usually in smaller offices. Experienced branch managers from smaller offices would then be selected to fill openings in larger offices. This process typically took eight to ten years.

Because of a rapid business expansion, a large number of new branch offices were to be opened. The traditional career path simply could not provide a sufficient number of qualified candidates in a timely way. Because of the length of time required to move along the traditional path, the company was forced to find alternative sources of branch manager candidates. It developed a staffing strategy that helped it to define the appropriate mix of targeted recruiting and accelerated development to meet its growing need for management talent. Since implementing these solutions required time, openings had to be identified well in advance of need.

Long-term staffing strategies may not need to be created for any other type of position, and certainly do not need to be developed for all positions. Remember that I am suggesting that you limit the number of jobs included in your *strategic* staffing process. It may be necessary to include more jobs (perhaps even all jobs) when you are defining required staffing in the near term (e.g., to specifically support budget preparation).

Keep Plans Separate, Not Consolidated

In many cases, organizations prepare staffing plans at a unit level, but these plans are then rolled up into some kind of consolidated plan (perhaps to display the results "on one sheet of paper"). Common templates are often used to gather staffing data in order to facilitate just this type of consolidation.

While on its face this summarizing seems to be helpful, the process of consolidation actually squeezes out of the plan the very detail that is most useful and sometimes hides significant differences. If one unit has twenty software engineers too many and another unit has twenty too few, a consolidated staffing plan would make it appear that there is no problem (i.e., the surplus of twenty and the gap of twenty would cancel out, implying that there are no issues that need to be addressed). However, if the units are not co-located (or if transferring individuals between their locations is not financially feasible), there may actually be forty issues to address (i.e., reducing twenty gaps and alleviating twenty surpluses).

It is also difficult (and sometimes actually impossible) to develop specific, implementable staffing plans to address consolidated, summarized staffing needs. Effective staffing plans may vary greatly depending on circumstances and situations. For example, a consolidated staffing plan might describe an overall need for 150 ''technical specialists.'' The staffing actions required to fill 150 openings in one unit, location, or job might be completely different from those needed to fill a single opening in each of 150 separate units or locations. Similarly, the consolidated category might actually include jobs with different skill requirements. The actions needed to fill 150 openings for one type of specialist would be quite different from those needed to fill 150 openings for different types, all of which were classified as specialists. Similarly, it would be difficult (and perhaps even impossible) to define recruiting plans based on a strategy that consolidated various engineering specialties into a single category. Key differences in engineering discipline would need to be considered if effective staffing plans were to be developed. In these and many other cases, it is unlikely that the information needed to create realistic, focused staffing plans could be discerned or inferred from summarized or compiled data.

When you create staffing strategies, keep the plans separate and distinct. This is especially important if you have developed plans that address separate issues, using different planning parameters. Create plans that are at the same level as your probable solution. Don't roll up data as a matter of course. Create a corporate view only if the staffing issues that can be identified should be addressed at a corporate level. If an integrated plan is required in certain cases (e.g., to manage IT across, not within, organizational units), create a stand-alone model that spans those units but includes only those jobs.

When it comes time to summarize (and develop that one-sheet overview), don't combine the numbers into a summarized chart. Instead, create a page that highlights the most critical staffing issues you have defined and summarizes the strategies you plan to implement to address those issues. Figure 3-1 shows what this summary might look like for the bank described in a case study in Chapter 8. If more detail is requested, provide the relevant staffing data and

Figure 3-1. Example of a One-Page Strategic Staffing Summary

ABC BANCORP
Summary of Strategic Staffing Issues and Recommendations

Critical Staffing Issues for the Unit

- Staff in the economic, education, and operations job streams are being asked to play the generic role of project manager and are not effectively applying the specialized expertise for which they were hired.
- Since they can't afford individual experts, many smaller regions have created positions that span or combine functional areas (e.g., education, health, and social programs), resulting in a general "lowering of the bar" regarding technical expertise.
- The company lacks sufficient high-level policy expertise to support the implementation of a more strategic focus.
- Current staffing programs are ineffective:

—Most staffing efforts begin only after specific openings are identified.

—Staffing programs are not specifically needs-based. In many cases, "promotions" were position upgrades based on performance; they do not "fill" actual openings.

—The company tends to implement one-size-fits-all approaches to staffing, not targeted, as-needed processes

Staffing Strategies to Be Implemented

- Differentiate job streams to support needed specialization.
- Position and develop the corporate unit as a "center of functional excellence."
- Recruit and develop high-level policy development expertise.
- Improve the effectiveness of staffing practices so that they are:

—Proactive

—Needs-based

—Tailored to address specific user needs

Note: The detailed staffing models and analysis on which these conclusions are based are available.

the specific staffing plans that you relied on in coming to these conclusions as attachments.

Define Issues on an Ongoing Basis; Don't Create an Event

As stated in Chapter 2, strategic staffing should be thought of as defining and addressing the staffing implications of *change*. Thus, whenever business changes are being discussed or anticipated, the staffing implications of those changes need to be defined. If your organization discusses and considers changes to its business plans and strategies just once each year, then an annual staff planning process may be appropriate. However, if your organization discusses, considers, and implements changes throughout the year, an annual staff planning process alone is probably insufficient. A discussion of the staffing implications of changes in business plans should be conducted each and every time such changes are discussed or anticipated—not at some set time during each planning period. Ideally, staffing issues should be identified and addressed as part of the ongoing business management process. Assuming that change is constant, this implies that strategic staffing is an ongoing process that is implemented and updated throughout the year, not a once-a-year event.

Here is an example: An engineering/construction company used an annual staff planning process that was driven by the budget cycle. However, rapid changes in competitive situations and quickly emerging opportunities meant that the company needed to mobilize and reallocate its staffing resources quickly, throughout the year, a process that could not be supported by the once-a-year staff planning process. As a result, the company now discusses the staffing implications of change at every management committee meeting (i.e., on a biweekly basis). Further, it has developed a performance expectation for managers that any proposal that requires additional resources (e.g., a new project or a change in technology used) has to include an analysis of staffing issues and a high-level staffing plan.

Focus on Planning and Acting, Not on Reporting

Many organizations spend far too much time creating staffing reports, tables, and listings that describe in detail past turnover, current staffing levels, basic demographic profiles, and other staffing-related data. Others document staffing movement (e.g., they identify openings and specify how each was filled). In some cases, these reports represent the bulk of the strategic staffing effort. What good are the data included in these listings and reports if they do not have a significant impact on decision making?

There's an old adage that describes a significant difference between *data* and *information*. Data are just that—facts, figures, numbers, and the like. Data that are used to make a decision are information. If, for example, you reallocate staff because of something you discern from a data table, then those data have become information. When it comes to staffing, make sure that you provide managers with information, not just data. Provide only information that affects decision-making. If your reports provide managers with data that are simply nice to know or interesting, but that don't directly influence decision making, you shouldn't be providing those reports.

Generally, information on past practices and results is useful only when it can serve as a basis for formulating assumptions that can be incorporated into future plans. For example, studies of past turnover should be conducted only when turnover assumptions are to be factored into future plans and models. Detailed information on employee movement might identify alternative career paths that can be exploited to fill staffing shortages that the model has identified, but it should not be used to estimate the number of moves of various kinds that are expected in the future.

Here are two examples in which organizations wrestled with the differences between "data" and "information." In the first example, the company spent too much time and too many resources reporting data. In the second, the company began to manage data, but later moved to an information management approach.

1. One high-tech company regularly published a detailed listing that addressed staffing activity throughout the corporation. The report (often more than one hundred computer-generated pages in length) identified existing openings and indicated how long each position had been open, what had been done in the last month to fill each opening, and any data on how each position would be filled. The report did not include any look forward and was not viewed by managers as an especially useful tool. Once the organization began to consider staffing from a more strategic perspective, the report was streamlined to provide only information on possible sources of needed talent. Its distribution was greatly reduced as well.

2. An automotive company was trying to establish a strategic workforce planning function. It elected to build its function on the foundation of providing information—accurately answering managers' questions regarding past staffing practices and patterns (e.g., defining annual turnover rates for specific categories of jobs in response to specific management requests). As it built credibility, the workforce planning unit began to add value by discussing with managers why they were requesting the data, suggesting alternative data, conducting analyses, and interpreting results. By asking these intelligent questions, the function built a reputation as a valued strategic partner, thus allowing it to participate actively in the business planning process.

Solve Problems; Don't Just Build Capability

Line managers want answers to their staffing problems and solutions to their issues. Yet some human resources functions focus their efforts on developing and supporting a standardized process, system, or tool that managers can use to develop staffing strategies, not on meeting the managers' need for action and answers.

The best deliverable of the strategic staffing process isn't a tool or a model—it is a solution to a staffing problem (i.e., a qualified individual filling an opening).

Generally, the development of a tool or model, while necessary in many cases, is by itself insufficient. The tool must be applied effectively to identify and address critical staffing issues. Managers must be trained (perhaps by human resources staff) to use the tool effectively and apply the results analytically. Make sure that implementation of your process or tool results in specific, implementable staffing plans (i.e., what will be done to address staffing shortages and surpluses), not just a better definition of the needs themselves.

Summary

If your organization understands the benefits of creating a staffing strategy but has had little or no success to date implementing a traditional process, consider the alternatives described in this chapter and summarized in Figure 3-2. Think of strategic staffing as creating a longer-term context within which more effective short-term staffing decisions can be made. Integrate staffing into business planning; don't think of it solely in terms of implementation. Create strategies that focus on particular issues, and vary planning parameters accordingly. Include only those jobs for which a longer-term perspective is really needed. Keep plans separate and distinct. Update staffing plans whenever significant changes in business plans are being considered. Work to provide managers with information, not data. And, most important of all, develop staffing strategies and plans that solve staffing issues and problems, don't just build a new tool or system.

Figure 3-2. Consider New Approaches

Instead of:	Consider:
Addressing staffing as an implementation concern	Addressing staffing from a proactive, planning perspective
Focusing on organizations and units	Focusing on issues and areas of particular concern
Defining a one-size-fits-all process	Tailoring the process and parameters for each issue
Including all positions	Focusing on positions where you need to be proactive or need time to react
Consolidating plans	Keeping plans detailed, separate, and distinct
Creating plans as a one-time event (e.g., annually)	Creating plans in response to changing strategies, whenever change occurs or is discussed
Creating reports and listings that describe what was	Focusing on planning and looking ahead, forecasting what will be
Building capability or tools	Solving staffing problems and addressing staffing issues

SECTION

2

Developing the Strategic Staffing Process

CHAPTER 4

The Strategic Staffing Process

An Overview of the Strategic Staffing Process

As defined earlier, strategic staffing is a process that organizations use to help them identify and address the staffing implications of business plans and strategies. By implementing this process, organizations can ensure that they will have the right number of people, with the right capabilities, in place at the right time. The strategic staffing process results in two major outputs or deliverables: staffing strategies (which describe what will be done in the long term to address critical staffing issues) and staffing plans (which describe specific, short-term tactical plans and staffing actions to be implemented in the near term).

These two components can be developed in many ways, but I have found one process to be particularly effective. This strategic staffing process has four steps:

1. **Define critical staffing issues/areas of focus.** To be effective, your strategic staffing efforts should focus on a relatively small number of particularly critical staffing issues or job categories, not on entire business units or organizations. The first step of the process is to identify and prioritize your most critical staffing issues and select those for which specific staffing strategies are required.

2. **Define staffing gaps and surpluses.** Once you have selected an issue (or an area on which your analysis will focus), the next step is to develop a staffing model that defines staffing requirements, forecasts staff availability, compares demand to supply, and calculates staffing gaps and surpluses for each job category for each period in your planning horizon.
3. **Develop staffing strategies.** The next step is to review the preliminary staffing gaps and surpluses, as calculated by your model, across all the planning periods in your planning horizon. Create a series of long-term, directional plans of action that describe what your organization should do to address those critical staffing issues most effectively (i.e., how to best align staffing demand and supply) across all planning periods, throughout the entire planning horizon. At this point, do not focus your efforts on any one planning period.
4. **Define staffing plans.** After you have developed staffing strategies that span all planning periods, examine the specific staffing needs for each period. Using the staffing strategies developed in the previous step as a long-term context, define the specific staffing actions that will allow you to meet the staffing needs effectively and efficiently in each planning period. Make sure that those actions are consistent with and fully support the staffing strategies that you developed in the previous step.

Finally, you will need to fully implement the plans, measure your results, and adjust your staffing strategies and plans as needed to reflect changing business conditions.

This chapter describes each step of the strategic staffing process in detail. Remember that while the process itself is relatively straightforward, it should be applied within the more focused context described in Chapter 3. It should be applied selectively, not to all units within an organization in a one-size-fits-all manner.

Step 1: Define Critical Staffing Issues

The identification of critical staffing issues is one of the most important steps in the strategic staffing process. As discussed in Chapter 3,

I strongly believe that staffing strategies should focus on critical staffing issues, not on organizations or business units. These staffing issues can be thought of as especially critical categories of jobs that warrant—and require—special attention (e.g., positions that are especially critical to effective strategy implementation or jobs that are traditionally hard to fill). To define critical staffing issues, it is necessary to understand the longer-term business context and define the staffing issues you will address.

Understand the Longer-Term Business Context

The identification of staffing issues requires a full understanding of your business objectives and plans as well as a mastery of the staffing process. Begin your search for possible staffing issues by reviewing in detail what your organization is trying to accomplish in the long term and how those things are to be done. Ideally, your company will have a well-defined business strategy that you can refer to. There may also be other components of the planning process that will deepen your understanding of the future direction of the business (e.g., definitions of mission, vision statements, and sets of strategic objectives).

It is not sufficient for you to be an expert in the staffing process. Those who are responsible for developing staffing strategies need to know as much about the business as the business unit heads do. It is not sufficient to have some knowledge of the business and in-depth expertise in the area of staffing—in-depth understanding of both is needed.

Do you understand your company's business plans and strategies well enough to serve as a true "business partner" and develop effective staffing strategies and plans? While many HR professionals have a full grasp of their company's business strategies, others may need to have a more robust understanding of these strategies before they can initiate or support a strategic staffing process. Here is a test that you can use to determine whether you do indeed understand your company's business strategy well enough. Suppose that on a Friday afternoon you were suddenly named to head up a business unit in your company (e.g., to run a plant if you are in a manufacturing company, or to be general manager of a region if you are in a service company), starting the following Monday. Would you welcome such an assignment? Do you think that you would be fully prepared to function in the new position when you reported to work that next Monday morning? Just before you fall asleep that night (when you are really fairly honest with yourself), would you think that you knew enough about the business to be successful on your own? If the answer is yes, you probably know enough about the business. If the answer if no, however, you may need to improve your understanding.

If you determine that you need a better understanding of your company's business objectives and plans, here are some low-cost, nonthreatening things that you can do to learn more:

- Review the company's business strategies, plans, and proposals (e.g., unit, financial, marketing, technical, and functional plans) on your own and ask unit managers for clarification of or expansion on points you don't understand.
- Examine planned capital investments, identifying what is to be invested, where, and why.
- Identify industry, competitive, and other external factors affecting the business and think about the impact that these will have on your company and its plans.
- Ask to meet with a planner or line manager, saying that you need a better understanding of business plans in order to determine the staffing implications or develop realistic staffing plans.
- Where specific plans are not available, create your own "what if" business scenarios that you can use as a foundation for strategic staffing.

Define the Staffing Issues You Will Address

First, identify (at least in a preliminary way) the particular aspects of your business plans that have (or may have) significant staffing implications. Identify key business initiatives, plans, and actions that may have a significant impact on required capabilities, staffing levels, or both. Next, define the specific staffing issues that you will focus on. Identify specific, critical job categories that will need the special attention that strategic staffing provides. You might choose to focus your analysis on staffing issues/implications such as these:

- Job categories that are critical to strategy implementation
- Job categories in which significant changes in required capabilities will be needed
- Job categories in which required staffing levels need to change significantly (e.g., additions are needed to support significant growth, or reductions are necessary because of a downsizing)
- Positions that are expected to be hard to fill
- Positions that have long learning curves (and thus should be filled well in advance of actual need)
- Emerging skill sets, especially those that you have not looked for previously
- Skill sets for which there is intense competition externally
- Areas in which specific staffing plans are needed (e.g., when identifying opportunities to redeploy surplus staff rather than resort to layoffs)

When you are identifying staffing issues and their implications, it is often helpful to focus on what will be changing in your organization (i.e., not just what is to be done, but what is to be done differently). In many cases, business strategies describe very specific changes that are to be implemented; often, these changes have an impact on required staffing levels, required capabilities, or both.

It may be helpful to think of these various changes as "staffing drivers," since they drive changes in required capabilities and staffing levels. These staffing drivers are really just categories of change that your business may be implementing. Staffing drivers might include:

- Changes in business focus or objectives
- Business expansion or contraction
- Changes in markets or customer base
- Major projects or capital expenditures
- Changes in technology
- Changes in product mix
- Productivity improvements
- Changes in organization

Since they are somewhat generic categories (rather than specific changes), many of these staffing drivers can be identified in advance. Create a list of the staffing drivers that typically affect staffing in your organization. Then use this list as "crib notes" when identifying staffing implications. When you read a business plan, highlight (perhaps literally, using a marker) the parts of the plan that describe the kinds of changes that are included on your list of staffing drivers. Remember that often these changes are described in financial sections and tables, so don't just read the text. Consider these highlighted sections to be rocks to look under—you will need to go back to these sections later and dig deeper to identify what the potential staffing issues or implications really are.

If you are participating in planning discussions (rather than reviewing written plans), staffing drivers can also be helpful. As planning discussions progress, specifically listen for the changes described on your list of drivers. When they are described, politely stop the conversation to ensure that the staffing implications of these changes are also discussed.

In some cases, business plans just don't provide the richness of detail that is needed to define critical staffing issues. In these cases, interviews with line managers and planning staff may provide the additional information you need. Prepare for the interview by learning all you can about that manager's business. Identify possible staffing issues or areas of concern. Define that manager's current staffing resources, in terms of both requirements and staffing levels. When conducting the interview, verify current staffing, talk about business plans and changes, and discuss the impact that those changes might have on required skills and/or staffing levels. A suggested format for such an interview (and an interview guide) is included in Chapter 12 of this book.

Another caution: Don't limit your analysis and efforts to the staffing data that might be included in the business strategy (if there are any) or the human resources section of your business plan (if your business plan includes such a section). In many cases, those plans and projections are inaccurate and unrealistic. They are simply management's best guess regarding staffing requirements. Create your own staffing plans instead, using the tools and techniques described in this book.

Once you have identified your staffing issues, set priorities and select those issues for which staffing strategies will be developed. Usually, it is not possible to address all the issues that you identify. In some cases, the order in which you address issues will be based on need (i.e., you first address those that are most critical). In other cases, it may be necessary to address issues in a particular sequence (i.e., less critical issues must be addressed first because they provide input that is needed in order to address more critical issues). Finally, you need to clearly document and define the staffing issues that you are going to address.

Step 2: Define Staffing Gaps and Surpluses

Once you have identified the staffing issues to be addressed, the next step is to define, for each issue, the staffing gaps and surpluses that must be eliminated (or at least alleviated) if that issue is to be addressed fully (and thus your business strategies implemented effectively). When you create a staffing strategy, you must define the staffing gaps and surpluses that are expected during each planning period of your planning horizon. These gaps are specific, quantifiable, and objective. There are three kinds of differences that you might identify:

- **Staffing levels.** You may have too many staff (a surplus) or too few staff (a gap or deficit) in some job categories to implement the company's business plans effectively.
- **Capabilities.** It may be that you have the right number of staff, but that these individuals lack particular capabilities that will be needed to implement the company's business strategies.
- **Mix.** It may be the case both that you have the wrong number of staff and that the staff you have lack critical capabilities. I call this a staffing mix problem.

In order to define these differences in sufficient detail, you will need to create a staffing model that allows you to define staffing requirements, forecast staff availability, and compare requirements to availability. Step 2a describes the overall approach that should be used to structure the staffing model process. Step 2b describes the steps involved in developing and implementing a specific, detailed staffing model. A separate staffing model will be required for each staffing issue that you are going to address.

Step 2a: Define Your Overall Staffing Model Process

To define staffing strategies and plans for each staffing issue, you will need to develop a staffing model that includes a definition of requirements (in terms of both skills and staffing levels), a projection of staff availability, and the calculation of specific gaps and surpluses for each of your planning periods. At the core of the strategic staffing process is a fairly traditional, quantitative model that defines required staffing levels (demand), identifies available staffing (supply), and calculates the gaps between supply and demand (net needs). Figure 4-1 shows this process at its simplest.

The simple (and often used) process shown in Figure 4-1 is perfectly appropriate as long as there are no changes in available staffing between "now" (whenever current staff availability was determined) and "then" (that point in the future for which demand has been calculated). In most companies, however, many actions that affect staffing will occur between now and then (especially

Figure 4-1. The Traditional Approach

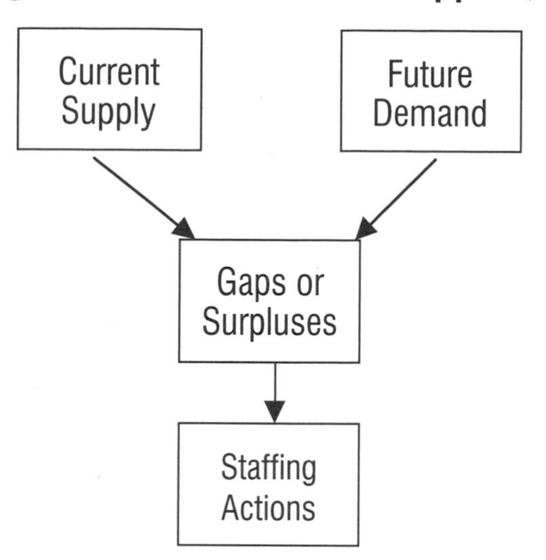

when you consider that my broad definition of *staffing* includes all movement into, around, and out of an organization). People will leave the organization through retirement and for other reasons. Those who stay may change jobs, be promoted, or be redeployed. New people may join the organization. There is simply no way to account for these actions in the simplistic model described in Figure 4-1, so a different version of the model is necessary.

A better process for defining staffing gaps and surpluses is one in which you first define how many people you have now and then use that information as a foundation for projecting the number and types of people you think will be available at the point for which requirements have been defined. To do this, you need to make assumptions regarding the losses, additions, and movement that you think will occur between "now" and "then." By using this technique, you can compare supply and demand at the same point in time and get a meaningful estimation of staffing gaps and surpluses. Figure 4-2 shows what this process looks like.

You still start by determining future requirements (both required skills and required staffing levels) at a particular point in time ("demand then"), but in this version of the process the supply side has two steps. First, you define the current staffing levels and capabilities, just as you did in the traditional approach depicted in Figure

Figure 4-2. A Better Approach

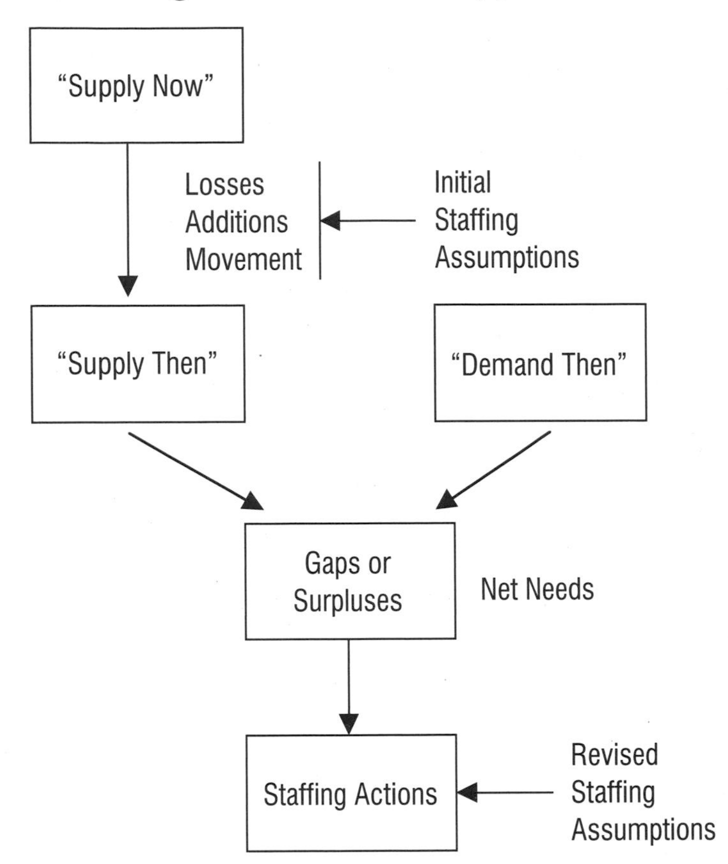

4-1. Next, you make specific assumptions about the staffing actions that you think are likely to occur between now and then. Make your "best guess" assumptions about the number of people you think will leave voluntarily, retire, be promoted, be redeployed, or be hired. Once you have made (and documented) these staffing assumptions, you apply them to the current population to see what you would end up with if all these staffing actions actually took place:

- Subtract from your current population the number of people you think will leave (e.g., through voluntary turnover, retirements, and other planned losses).
- Add in the number of people that will be hired or that will be added from sources not included in your model.

- Account for promotions and other movement (e.g., redeployment) by subtracting that number of people from the jobs they are leaving and adding them to the jobs they will be entering.

Chapter 7 includes a specific example of what these calculations might look like. Once you have applied all your assumptions, you will end up with a "snapshot" or forecast of the numbers and types of employees that will be available at that point in the future ("supply then"), given that all the staffing actions you assumed really do take place.

Now compare "supply then" to "demand then" and calculate staffing gaps and surpluses. Finally, define the staffing actions needed to eliminate these gaps and surpluses. This process usually entails a revision of the staffing assumptions you made initially. If you assumed that some hiring would take place, but there are still some gaps, you may need to hire even more people. Alternatively, you may need to promote or redeploy additional people to meet that need. Conversely, there may be surpluses in jobs where the number of people you assumed would be hired or promoted was greater than the number actually needed. In these cases, you might need to reduce the number of people you assumed would be hired or promoted. In other cases where there are surpluses, you may need to assume that more people will leave than you projected in the first place (e.g., through layoffs or early retirement). In the end, your objective is to create a set of staffing assumptions (actions) that most effectively matches supply and demand.

While this approach is certainly better than the first one (because it factors in the staffing changes that will occur between now and then), it too can be improved. The problem with this version is that it is iterative in nature: You make assumptions regarding the staffing actions that are needed and then test those assumptions to see if in fact the staffing gaps and surpluses are eliminated. If they are, you have arrived at a good solution. If, however, there are still differences between supply and demand (a scenario that is quite likely), you must revise your staffing action assumptions and recalculate the gaps and surpluses. It may be necessary to repeat this process (perhaps many times) until an acceptable solution is reached.

Thinking of it another way, the staffing ''assumptions'' that you make are often just guesses. In using this particular approach, we guess at a solution, try it, and if it is not correct, we guess again. For example, we may not know the actual number of people that need to be promoted from one job to another, so we guess at that number (calling it an assumption, of course), plug in our guess, and see if we were right. If we weren't, we will need to revise our promotion assumptions (in fact guessing again) until we get supply to equal demand. While we eventually will arrive at the right answer, the process is very iterative and is not very efficient.

By making a relatively small change in our model, we can largely eliminate the guesswork. The difference lies in the nature of the assumptions that are made. This third, ''best'' version begins the same way as the second version (see Figure 4-3). You start by defining ''demand then'' and ''supply now,'' just as you would have done in the previous process. This time, however, you make assumptions only about the staffing actions that you really can't control—that is to say, those staffing actions that are likely to happen no matter what you do. Usually, these uncontrollable actions include:

- Voluntary turnover
- Normal retirements
- Seniority- or tenure-based promotions
- Completion of hiring plans that are already in motion (e.g., openings that will be filled during the period in which candidates have accepted offers but have not yet started work)

Create your first version of ''supply then'' by considering *only* uncontrollable actions like these. At this point, specifically do not include any assumptions regarding other staffing actions. Compare this preliminary ''supply then'' to ''demand then'' to determine the preliminary gaps and surpluses that result.

Now you can begin to define staffing actions that you will take to eliminate these gaps and surpluses. However, you will do it in a slightly different way from the way you did it in the previous ver-

Figure 4-3. The "Best" Approach

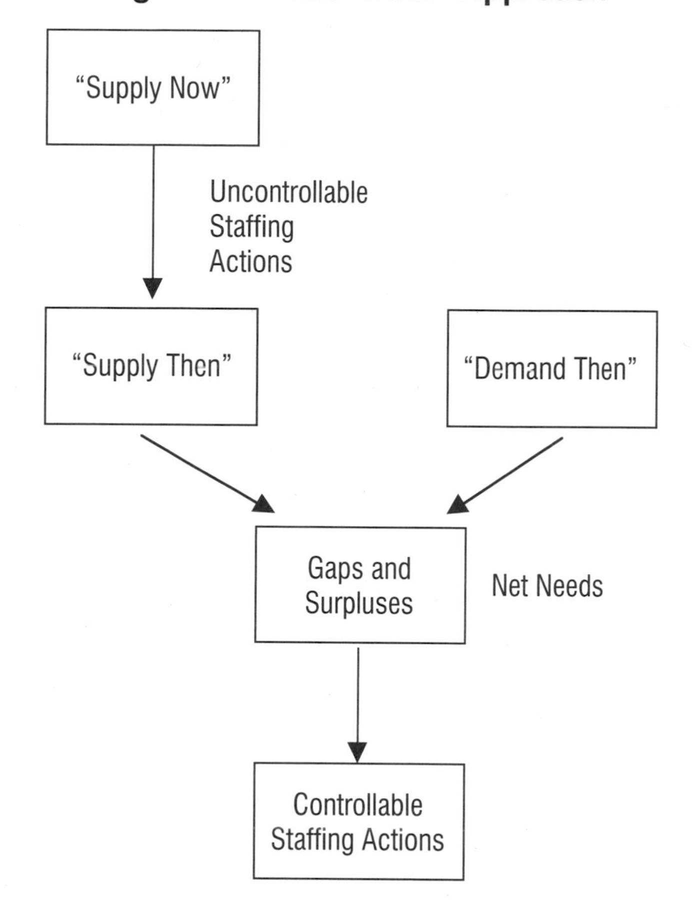

sion. Consider at this point all of the controllable staffing actions that are needed in order to eliminate the preliminary gaps and surpluses you just identified. Controllable staffing actions are all those that happen because you make them happen—they would not happen otherwise. Controllable staffing actions include virtually all:

- Hiring
- Promotions
- Transfers and redeployments
- Planned staff reductions

Each of these staffing actions is a specific move that is made in an intentional way to meet a particular need that has been identified. The advantage of this approach is that it eliminates the guesswork that is part of the second approach described previously. For example, rather than guessing how many promotions to a particular job will be needed, first determine the number of openings that will be created as a result of uncontrollable actions and then decide how many of those openings can and should be filled through promotion. Similarly, don't estimate the number of new hires at first. Instead, use this technique to figure out how many openings are expected, then determine how many of those openings can and should be filled with new hires. In fact, this technique allows you to identify talent surpluses from which employees might be redeployed, eliminating the need for some hiring or promotion. With this process there is no need to guess, test, and guess again until you arrive at an acceptable solution. Instead, you get that solution in a single iteration.

In summary, it is typically most effective to adopt an overall approach to strategic staffing that takes into account the staffing actions that are anticipated between the current time and that point in the future for which demand has been calculated. The efficiency of the process can be improved (and the guesswork eliminated) by first considering the uncontrollable staffing actions and then determining the mix of controllable staffing actions needed to eliminate the resulting gaps and surpluses.

Step 2b: Create a Detailed Staffing Model

Using the approach described in Figure 4-3 as your road map, you will now need to develop a detailed staffing model that will define specific staffing gaps and surpluses. A separate model will be needed for each staffing issue that you will focus on. Again, Chapter 7 includes a worked-out example of this process. Here are the steps in the process:

Define Staffing Model/Planning Parameters

Once business plans have been defined and understood, you should begin to define and quantify staffing requirements and availability. As discussed earlier, it is usually best to build a separate model for each issue, so that you can vary the planning parameters accordingly. For every model that you build, you must define three sets of parameters: the time frame, the population, and the model structure.

Time Frame. This parameter has two components. The first, the *planning horizon*, describes how far out you will plan (e.g., three years). The second, the *planning period*, describes how frequently you will plan or update within your planning horizon (e.g., annually or quarterly). Each of these two components should be determined (and may differ) for each staffing issue that you are addressing.

It is important that you match the planning horizon to the staffing issue you are addressing. There is no need to force every unit to use the same time frame, nor it necessary to use the time frame and planning horizon of your strategic planning process ''just because.'' If you are looking at jobs in which requirements and technology change quickly, you might use a one-year time frame, creating plans for each of the four quarters in that year. If you are analyzing management depth, you might need to use a three- to five-year planning horizon (it will take that long to get any measurable results), updating the plans annually within that framework.

Never create a staffing plan that has a planning horizon longer than your management's willingness to allocate resources. If managers won't act on the longer-term results of your work, why create such a long-term plan in the first place?

Here is an example of how planning horizons are determined. Suppose that your managers were willing to change resource allocations to avoid an issue that was two years out but would do nothing more than cast a watchful eye on issues that were three years away. What would be the proper planning horizon? At first glance, a two-year plan would seem appropriate, since that matches management's proclivity to act. However, remember that the objective of a staffing strategy is to create a longer-term context that can be used to guide short-term decision making. How would you determine the best staffing plan for year 2 without creating a plan for year 3 as well? I would create a three-year plan, using year 3 as the context for defining the right actions for year 2. However, I would share only the first two years of that plan with managers, given that they would probably be unwilling to implement the plan for year 3.

Population. What jobs/staff should be included in your plan? Remember that there is no need to create a single model that includes all jobs or people. You need to include in each model only those positions (or staff) that are directly affected by the issue you are addressing. When you build a model, you should include three groups of people/jobs:

- *The target population*—those who are directly affected by the issue you are addressing
- *Sources*—those jobs that might be likely sources of talent if there is a need in your target population. Are there other jobs in the organization that require similar skills and capabilities from which you might draw talent?
- *Uses*—those jobs that might be users of talent if there is a surplus in the target population. Are there other areas of the company that might need people with these skills and capabilities?

Once you have determined the job categories to be included from an overall perspective, try to separate those specific positions that must be addressed strategically from those that can be addressed primarily from a tactical perspective. Include in your model only those jobs that must be analyzed from a strategic perspective—those for which staffing needs must be addressed proactively or those for which it will take considerable time to address staffing needs.

If you are unclear as to whether or not a job category should be included in your strategic staffing process, think about the nature of the staffing actions that you would be likely to apply if a gap in that area were to be defined. Consider each of the four categories of staffing action and try to reach a consensus as to whether the job is more strategic or tactical in nature. As you review each category, think about the following questions:

• *Recruiting.* If you were to rely on recruiting to meet the need, could you wait until an opening occurs and just react (e.g., simply posting the job on an Internet job board will identify a sufficient number of qualified candidates)? If so, it's likely that this job can be addressed tactically, and it may not be necessary to include it in your process. On the other hand, would you really need to anticipate that opening and be more proactive (e.g., where competition for people with those skills is intense and the number of qualified candidates is relatively low)? If so, it's likely that a more strategic approach will be needed.

• *Internal movement.* Think about filling an opening in this job category through normal channels or career paths. Does there tend to be a relatively large pool of qualified candidates available? If so, a tactical approach may be sufficient. If that pool is not large enough, or if the candidates require additional development before they can be placed, then the opening should be addressed from a strategic perspective.

• *Redeployment.* Will it be possible to meet staffing needs in this category through redeployment? Are there qualified candidates available (allowing you to be tactical), or would such redeployment require advance planning (requiring you to be more strategic)?

• *Development.* Think about closing a staffing gap in this category by providing existing staff with the required skills. How large are the skills gaps? Can these gaps be dealt with through training in the time available? Is it possible that the missing skills can be developed after the job moves are made? If so, then a tactical approach is probably adequate. On the other hand, if development needs are substantial, involve core functions, and/or cannot be met in a short-term time frame, then it's better to include these jobs in the strategic category.

Following is a worksheet that you can use as a guide to help you determine whether a job should be addressed strategically (and thus should be included in your model) or tactically (and thus can be excluded). In each cell of the worksheet, jot down likely staffing actions, whether strategic or tactical. Review your probable actions and determine whether you are more likely to implement the strategic options or the tactical options. Indicate your choice in the fourth column.

Worksheet
Should a Job Be Included in the Strategic Staffing Process?

Job Category: ______________________________

Staffing Action	Strategic	Tactical/Operational	Most Likely Option
	Need time to respond? Need time to be proactive?	Can you respond quickly? Can you be reactive?	
Recruiting			☐ Strategic ☐ Tactical
Internal movement			☐ Strategic ☐ Tactical
Redeployment			☐ Strategic ☐ Tactical
Development			☐ Strategic ☐ Tactical

Model Structure. You will need to create some kind of model structure or framework to keep track of and organize your data. Usually, a two-dimensional matrix works well. Try using the columns of the matrix to capture organization units, functions, job groups/families, or locations. Use the rows to differentiate levels of experience or accountability.

Remember that whatever matrix you build, you will be using it to structure each component of your model. Use the same matrix format to capture required staffing (''demand then''), current staffing (''supply now''), losses (e.g., voluntary turnover for each category), hiring, transfers in and out, and future availability (''supply then''). When you compare ''supply then'' to ''demand then'' (as described below), you will end up with a gap, a surplus, or zero in every cell of this matrix.

When defining model structure, don't limit your choices to those titles and levels that exist currently. I often find it helpful to define various roles that individuals play. Frequently, technical or functional areas can be defined using just three roles: senior (those with particularly deep experience in a particular area), individual contributor (those who have some specific capabilities and can function independently), and entry level (those who have basic capabilities and aptitudes, but no significant expertise or experience). Usually, a vast number of individual position titles can be combined into a very small number of roles. Not only is this a more realistic way to describe the work that is being done (or needs to be done), but it has the added benefit of keeping the size of the model manageable.

Sometimes it is necessary to keep track of more than two dimensions (e.g., it may be necessary to define staffing needs by function, location, and level of experience). Often, a two-dimensional model can still be used to track three (or more) variables. Suppose that there are three locations (e.g., New York, Chicago, and Los Angeles), four functions (e.g., Manufacturing, Sales, Finance, and HR), and three roles (e.g., manager, senior, and individual contributor). Create a column for each location and a separate row for each combination of function and level (e.g., HR/manager, HR/senior, HR/individual contributor, Sales/manager, etc.). In this way you can create a model that uses a two-dimensional format to track three variables. While this is a little unwieldy, it is usually preferable to somehow creating a three-dimensional array or spreadsheet. Figure 4-4 shows one way in which that model might be structured.

There may also be cases (such as those where required capabilities are expected to change significantly) in which it is necessary to create categories for jobs that are expected to exist in the future but that do not exist currently. If this is necessary, include both old and new job categories in your matrix. However, it is likely that there will be no staff that currently have all the skills that will be necessary in the future; further, it is just as likely that you will need no one in the future that has only the skills that are needed now. Later on in the modeling process, your "supply now" matrix will probably show those with the skills that are currently required but will include no one with the skills needed in the future. Conversely, your "demand then" matrix will show your requirements for the

Figure 4-4.

Function/Role	New York	Chicago	Los Angeles
Manufacturing/manager			
Manufacturing/senior			
Manufacturing/individual contributor			
Sales/manager			
Sales/senior			
Sales/individual contributor			
Finance/manager			
Finance/senior			
Finance/individual contributor			
HR/manager			
HR/senior			
HR/individual contributor			

new skills, but will define no requirements for the obsolete skills. Figure 4-5 is a simple example of what that type of matrix might look like for just two job families.

Define Staffing Requirements

Once you have defined the parameters, you can begin building your model. While you can start with either the supply side or the demand side, I almost always start with demand for the following reasons:

- In virtually every case, it is more difficult to define the required capabilities and staffing levels than it is to describe the anticipated supply. If you start with demand, you will get the hard part done first.
- Usually, less information is available about demand, and the information that is available is at a more "macro" level than that available for the supply side. If you start with the supply side, it can be easy to develop a very detailed model, if only because a human resource information system usually con-

Figure 4-5.

Supply Now

Role	Networking (Current Skills)	Data Management (Current Skills)	Networking (Future Skills)	Data Management (Future Skills)
Team leader	5	10	0	0
Individual contributor	25	21	0	0
Entry-level	15	6	0	0

Demand "Then"

Role	Networking (Current Skills)	Data Management (Current Skills)	Networking (Future Skills)	Data Management (Future Skills)
Team leader	0	0	7	12
Individual contributor	0	0	30	27
Entry-level	0	0	18	10

tains a lot of detailed data. Rarely, however, is that same level of detail available about future plans (e.g., longer-term forecasts or business volumes). Since the model can be built only to the lowest level of detail available on both the supply and demand sides, it is more likely that the level of detail on the demand side will become the design parameter. Thus, any time spent or resources expended on gathering additional detail will be wasted.

- Most managers are more interested in requirements than they are in availability. If you are trying to build interest in the process, start by defining requirements.

You will need to define both the capabilities and the staffing levels that will be needed in each job category (or cell of your model/matrix) in order to implement the business plan. It is not possible to define staffing levels until you determine the roles and capabilities that will be needed, so start there. Don't try to identify all the capabilities that are required in each category. Instead, try to focus on a very small number of capabilities (usually five to ten) that are really important, including:

- Those that are especially critical (e.g., those that are needed to win, not just to play the game)
- Those that differentiate one job, category, or level from another
- Those that are changing (e.g., newly emerging capabilities)

If your company uses competency models or some kind of skills database, use this as your starting point. Remember to select only those skills that are absolutely critical, however. If you choose skills from a predefined list, you are apt to choose too many.

Once you have identified the required capabilities, define the required staffing levels. There are many techniques that can be used to do this, including statistical techniques, staffing ratios, project-based staffing, and staffing profiles. Rather than describe these techniques here, I've provided detailed descriptions of each (including specific examples with solutions) in the next chapter of this book.

It may be necessary to combine several of these techniques in order to create a complete picture of the requirements. For example, when defining staffing requirements for new bank branches, you might combine the following techniques:

- The number of branch managers might be constant (e.g., one per branch).
- The number of loan officers might be determined by a staffing profile (e.g., ten officers for a large branch and six for a small branch).
- The number of tellers or personal bankers might be defined using staffing ratios (e.g., relating the number of tellers or officers to the anticipated number of customers or transactions).

Regardless of the technique you use, you will end up with a definition of the critical capabilities and required staffing levels for each cell of the matrix/model you have developed.

Forecast Staffing Availability

Once you have defined the demand, the next step is to forecast the supply side. First, define the number and types of staff that are *cur-*

rently available in each job or category (i.e., each cell of your model/matrix). Where possible, first document the overall, existing capabilities in each category/cell. Capture the common or core skills of the group as a whole (i.e., by cohort), not the specific capabilities of each individual in that group. Individual skills and capabilities are not helpful at this point (although they may be later on when you identify the specific individuals who will be promoted, redeployed, etc.).

The information you need in order to produce this "supply now" component can usually be extracted from your human resource information system (HRIS). Access the system to determine the number of individuals you currently have in each job category (i.e., each combination of row and column heading). It may be necessary to "map" the HRIS data into the categories you have created (e.g., to define a role that you are using as consisting of several actual titles or a given experience level as a group of salary grades).

Next, forecast the number of staff that you think will be available at that point in the future for which you have calculated demand. Make assumptions regarding the staffing actions involving current staff that will occur between the current time (now) and that point in the future for which demand has been calculated (then). Remember to consider only those staffing actions that are uncontrollable. In this context, what staffing actions should be considered controllable and which are uncontrollable? It may be helpful to think of the difference this way:

- **Uncontrollable staffing actions** are those that are likely to occur anyway (i.e., whether or not your organization creates and implements staffing strategies and plans).
- **Controllable staffing actions** are those that you will define and implement specifically to meet the staffing needs that your strategic staffing process identified.

Table 4-1 lists some common examples of both uncontrollable and controllable staffing actions.

Calculate the number of staff that will be available in each category if your assumptions concerning uncontrollable actions actually occur, including:

Table 4-1. Examples of Uncontrollable and Controllable Staffing Actions

Staffing Action	Uncontrollable	Controllable
Recruiting	• Positions for which candidates have accepted offers but are not yet working • Positions for which candidates are being actively considered and the openings will be filled in the planning period (even though particular candidates may not yet have been selected)	• Any opening for which specific candidates have not been identified • Openings that have been "approved" but for which no candidate will be placed • Most openings that are to be filled by implementing the staffing plans you are preparing
Promotions, transfers, and other internal movement	• "Lock step" promotions (e.g., those defined by labor agreements) • Seniority- or tenure-based promotions that are not at the discretion of management • Any move where an employee has been selected but not yet placed (assuming that the placement occurs during the planning period in question)	• Any opening for which specific candidates have not been identified • Most openings that are to be filled by implementing the staffing plans you are preparing
Losses	• Voluntary turnover • Normal retirement • Temporary/contingent staff whose contracts will expire during the planning period	• Early retirement programs • Termination for cause • Layoffs or reductions in force • Temporary/contingent staff whose contracts will be terminated prematurely

- Subtracting out anticipated turnover, retirements, transfers out, and other planned losses
- Adding in anticipated hires and transfers in
- Adjusting for promotions and movement (i.e., subtracting from the source jobs and adding that same number to the target jobs), including retirements, internal movement, hiring, and other staffing actions that are anticipated between now and then

Don't forget to document changes in capabilities, too. If, for example, you have a major development initiative that will be completed between now and then, capture the new skills that you assume the group will gain as a result of the training that is to occur.

What role do historical rates and performance (e.g., turnover rates and promotion patterns) play in making these assumptions? The objective here is to develop a realistic set of assumptions that reflects what you think will actually happen between now and then on the supply side of your model. If considering historical performance helps you to develop these assumptions, feel free to use those data. If, however, you think the future will be different from the past, make new assumptions that reflect what you think will occur—don't simply rely on past patterns that probably won't recur in the future. If, for example, the average voluntary turnover rate for the last five years has been 5 percent, and you think that that trend will continue, assume the same turnover rate for the future. However, if you think that changing economic conditions will affect that rate (e.g., times will get better and turnover will increase somewhat), use the rate that you think will occur, not the historical rate. As another example, a historical promotion rate from one job to another of 10 percent probably reflects the way the organization chose to fill openings at that point in the past. Since it is unlikely that a similar number of openings will be filled in that manner in the future, it would be better to make new assumptions regarding promotions (between now and then) that show what you think will occur. Don't blindly assume that past trends will continue.

In forecasting the number of retirements, two approaches are particularly helpful:

- Calculate the average retirement age, then count the number of individuals in each job category that will reach that age in each period.

- Forecast retirements based on actual eligibility. Access the data in the HRIS to determine the individuals in each job category that will become eligible for retirement. Next, create an assumption that describes how many of those who are eligible will retire in each period. Here are three possible assumptions:

1. All will retire as soon as they are eligible. Under this assumption, simply count the number that become eligible to retire in each planning period and assume that they all will leave during that period.
2. Spread retirements evenly over the five years following eligibility, with 20 percent of those eligible retiring in each year. Thus, if twenty employees become eligible to retire in period 1, assume that four of them (i.e., 20 percent of the twenty) retire in period 1, four more in period 2, and so on for the five periods.
3. Spread the retirements out unevenly over six or more years (e.g., 20 percent of those eligible will retire as soon as they can, 15 percent will stay one period longer than they need to, 10 percent will stay two periods longer, etc.).

When using a process similar to that described for the second and third assumptions, remember to add up all those that are projected to retire across all eligibility distributions. Look at the third assumption. Let's suppose that for the jobs in question, 20 percent of those that become eligible in period 1 will retire. In period 2, 15 percent of those in that same category who became eligible in period 1 will retire, along with 20 percent of those who first become eligible in period 2. Similarly, retirements in period 3 will be the sum of 10 percent of those that became eligible in period 1 plus 15 percent of those that became eligible in period 2 plus 20 percent of those that first become eligible in period 3. This logic continues for each period. A separate spreadsheet can easily be developed to model these retirement scenarios and calculate the total number of people in each job category that will retire in each planning period. Figure 4-6 is a sample of what that might look like for a given job (the results of the calculations have been rounded to the nearest whole number).

Your HRIS may include valuable data that you can use to de-

Figure 4-6. Sample Retirement Projection

Percent retiring in the first year of eligibility: 20 percent
Percent retiring in the second year of eligibility: 15 percent
Percent retiring in the third year of eligibility: 10 percent
Percent retiring in the fourth year of eligibility: 25 percent
Percent retiring in the fifth year of eligibility: 30 percent

Model Year	Number Becoming Eligible	Retire in Year 1	Retire in Year 2	Retire in Year 3	Retire in Year 4	Retire in Year 5
Year 1	50	0.20 × 50 = 10	0.15 × 50 = 8	0.10 × 50 = 5	0.25 × 50 = 13	0.30 × 50 = 15
Year 2	60		0.20 × 60 = 12	0.15 × 60 = 9	0.10 × 60 = 6	0.25 × 60 = 15
Year 3	40			0.20 × 40 = 8	0.15 × 40 = 6	0.10 × 40 = 4
Year 4	55				0.20 × 55 = 11	0.15 × 55 = 8
Year 5	35					0.20 × 35 = 7
Total retiring		10	20	22	36	49

velop these assumptions. You may be able to calculate historical voluntary turnover rates that you can use as a foundation for estimating future rates. Your HRIS can also provide retirement eligibility data. Ask the HRIS staff to produce a listing of employees by retirement eligibility date. Make sure that the listing also includes the information you need in order to identify the job category (in your staffing model) that each employee is in currently. Then simply count the number that become eligible in each of your planning periods and enter that number in the appropriate cell of your model.

Here is a quick example of how "supply then" might be calculated for a given job category. Suppose that there are forty people in a job right now. Suppose also that the following uncontrollable staffing actions are expected:

- The voluntary turnover rate for this job is 5 percent.
- Two people are expected to retire.
- One person will be promoted from this job to a higher level (a move based on seniority).
- One person has accepted a job offer and will join the company in two weeks.

What is "supply then" in this case? Your calculation will look like this:

"Supply now"	40	
Minus voluntary turnover	− 2	(i.e., 5 percent of the 40 staff)
Minus retirements	− 2	
Minus promotions to other jobs	− 1	
Plus planned hires	+ 1	
Equals "supply then"	36	

This calculation assumes that no other uncontrollable staffing actions will take place and that all controllable staffing actions will be defined and applied later in the modeling process. A similar calculation would be made for every cell of your model/matrix.

Define Staffing Gaps and Surpluses for the First Period

For each cell of your model, compare staffing requirements (demand) to staffing availability (supply) and calculate gaps (where demand exceeds supply) and surpluses (where supply exceeds demand). When you make this comparison, subtract demand from supply. If you use this convention, gaps will be defined as negative numbers and surpluses will be defined as positive numbers. Remember to identify capability gaps as well, not just differences in staffing levels. For example, if you will have ten staff in a job category that will require twelve, you will have a gap of two people. On the other hand, if you will have fifteen people in a job that will require ten, you will have a surplus of five staff. Figure 4-7 shows a simple example.

Figure 4-7.

Demand Then

	Project 1	Project 2
Engineering manager	10	12
Engineer	25	40

Supply Then

	Project 1	Project 2
Engineering manager	11	10
Engineer	23	43

Expected Staffing Gaps/Surpluses

	Project 1	Project 2
Engineering manager	11 − 10 = +1	10 − 12 = −2
Engineer	23 − 25 = −2	43 − 40 = +3

Define Staffing Gaps and Surpluses for All Remaining Periods

When you have calculated gaps and surpluses for all the job categories in the first period of your model (considering only the uncontrollable staffing actions), you will be ready to calculate gaps and surpluses for the second period. Use your "supply then" matrix from period 1 as the "supply now" matrix for period 2. Calculate "supply then" for period 2, factoring in any uncontrollable staffing actions that you think will happen during period 2. Compare the result to staffing requirements for the end of period 2 (which obviously could be different from the requirements for period 1) and calculate the staffing gaps and surpluses that you expect in each job category for the end of period 2. Repeat this process for all remaining planning periods, always remembering to:

- Use "supply then" from the previous period as "supply now" for the subsequent period.

- Define and include the uncontrollable staffing actions that you think will occur during the period.
- Define a new set of staffing requirements for each period.

These gaps and surpluses are preliminary, of course, because they do not take into consideration the staffing plans that you will implement (i.e., the controllable staffing actions). They are a necessary interim step, however.

Note that this approach represents a significant departure from common practice. Usually, the staffing actions needed to address gaps and surpluses are defined for a given period before the analysis for the subsequent period begins. This practice precludes any longitudinal view of staffing needs (i.e., analyzing needs across periods), and this longitudinal view is absolutely required if effective staffing strategies are to be developed.

Step 3: Develop Staffing Strategies

Staffing strategies are longer-term, directional plans of action that describe what an organization is actually going to do to address staffing needs across all planning periods throughout its planning horizon. Examples of staffing strategies include:

- Meet needs at senior levels through a 75 percent/25 percent blend of promotion from within and external recruiting.
- Focus recruiting and development on core positions that generate significant competitive advantage.
- Meet needs for specific technical skills by using contractors.
- Redeploy individuals that are surplus in one area to a different area, providing accelerated development.
- Reorganize work to better utilize the available talent.
- Initiate intern programs at local high schools to develop pools of qualified technicians to meet future needs.

By definition, an effective staffing strategy can be defined only across planning periods (e.g., across all five years of a five-year business strategy). Consequently, then, meaningful staffing strategies can be developed only after the initial differences between staffing supply and demand have been defined for *all* planning periods in the planning horizon. The best staffing strategy can be developed only after you have developed a full understanding of the staffing gaps and surpluses that are expected in *each* period in your planning horizon and analyzed those needs from an integrated, holistic perspective.

Once you have calculated gaps and surpluses for each period, review your needs *across* those periods (as opposed to looking at each period by itself) and develop staffing strategies that will most effectively eliminate or reduce those particular staffing gaps and surpluses in the long run. Don't simply choose an action that seems to meet a need in a particular planning period. Instead, review needs across all periods and define the actions that will best eliminate staffing gaps and surpluses when all planning periods are considered.

There are two main reasons why such a specific definition of staffing needs must be completed for all planning periods before staffing strategies can be developed:

1. **Staffing strategies must address actual needs.** While staffing strategies are long-term and directional, they are not simply general approaches that seem to make sense. The strategies that you choose to develop and implement must be those that most effectively address your actual staffing needs. Consequently, it is not possible to develop staffing strategies until staffing needs have been defined in very specific terms. At a minimum, needs must be defined in terms of what (i.e., particular capabilities and staffing levels), where (i.e., function or location), and when (i.e., a given period of your planning model). If you do not define your staffing needs at this level of detail, it will not be possible for you to develop the specific, targeted staffing strategies that will meet those needs most effectively.

2. **Staffing strategies span planning periods.** Staffing strategies define what will be done throughout your planning horizon, across all planning periods. It doesn't make sense to develop a strategy

that addresses needs in a single period; instead, you must determine the staffing approach that works best when all planning periods are considered. A staffing action that seems to make sense within the bounds of a single period may actually prove to be inappropriate when staffing needs in subsequent periods are considered. Here are some examples:

- A plan for hiring in period 1 may seem to be a good alternative if analyzed by itself, but its effectiveness needs to be evaluated in light of the needs of later periods. It makes no sense to hire individuals into full-time roles to meet a gap in period 1 of your plan if those individuals are not also required in periods 2 and beyond.
- It may be possible to balance staffing needs by moving work from one period to another. If there is a shortage of a particular skill in period 1 and a surplus of that skill in period 2, it may be best to move some of the work from period 1 (thus reducing the need for that skill during that period) into period 2 (thus eliminating the surplus). This kind of cross-period change in work allocation allows needs to be met without staffing changes of any kind. However, such a reallocation cannot be considered if staffing needs and plans are defined for one period at a time.
- It may be that a staffing gap in a critical role (e.g., one of the core roles that provide competitive advantage) in a future period (e.g., period 4) can best be met by redeploying current employees. However, some of those to be redeployed may have particular training or development needs that must be addressed before such movement is possible. A staff plan that addressed only period 4 might have indicated that, because the required talent was not available internally, external hiring was the only option.

Here is an example of how this approach might work. Suppose that a staffing analysis for period 1 identified several staffing needs in a job category that is normally contracted out. Looking at period 1 alone, it seems reasonable to continue to contract for those services, and if only period 1 were considered, that staffing action would probably be the one selected. However, when gaps and surpluses were calculated for periods 2 through 4, it was determined that there would be several openings in that category in each period. Though contracting made sense when period 1 was analyzed by itself, it was no longer the most appropriate option when the needs in all four periods were viewed longitudinally. When staffing needs were viewed across all four periods, it made more sense to hire full-time staff than to continue to contract that work out. It would simply be cheaper to hire full-time staff. In addition, the continuity that full-time staff allows would result in a significant competitive advantage. Further, full-time hires would be of higher quality than contract staff. Regardless of the reasons for this, the staffing actions that were defined when all four periods were considered differed significantly from what would have been done if the needs were defined and met one period at a time.

As this example shows, it is quite possible that the particular strategy that best meets staffing needs in a particular planning period may not be the most effective approach when needs are viewed across all periods. Here are four examples of staffing strategies that might be developed after reviewing staffing gaps and surpluses across multiple periods:

- An organization is expecting a staffing gap in a critical job category in the first planning period. Given that the required capabilities are indeed critical, it would seem to make sense to fill these first-period openings with full-time hires. Suppose, though, that this need was expected to disappear in subsequent periods as demand for the services provided by these people lessened. If the jobs were filled through hiring in the first period, these new employees would become surplus in period 2 and beyond. Consequently, it might make more sense to contract the work out in period 1 so that the company can avoid the payroll expense of carrying these unneeded employees in periods 2 through 4.

- A need for a "commodity" type skill in the first planning period is identified. Normally, these skills are contracted out. However, a review of periods 2 through 4 shows that these skills will be needed in each period. While in general the strategy is to contract out commodity skills, it may make more sense in this case to hire these people full-time, since the need is ongoing (i.e., to provide continuity and lower costs).

• A surplus is defined in a particular job category in the first planning period. A deficit in this same category is forecast in period 3. If these skills can be obtained easily, it might be acceptable to lay off these people at the end of period 1 and hire new staff at the beginning of period 3. However, if the skills are difficult to find (or if competition for people with these skills is intense), it might be better to retain these individuals at the end of period 1 so that they will be available in period 3:

—It may be cheaper to maintain the employees on the payroll than it is to pay them severance and incur the additional expense of hiring new people.

—If people with these skills really are hard to find, the company may not want to take the risk that it will not be able to find and attract individuals with the needed skills at the beginning of period 3.

• In a project-based environment, a company forecasts that there will be a deficit in a technical area in the first quarter of a four-quarter model and a surplus of that very same capability in the second quarter. Hiring to meet this need in period 1 would only increase the surplus in the second period. Using contractors in the first period would also eliminate the deficit, but it would do nothing to alleviate the surplus that is expected in period 2. The best staffing strategy in this case might be to identify a project in period 1 that requires these skills and defer it to period 2. This action would meet both needs.

It may take more than one strategy to address a give issue. For example, if you determine that your company lacks sufficient management depth, you may need to develop and implement a strategy that integrates succession, development, and targeted recruiting (where any of those strategies alone would be necessary but insufficient). Obviously, these strategies will provide the context within which you can define effective near-term staffing plans.

Step 4: Define Staffing Plans

The final "take-away" or deliverable of the strategic staffing process is usually a set of well-documented staffing plans that define all the staffing actions that must be implemented in each planning period if supply is to equal demand for all periods. Once you have defined particular staffing needs and developed your overarching staffing strategies (following steps 2 and 3 above), you will be able to define specific staffing plans for each planning period within your planning horizon.

Regardless of its particular format, any staffing plan must provide a list of specific actions to be implemented to eliminate staffing gaps and surpluses for a given planning period. This is actually where the rubber hits the road. Since they define exactly what you will do, in very specific terms, staffing plans may actually be the most important component of the strategic staffing process. The following process can be used to create staffing plans.

Define Required Staffing Plans and Actions

I usually define staffing *plans* in terms of the numbers of moves to be made (e.g., ten individuals should be promoted from Senior Sales to Sales Manager) and staffing *actions* as the names and faces (e.g., identifying the ten individuals who will actually be promoted). First, define the specific staffing plans that will most effectively eliminate the staffing gaps and surpluses you have identified. Remember that the plans and actions that you develop must be consistent with, and fully support, your staffing strategies. Staffing plans might include:

- Redeployment that eliminates a gap in one area while also reducing a surplus somewhere else

- Promotions
- Lateral moves
- Hiring to reduce a gap
- Accelerating internal movement (and defining the development that such movement entails) to reduce a future gap
- Using contractors
- Increasing or decreasing the use of overtime
- Encouraging turnover or early retirements to reduce a surplus
- Reductions in force (or other planned losses)

Once the staffing plans are completed (on a tentative basis), staffing actions can be defined (i.e., specific individuals can be identified). This level of detail requires more in-depth information on the skills and capabilities of the individuals being considered. Staffing actions give your efforts teeth. It is impossible to implement a plan that simply says that someone should be promoted—you need to identify which person that is. The definition of staffing actions can also ensure that your staffing plans are realistic.

Here is an example: A staffing plan might state that a staffing need should be met by promoting ten people from one job to another along traditional career paths. This might appear to make sense, but it would be impossible to implement such a plan if all the individuals in that source pool happened to be recent hires who lacked the required skills or experience. This important distinction could not be made if you were operating only at the level of staffing plans (i.e., the numbers).

Here is another hint: If your model is hierarchical (e.g., if more senior positions are at the top of a column), create your solution by starting at the top of each column and working your way down. Determine the staffing actions needed to address gaps and surpluses at the most senior level. Next, work down a level. Continue the process until you resolve staffing issues at the lowest level of your model (usually through hiring, since there are rarely other sources of qualified talent at the entry level).

Here is an example of how gaps and surpluses might be translated into a staffing plan. Suppose that your analysis yielded the following gaps and surpluses:

	District A	District B
Managers	−4	+2
Engineers	−8	−1

Start by addressing the gap of 4 managers in District A. Let's say that we could redeploy the 2 surplus managers from District B to District A (assuming that there would be 2 qualified individuals who would be willing to make such a move). This would eliminate the surplus of managers in District B (a surplus of 2 less the 2 that are moved = 0) and reduce the deficit in District A to 2 (the gap of 4 plus 2 transfers in = gap of 2). One way of addressing that gap of 2 would be to promote 2 engineers in District A to manager. This would eliminate the gap in District A managers (gap of 2 plus 2 promoted in = 0) but would increase the deficit at the engineer level to 10 (-8 less the 2 that were promoted). The gaps of 10 engineers in District A and 1 engineer in District B occur in separate, distant districts. Therefore, they would probably be addressed though hiring.

Thus, your final staffing plans would show that the following staffing actions should be taken in District A during the planning period in question:

- A redeployment of two managers from District B to District A
- The promotion of two engineers from District A to manager positions in District A
- The hiring of ten engineers into District A and one engineer into District B

Document Your Plans

Document your staffing actions in detail. Consider creating a table to capture this information. The columns can capture key information on each action; each type of action is a row on the table. If you have created a model, use the row and column headings to describe the needed moves. Note the number of staff making each move and the type of move. Further, make sure that you note the date by which the action is to take place and the individual(s) responsible for making it happen.

Figure 4-8 is an example of what a staffing plan using this format might look like.

Define Supporting Actions

Remember also to define and document any actions that support or are directly related to required staffing. Such actions might include:

- Development needed to support accelerated promotions or redeployment
- Changes in compensation needed to increase the company's ability to attract outside hires

Figure 4-8. Sample Staffing Plan

Type of Action	Number of Staff	From		To		Completion Date
		Row	Column	Row	Column	
Promote	10	Senior	Sales	Manager	Sales	12/31/01
Promote	5	Staff	Sales	Senior	Sales	12/31/01
Hire	8			Staff	Sales	12/13/01
Promote	3	Supervisor	Project 1	Manager	Project 1	4/15/02
Redeploy	6	Supervisor	Project 1	Supervisor	Project 2	4/15/02
Promote	2	Staff	Project 1	Supervisor	Project 1	4/15/02
Promote	3	Staff	Project 2	Supervisor	Project 1	4/15/02
Transfer	9	Staff	Project 2	Staff	Project 3	4/15/02
Lay off	6	Staff	Project 2			12/31/02

- Changes in relocation policies or practices to support redeployment
- Changes in staff or resources in the recruiting infrastructure
- Identifying new sources of talent and proactively finding sources of skills that were not previously needed
- Developing or improving relationships with outside suppliers of talent

Define Accountabilities and Time Frame

Define who is responsible for implementing or completing each staffing action that you define. Determine when each action needs to be completed (in most cases, the time frame will be defined in terms of the planning period of your model).

Define Support Activities and Infrastructure

Once your plans are completed, review the volume of required staffing actions and define the support and infrastructure that will be needed to implement those plans. Make sure that you have the number of recruiters that you need in order to source, contact, and evaluate a sufficient number of qualified candidates. Ensure that your training department has the staff and resources required to provide the development needed to support accelerated promotions and redeployment.

Repeat

All of the components of Step 4 must be completed for each period of your analysis. For example, if you are developing a three-year plan, these steps must be completed for each of those three years. Once you have defined the appropriate staffing plans and actions for period 1, enter that information into your model and calculate a new set of staffing gaps and surpluses for period 2. Define the staffing plans and actions that best address the staffing gaps and surpluses that remain. Remember to keep your plans and actions consistent with the staffing strategies that you developed. Document the plans, actions, accountabilities, time frame, supporting activities, and infrastructure, just as you did for period 1. Then repeat this process for all remaining planning periods.

Review Plans and Progress

Once plans have been prepared for all periods, they must of course be implemented if the gaps and surpluses are to be reduced as expected. Carefully track your plans to ensure that the required staffing actions are actually taking place and that anticipated gaps and surpluses are being addressed. Follow up as quickly as possible on actions that do not occur. Similarly, identify and amend those actions that have not had their desired effect (e.g., specific recruiting plans that have been implemented, but that have not attracted and retained key talent).

CHAPTER 5

Defining Required Staffing Levels

Defining staffing requirements is often the most difficult and time-consuming part of the strategic staffing process. There are many techniques that can be used to estimate or project the numbers and types of staff that will be needed to support business plans and strategies. Some are quantitative and at least somewhat objective (especially those that focus on staffing levels); others are primarily qualitative (including most of those that address required capabilities) and rely primarily on the subjective judgments of managers. This chapter describes several of the more common techniques and provides an example of each (including the solution).

Remember that when you are trying to estimate staffing requirements, you are not trying to predict the future with certainty. You are simply trying to define the staffing levels (and capabilities) that will probably be needed to implement your company's business strategies and plans. If you know what all of the staffing requirements are, define them specifically and create staffing plans accordingly. If you are certain about some portion of those requirements, create specific plans for the portion you are sure of and contingency or "what if" plans for the remainder.

Finally, when it comes to estimating requirements, do the best job you can with the data that are available. Don't try to find, or wait to get, full, complete data on staffing requirements—they probably don't exist. Instead, make full use of the data that you do have, even if they address only part of an issue. It's far better to completely address part of an issue than to do nothing at all. Specific techniques for defining staffing needs when plans are uncertain are discussed in Chapter 6.

Regression

Traditionally, statistical techniques, including regression analysis, have been used to define required staffing levels. With these techniques, statistical analyses are usually conducted to define the historical relationships between staffing levels and other variables (e.g., developing an equation that relates actual sales volume achieved to the number of sales staff employed). The use of regression requires historical data on both the independent variable(s) (e.g., sales, number of products produced, number of customers served) and the dependent variable (usually staffing levels or full-time equivalents. There are several types of regression analysis, including:

- **Simple, or single.** This technique defines a straight-line relationship between one independent variable and one dependent variable (e.g., relating sales to the number of sales staff).
- **Multiple.** This technique defines a straight-line relationship among two or more independent variables and the dependent variable (e.g., relating both total sales and the number of accounts served to the number of sales staff).
- **Curvilinear.** This technique defines nonlinear relationships between independent and dependent variables. Because of its complexity, it is less commonly used (and won't be discussed here).

To develop a single regression model, create a table that captures actual historical data. Each row of the table should include the value of the independent variable (e.g., actual total sales) at a particular point in time and the value of the corresponding dependent variable (e.g., the number of staff actually on board and supporting that work) at that same point in time. An eight-quarter model would thus include eight rows or data points. Here is what a simple one might look like:

Quarter	Total Sales ($000)	Number of Sales Staff
1Q 2000	2,000	5
2Q 2000	2,125	5
3Q 2000	2,403	6
4Q 2000	2,599	6
1Q 2001	2,680	6
2Q 2001	2,598	7
3Q 2001	2,821	7
4Q 2001	3,011	8

Next, enter these data into a program that includes a regression routine. Both Excel™ and Lotus™ include such routines, and virtually all statistical packages include a regression capability as well. Many business-oriented calculators also include simple regression capability.

The output of the analysis is an equation that describes the best fit between your independent and dependent variables. In the case of single regression, the equation is of the form:

$$y = ax + b$$

where y is the dependent variable (e.g., staffing levels), and x is the independent variable (e.g., sales), and a and b are values determined by a regression analysis. A regression analysis of the simple eight-quarter model (above) produces this equation:

$$\text{Number of Sales Staff} = 0.0027896 \times \text{Sales (in thousands)} + 0.8067036$$

To use this equation to forecast staffing levels, you simply obtain projections for the independent variables you have used (e.g., get projected sales from sales forecasts), enter these in the equation you have created, and calculate the required staffing level. In this simple example, if expected sales for the coming quarter were projected to be $3,000,000, then the expected number of sales staff needed to support that level of activity would be 7.56 (i.e., $0.0027896 \times 3{,}000 - 0.8067036$).

Multiple regression is similar, but it includes more than one independent variable. If there are two independent variables, the regression equation is of the form:

$$s = ax + by + z$$

where s is the dependent variable (e.g., staffing levels), x and y are the independent variables (e.g., total sales and number of accounts), and a, b, and z are values determined by the regression analysis. Again, Excel™ or Lotus™ can be used to produce multiple regression analyses, and most statistical packages include multiple regression routines as well. To develop a multiple regression model, create a table that captures actual historical data. Each row of the table should include the value of each independent variable (e.g., actual total sales and actual number of accounts) at a particular point in time and the value of the corresponding dependent variable (e.g., the number of staff actually on board and supporting that work) at that same point in time. A twelve-quarter model would thus include twelve rows. To use a multiple regression equation to forecast staffing levels, simply obtain projections for the independent variables you have used, enter these in the equation you have created, and calculate the staffing that will be needed.

Suppose, for example, that your equation was in this form:

$$\text{Number of Sales Staff} = [0.100 \times \text{Sales (in millions)}] + (0.01 \times \text{Number of Accounts}) + 2$$

In this example, if expected sales were $100 million and the number of accounts was 200, then the expected number of sales staff needed to support that level of activity would be fourteen:

$$\text{Number of Sales Staff} = (0.100 \times 100) + (0.01 \times 200) + 2$$
$$= 14$$

All regression techniques work best in situations in which "the past is prologue"—that is, those situations in which the expected work and conditions in the future resemble those of the recent past. If you think the future will differ significantly from the past, don't use this approach. A second caution is also in order: Technically speaking, regression relationships (and thus regression models) are valid only within the range of the data that were used to construct the model in the first place. In our examples, the regression equations should be used to forecast required staffing levels only if the sales projections fall within the range of sales that has actually been observed in the past. For example, suppose you built a regression model that related actual sales for a quarter to the number of sales staff that supported that volume. If the lowest level of quarterly sales actually observed was $20 million and the highest was $40 million, the model would be valid only for this particular range of quarterly sales. It should not be used to forecast the number of staff that would be needed to support anticipated sales of $50 million (or $10 million, for that matter).

Regression is best applied where there are direct relationships between the amount of work that is done and the number of staff doing that work. Further, you must be able to define work or output in quantifiable terms. The technique should also be applied primarily to job categories that have relatively large numbers of staff that are doing substantially similar work.

There is another case in which regression works quite well. Instead of building a historical database for a given unit, you can use the process to analyze staffing across units at a given point in time. Suppose that your organization has branch offices of various sizes that are handling different workloads. Regression can be used to define the relationship between staffing and workload across branches or locations. Once the regression equation has been developed, it can be used to define the "ideal" staffing level for any given workload for any branch. Figures 5-1 and 5-2 show how this might work. Figure 5-1 defines the problem; Figure 5-2 provides the solution.

Figure 5-1. Regression

The Packer Insurance Company would like to determine the number of additional underwriters that will be needed to support the acquisition of a "book of business" that is being spun off by a competitor. Packer has determined that the number of underwriters needed is most dependent on the mix of auto, home, and life polices. Over the last ten quarters, the following data have been reported:

Quarter	Number of Auto Policies	Number of Home Policies	Number of Life Policies	Number of Underwriters
1	2,123	1,722	991	45
2	2,241	1,821	1,003	47
3	2,302	1,901	1,098	52
4	2,605	2,011	1,187	53
5	2,771	2,198	1,251	55
6	2,803	2,347	1,376	57
7	3,009	2,290	1,434	60
8	3,107	2,401	1,563	63
9	3,229	2,551	1,479	70
10	3,398	2,612	1,501	71

The new book of business is expected to include 2,200 auto polices, 1,851 home policies, and 1,434 life policies. How many underwriters will be needed?

Figure 5-2. Solution to Regression Problem

First, we need to determine the equation that defines the relationship between the number of underwriters and the various types of business. Because there are three different types of policies to be considered, we will need to use multiple regression. Using any available statistical package, we determine the regression equation for these data. That equation turns out to be:

$$\begin{aligned}\text{Number of Underwriters} &= (0.01504)(\text{Number of Auto Policies}) \\ &+ (0.01344)(\text{Number of Home Policies}) \\ &- (0.01042)(\text{Number of Life Policies}) \\ &- 0.1642\end{aligned}$$

To obtain an estimate of the number of underwriters needed to support the given book of business, we need to insert into this equation the number of each type of policy that is to be supported (i.e., 2,200 auto policies, 1,851 home policies, and 1,434 life policies, as stated at the end of Figure 5-1). Entering our data, the equation becomes:

$$\begin{aligned}\text{Number of Underwriters} &= (0.01504)(2{,}200) \\ &+ (0.01344)(1{,}851) \\ &- (0.01042)(1{,}434) \\ &- 0.1642 \\ &= 42.86 \text{ Underwriters}\end{aligned}$$

Thus, 42.86 underwriters (if full-time equivalents) or 43 underwriters (if whole bodies) would be needed to support Packer's anticipated book of business.

Staffing Ratios

It is often possible to define simple, specific numerical relationships between work volumes or output and the number of staff required to do that work or produce that output. Usually, these relationships are expressed as a ratio of volume or output per person (e.g., 270 policies per underwriter or 10,000 barrels of oil refined per petroleum engineer). Not surprisingly, ratios that directly relate work to required staffing levels are called *direct ratios*. Once the ratio has been defined, it can be applied to the projected output or workload to define the number of staff that would be needed to support that effort. For example, if each underwriter can handle 270 policies in a month, and 2,700 policies are expected to be in force in a given month, then 10 underwriters would be needed (i.e., 2,700 policies divided by 270 policies per underwriter). Usually, it will be necessary to define a separate, distinct staffing ratio for each job category in your model (at least those to which staffing ratios will be applied).

There are also cases in which the required staffing in one area relates not to the work being done, but to the number of workers in another area. These ratios are called *indirect ratios*. Span of control is an example of an indirect ratio. Span relates the required number of supervisors not to the work being done but to the number of staff being supervised (e.g., 1 supervisor per 10 staff). To define indirect ratios, first apply the appropriate direct staffing ratios to determine the number of staff of the first type that are required (e.g., 1,000 engineers are needed). Next, apply the indirect ratio (e.g., 1 supervisor per 10 engineers) to determine the required number of staff of the second type (e.g., 1,000 divided by 10 equals 100 supervisors).

When using this technique, you must first determine what is actually driving staffing in each job category. Different jobs will have different drivers. Here is an approach that you can use to define staffing drivers:

- Make a table that has two columns. In the first column, simply list the job categories or titles for which staffing ratios are to be determined. Give each job category a separate row.

- Analyze each job category separately, on a row-by-row basis. For each job, identify all the inputs, work activities, and outputs that may drive staffing levels. Document these possible drivers in the second column. List as many as you can think of that may have a significant impact on staffing.
- Review the list of drivers for each job and identify those for which information is available. Cross off your list any drivers for which data are not available or are too difficult to gather and maintain on an ongoing basis.
- Develop staffing ratios for those drivers that remain on your list. Start by gathering data for each driver at a particular point in time. Then, for each job category, determine the number of staff that were employed in that job category at that same point in time. Calculate an initial ratio by dividing the value of the driver by the number of staff. Finally, use future data or management judgment to modify this ratio (if necessary) so that it can be applied on a looking forward basis (e.g., raise the ratio of driver to staff to account for productivity increases). You may want to talk with line managers and supervisors in each area to fine-tune your estimates.

Figure 5-3 shows examples of possible staffing relationships that were proposed in a manufacturing environment.

Each of the possibilities included in Figure 5-3 (along with some others) was considered. After some detailed analysis, the best relationship was identified and a specific staffing ratio was determined for each job category. In a few cases, required staffing levels were a function of two staffing ratios. For example, with production workers, it was necessary to develop one ratio linking staffing to the number of production runs and a second ratio linking staffing to the number of production slots, and then summing the results. Data for the drivers came primarily from production plans and schedules; additional information came from other planning systems and the company's human resource information system.

The staffing ratio technique works best where specific relation-

Figure 5-3. Possible Staffing Ratios

Job Category	Possible Staffing Drivers
Production workers	Number of production runs by type Number of slots
Facilities workers	Number of work orders Number of projects Number of critical systems Number of noncritical systems Number of operating production lines Number of shut down production lines Number of shutdowns Number of changeovers
Equipment cleaning crews	Number of operating production lines Number of shut down production lines Number of changeovers
Project managers	Number of projects by type and complexity Project duration
Other management	Number of staff Number of shifts Number of work centers
Administrative	Number of staff Number of managers Number of work centers

ships exist (or can be inferred or determined) between staffing and workload (e.g., in sales, manufacturing, production, and customer service). Ratios can be based on history (what the ratios have been in the past), current practice (what they are now), or desired future performance (future target ratios that reflect needed increases in productivity).

Here is a simple example of how staffing ratios are applied: An insurance company needed to forecast the number of claims adjusters, support staff, and supervisors that would be needed to support its workload of claims. The company had a performance or productivity target of 200 claims per adjuster per month. It used an indirect ratio to determine the required number of support staff (i.e., 1 support staff per 5 claims adjusters). The desired span of control was 1 supervisor per 6 staff (of all types). The company expected that there would be 2,000 claims in the last month of the fourth quarter. Applying staffing ratios, we would estimate required staffing as follows:

- **Adjusters.** This involves a direct ratio. Divide the expected value of the driver at the desired point in the future (i.e., 2,000 claims) by the ratio (i.e., 200 claims/adjuster) to determine the required number of adjusters (2,000/200 = 10 adjusters).
- **Support staff.** This involves an indirect ratio. Divide the required number of adjusters (i.e., 10) by the indirect ratio (1 support staff per 5 adjusters) to determine the required number of support staff (10/5 = 2 support staff).
- **Supervisors.** Calculate total staffing (i.e., 10 adjusters plus 2 support staff = 12 total staff) and divide this by the desired span of control (1 supervisor per 6 staff) to define the required number of supervisors (12/6 = 2 supervisors).

This technique is particularly appropriate for determining staffing levels in call centers. Define the overall operational parameters for the centers (e.g., the hours that the center will be open), key volume parameters for the center (such as number of calls expected and average length of call), and quality indicators (e.g., answer on x rings, keep caller on hold for no more than y seconds). Next, define the relationships among these parameters. Keep developing and linking these relationships until you determine the number of staff that will be needed to meet your standards. Here is a simple example.

Suppose that your call center will be open twenty-four hours per day and that you expect that on average the center will field 4,800 calls per day. That means that on average you can expect 200 calls per hour (this is just an example, of course; it is unlikely that in reality calls will be spread evenly over the whole twenty-four-hour period). If each call lasts 10 minutes, then you will need 2,000 staff minutes per hour (i.e., 200 calls times 10 minutes per call) to handle that volume of calls. Given that each customer service representative works 50 minutes per hour (factoring in break time), you will need 40 staff on duty each hour (i.e., 2,000 staff minutes divided by 50 minutes per staff member). This calculation assumes that all customer service reps are busy all the time and that call volume perfectly matches staffing patterns. Since this is unlikely, you will probably need to adjust staffing levels upward, based on the quality standards that you set (e.g., more staff will be needed if callers are to be kept on hold for no more than five minutes than will be needed if the standard is ten minutes).

I have both led and participated in many strategic staffing projects over the years. Quite possibly, staffing ratios is the technique that has proved to be most valuable when defining required staffing levels. It is direct and simple, yet not simplistic. The technique is easy to use, understand, and explain to others. It is flexible and can easily be tailored to reflect the specific needs of individual jobs or organization units. When appropriate, it can be based on historical data, but it can also easily reflect "what needs to be" rather than "what has been." While it can't be used in all cases, it is especially useful in those cases where it can be applied.

A more detailed example of staffing ratios can be seen in Figures 5-4 and 5-5. Figure 5-4 gives the facts of the problem, and Figure 5-5 provides the solution.

Figure 5-4. Staffing Ratios

To increase revenues and improve service to its members, Blair Healthcare (formerly known as Blair General Hospital) is considering opening a second full-service facility in the suburbs, twenty-five miles from its present urban location. By opening this facility, Blair expects to attract new members as well as to better serve existing members who are moving out of the city. Currently, Blair has 50,000 members.

The Medical Economics group expects that this move will increase membership in Blair Healthcare significantly. In fact, the group expects that Blair will add as many as 30,000 new members in the first year and an additional 20,000 in the second.

Based upon an analysis of historical and desired future staffing levels, Blair developed the following staffing ratios:

Job Category	Ratio
Family practice physicians	1:2,000 members
Cardiologists	1:15,000 members
Psychologists	1:8,000 members
Physical therapists	1:10,000 members
RNs	(# of physicians) × (0.8) × (0.5)
LPNs	(# of physicians) × (0.8)
Lab staff	1:25,000 members
Appointment clerks	(# of family practice physicians) × (0.6) + (# of specialty physicians) × (0.4)

James Kildare, the CEO, recently stated that 40,000 new members must be added next year if revenue projections are to be met. Consequently, the marketing targets have been set at this level, and programs are under way to try to attract these new members.

Define the required staffing levels for each of the above job categories for the coming year.

Figure 5-5. Solution to Staffing Ratios Problem

First, we need to define the scenario we are analyzing. There are two possibilities:

- We can determine the staffing needed to support the projections of the Medical Economics group (i.e., 50,000 current members plus the increase of 30,000 members that is expected, for a total of 80,000 members).
- We can determine the staffing needed to meet the targets the CEO set in order to meet revenue projections (i.e., 50,000 current members plus an increase of 40,000 members, for a total of 90,000 members).

If we know which one of these two scenarios is actually going to be implemented (or is more likely), we will probably define only the staffing requirements for that scenario. In some cases, however, it may make sense to define the staffing requirements for each scenario. By defining each, we will be able to:

- Analyze the difference in staffing requirements between the two (e.g., determine whether one is more effective or less expensive than the other).
- Define the lower of the two and create:

  Foundation staffing plans that define what should be done to obtain and deploy the minimum number of staff

  Contingency staffing plans, defining what could be done to obtain and deploy the additional staff needed to support the more aggressive strategy

The following solution assumes that total membership will be 80,000. The process will simply be repeated, using 90,000 members in place of 80,000, if the staffing requirements of the second scenario are needed.

Now we can define the staffing needed to support this number of members. The solution requires a combination of direct and indirect staffing ratios:

- For all direct ratios (e.g., the number of family practice physicians), simply divide 80,000 by the appropriate ratio.

- For all indirect ratios (e.g., the number of LPNs), first define the number of each type of physician that will be needed (using a direct ratio), then calculate the total number of physicians required (by adding up the results for each type) and apply the appropriate ratio.

Our solution would look like this:

Category	Required Number of Staff
Family practice physicians	80,000/2,000 = 40
Cardiologists	80,000/15,000 = 5.33
Psychologists	80,000/8,000 = 10
Physical therapists	80,000/10,000 = 8
RNs	(40 + 5.33) × (0.8) × (0.5) = 18.13
LPNs	(40 + 5.33) × (0.8) = 36.26
Lab staff	80,000/25,000 = 3.2
Appointment clerks	(40 × 0.6) + (5.33 × 0.4) = 26.13

Project-Based Staffing

Sometimes we need to know the total number of staff of a particular type that will be needed (e.g., a particular category of engineers), but the information that is available defines required staffing on a project-by-project basis (the number of engineers that are needed for a given engagement). Often this staffing information is defined in project proposals or plans. Complicating the issue further is the fact that the projects start and finish at different times.

The project-based staffing technique simply aggregates the required staffing for each job group for each project, at a particular point in time, across all projects to determine overall staffing requirements. There are two approaches, the zero-based approach and the incremental approach.

Regardless of which of these approaches is used to define staffing changes, the basis of this technique is to simply determine the number of staff of each type needed to support each project and aggregate those estimates across all projects to determine the total number of staff needed.

The Zero-Based Approach

This approach is used when project plans typically define the total number of staff of each type that are required at various points in time, independent of how many such staff are currently working on that job (e.g., ten apprentice-level engineers will be needed on a particular project at the beginning of the second quarter). To use this technique, take these steps:

- Identify the points in time for which you are defining staffing requirements.
- Determine which projects will be underway at each point.
- Define the staffing required for each project at each point in time.
- Sum the requirements for a given point in time across all projects to determine total requirements.

This approach works best when projects are starting from scratch and when project managers have a good understanding of the staffing that will be required. Figures 5-6 and 5-7 provide an example of this approach.

Figure 5-6. Project-Based Staffing: Zero-Based

Nelson Motorsports is currently staffed effectively; that is, the current staffing will allow the firm to complete all the assignments it has "in house" for the remainder of the year (i.e., Projects 1, 2, and 3). The current headcount is as follows:

	Team A	Team B
Engineering managers	15	14
Engineers	30	40
Apprentices	30	25

Next year, the following work plan is anticipated:

- Project 1 will continue and will require

  5 engineering managers on Team A and 3 on Team B
  12 engineers on Team A and 8 on Team B
  15 apprentices on Team A and 10 on Team B

- Projects 2 and 3 will be completed in the current year and will require no staff.

- Project 4 is a new project that will require

  4 engineering managers on Team A and 4 on Team B
  10 engineers on Team A and 9 on Team B
  8 apprentices on Team A and 11 on Team B

- Project 5 is also a new project and will require

  6 engineering managers on Team A and 2 on Team B
  9 engineers on Team A and 10 on Team B
  9 apprentices on Team A and 8 on Team B

What will be the staffing demand for Nelson Motorsports in the coming year?

Figure 5-7. Solution to Zero-Based Staffing Problem

In this example, we need to identify the staffing requirements for each project in each of the six categories (i.e., the three job categories for each of the two teams). The data that we need are provided in the case. In a "real-life" situation, this staffing information would probably be extracted from a project plan or unit business plan. It might also be provided by a manager through some kind of structured interview. Note that since this is a zero-based technique, the starting headcounts that are provided are not relevant and should be ignored.

For each of the six categories, we simply need to define the needs for each project and sum the requirements across all projects.

Category	Team A		Team B	
Engineering managers	Project 1:	5	Project 1:	3
	Project 2:	0	Project 2:	0
	Project 3:	0	Project 3:	0
	Project 4:	4	Project 4:	4
	Project 5:	6	Project 5:	2
	Total	**15**	**Total**	**9**
Engineers	Project 1:	12	Project 1:	8
	Project 2:	0	Project 2:	0
	Project 3:	0	Project 3:	0
	Project 4:	10	Project 4:	9
	Project 5:	9	Project 5:	10
	Total	**31**	**Total**	**27**
Apprentices	Project 1:	15	Project 1:	10
	Project 2:	0	Project 2:	0
	Project 3:	0	Project 3:	0
	Project 4:	8	Project 4:	11
	Project 5:	9	Project 5:	8
	Total	**32**	**Total**	**29**

The Incremental Approach

With this approach, staffing requirements are defined in terms of increments above or below current staffing (e.g., four more apprentice-level engineers will be needed, over and above the six that are already working on that project). The incremental method is especially helpful where no information exists regarding required staffing.

As with the zero-based approach, you will need to take these steps:

- Identify the points in time for which you are defining staffing requirements.
- Determine which projects will be underway at each point.
- Define how many more (or fewer) staff will be needed in each category than are currently available.
- Define the staffing required for each project at each point in time, adjusting staffing levels by the increments defined above.
- Sum the requirements for a given point in time across all projects to determine total requirements.

One advantage of this technique is that it can be used even if the staffing information you require is not readily available (e.g., specific project plans either do not exist or do not define staffing requirements explicitly). When you use this method, follow a structured interview format (you may find the interview guide in Chapter 12 helpful here). Define current staffing levels and capabilities before you meet with each manager. When you meet with a manager, review this information first. Next, discuss how the business is expected to change during the planning period (e.g., expansion, contraction, implementation of new technology, introduction of new products or services). As you discuss these changes, work with the manager to define how current staffing levels will be affected (e.g., there will be a need for more staff, fewer staff, or staff with different capabilities). Figures 5-8 and 5-9 provide an example of this technique.

Figure 5-8. Project-Based Staffing: Incremental

The current headcount for Nelson Motorsports is as follows:

	Team A	Team B
Engineering managers	15	14
Engineers	30	40
Apprentices	30	25

Based on interviews with senior managers, the following changes are expected in Team A:

- GT Motorsports will continue to run Ford engines and will need additional staff, including 1 engineering manager, 3 engineers, and 4 apprentices.
- Drew Racing will begin to use Ford's Zetec engine. To support the team, Nelson Motorsports will add 2 engineering managers, 4 engineers, and 6 apprentices
- The Schumacher team has decided to use Ferrari engines, thus freeing up 3 engineering managers, 10 engineers, and 15 apprentices.

The following changes are expected in Team B:

- Project A will expand and will require additional staff of 1 engineering manager, 4 engineers, and 2 apprentices.
- Project B has proved unrealistic and will be dropped, resulting in a reduction of 2 engineering managers, 5 engineers, and 3 apprentices.
- Project C has been reengineered; it will require 1 additional engineering manager but 2 fewer engineers and 3 fewer apprentices.

Calculate all staffing requirements for the coming season.

Figure 5-9. Solution to Incremental Staffing Problem

Because this technique is incremental (rather than zero-based), the starting populations in each category are relevant—in fact, they are the foundation of our calculations.

First, define current staffing levels for each category. Next, identify the changes that will occur in each category (based on the information provided in the case) and sum the totals across projects.

Here is the solution:

Category	Team A		Team B	
Engineering managers	Initial headcount:	15	Initial headcount:	14
	GT Motorsports:	+1	Project A:	+1
	Drew:	+2	Project B:	−2
	Schumacher:	−3	Project C:	+1
	Total	**15**	**Total**	**14**
Engineers	Initial headcount:	30	Initial headcount:	40
	GT Motorsports:	+3	Project A:	+4
	Drew:	+4	Project B:	−5
	Schumacher:	−10	Project C:	−2
	Total	**27**	**Total**	**37**
Apprentices	Initial headcount:	30	Initial headcount:	25
	GT Motorsports:	+4	Project A:	+2
	Drew:	+6	Project B:	−3
	Schumacher:	−15	Project C:	−3
	Total	**25**	**Total**	**21**

Staffing Profiles

In some cases, a series of "profiles," or templates, can be developed to estimate the staffing that a unit (or project) will require given certain combinations of parameters (such as project size and type). Each such profile will include the same rows and columns that you included in your staffing model. A different profile is created for each unique combination of parameters. Taken together, these different profiles form a set or "reference library" that can be used to define the staffing needed to support business plans. Once the profiles are developed, you would take these steps:

- Review business plans and strategies to identify the projects that will be underway.
- For each project described in the plans, identify the actual values for the key parameters that you have used to differentiate profiles (e.g., project size and type).
- For each project, select from your library of profiles the one that corresponds to each of the projects described in the plans.

Similar projects (e.g., those of a similar size and type) might use the same profile.

- Sum the staffing across all projects to determine the required staffing for each job category.

Here is a simple example that describes how profiles can be used to define the required staffing for a bank. First, the critical parameters that drive the bank's staffing are identified. For this example, let's assume that the bank has determined that branch staffing for tellers and loan officers depends primarily on branch size (i.e., small, medium, or large, expressed in terms of assets) and type of lending (i.e., primarily retail or primarily commercial). Next, the institution will develop six staffing profiles, one for each unique combination of size and type (small/retail, medium/retail, large/commercial, etc.). Each profile will specify the number of tellers and loan officers needed in that environment (e.g., a small/retail branch requires two officers and three tellers, a large/commercial branch requires six officers and six tellers, etc.). The profiles might look like the matrixes in Figure 5-10.

Figure 5-10.

Retail Branch Staffing

Job Category	Small Branch	Medium Branch	Large Branch
Officers	2	2	3
Tellers	3	4	5

Commercial Branch Staffing

Job Category	Small Branch	Medium Branch	Large Branch
Officers	3	4	6
Tellers	4	5	6

The institution will now review its business plans to see how many branches of each combination of size and type it expects to operate in the coming year (e.g., five small/retail, eight large/commercial, etc.). To determine the required staffing, the institution will:

- Define the total number of branches of each size and type that will be operated.
- Select the profile that corresponds to each combination of size and type (e.g., in this example, the profile for small/retail shows that two officers and three tellers are needed).
- Multiply the staffing requirements defined in each profile by the number of branches of that size and type to be operated.
- Calculate the total needs for officers and tellers by adding up the needs for each category across all types and sizes of branch.

Suppose there were to be four branches in a region in the coming year:

- One small/retail
- One large/retail
- Two medium/commercial

To calculate the staffing needs across all four branches, select the three appropriate profiles, determine the staff required from each, and sum the results:

- Officers: 2 + 3 + 2(4) = 13 staff
- Tellers: 3 + 5 + 2(5) = 18 staff

Staffing profiles are particularly applicable to retail establishments (e.g., where staffing is determined for each of three standard store sizes/"footprints") and to engineering/construction projects (e.g., where projects of a given size, complexity, and type might typically require a certain number of project managers and technical staff).

The example in Figures 5-11 and 5-12 uses profiles generated for an oil company, where the number of geologists and engineers needed depends on a project's type (i.e., offshore or onshore), size, and stage (i.e., initial exploration versus testing for commercial viability). Based on past performance and desired future effectiveness,

(text continues on p. 104)

Figure 5-11. Staffing Profiles.

The McLaughlin Oil Company is involved in oil exploration and production. The company is preparing a staffing strategy and needs to determine the number of geologists and engineers that will be required. It has been determined that staffing of exploration projects depends on:

- The size of each project (i.e., the potential number of barrels to be found)
- The stage of each project (i.e., the degree to which each phase has been completed)
- The type of the project (i.e., whether the project is onshore or offshore)

McLaughlin has created a series of staffing profiles that define the required staffing levels for geologists and engineers for various combinations of these variables. These profilcs are shown on the following pages. Business plans call for the following activity:

Project	Size	Stage	Type
Exploration Project 1	350	1	
Exploration Project 2	190	2	
Exploration Project 3	460	3	
Production Project 1	270	3	Onshore
Production Project 2	150	2	Offshore
Production Project 3	360	1	Onshore
Production Project 4	420	2	Offshore

Your analysis should assume the following structure:

	Geology	Engineering
Manager		
Technician		
Trainee		

The profiles that follow also use this format. What is McLaughlin's total need for geologists and engineers, across all projects?

Figure 5-11. (Continued)

Exploration

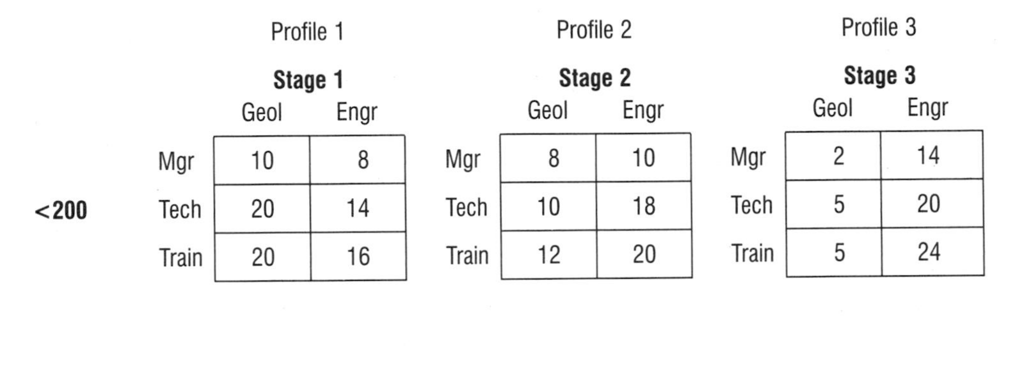

<200

Profile 1 — **Stage 1**

	Geol	Engr
Mgr	10	8
Tech	20	14
Train	20	16

Profile 2 — **Stage 2**

	Geol	Engr
Mgr	8	10
Tech	10	18
Train	12	20

Profile 3 — **Stage 3**

	Geol	Engr
Mgr	2	14
Tech	5	20
Train	5	24

200 to 400

Profile 4 — **Stage 1**

	Geol	Engr
Mgr	10	9
Tech	22	16
Train	24	19

Profile 5 — **Stage 2**

	Geol	Engr
Mgr	9	12
Tech	11	21
Train	13	25

Profile 6 — **Stage 3**

	Geol	Engr
Mgr	3	16
Tech	6	24
Train	6	30

>400

Profile 7 — **Stage 1**

	Geol	Engr
Mgr	12	10
Tech	24	17
Train	28	20

Profile 8 — **Stage 2**

	Geol	Engr
Mgr	9	13
Tech	13	22
Train	16	26

Profile 9 — **Stage 3**

	Geol	Engr
Mgr	3	18
Tech	7	26
Train	8	32

Onshore Production

<200

Profile 10 — **Stage 1**

	Geol	Engr
Mgr	8	10
Tech	14	20
Train	16	20

Profile 11 — **Stage 2**

	Geol	Engr
Mgr	10	8
Tech	18	10
Train	20	12

Profile 12 — **Stage 3**

	Geol	Engr
Mgr	14	2
Tech	20	5
Train	24	5

200 to 400

Profile 13 — **Stage 1**

	Geol	Engr
Mgr	9	12
Tech	16	22
Train	19	24

Profile 14 — **Stage 2**

	Geol	Engr
Mgr	12	9
Tech	21	11
Train	25	13

Profile 15 — **Stage 3**

	Geol	Engr
Mgr	16	3
Tech	24	6
Train	30	6

>400

Profile 16 — **Stage 1**

	Geol	Engr
Mgr	10	12
Tech	17	24
Train	20	28

Profile 17 — **Stage 2**

	Geol	Engr
Mgr	13	9
Tech	22	13
Train	26	16

Profile 18 — **Stage 3**

	Geol	Engr
Mgr	18	3
Tech	26	7
Train	32	8

Figure 5-11. (Continued)

Offshore Production

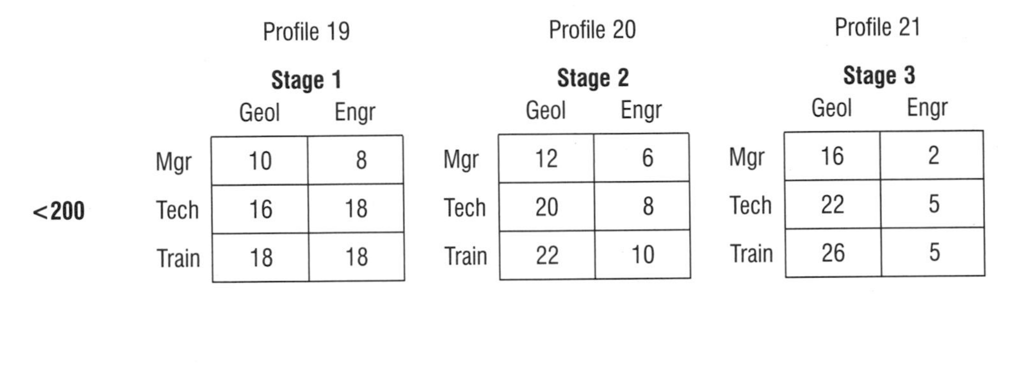

<200

Profile 19 — **Stage 1**

	Geol	Engr
Mgr	10	8
Tech	16	18
Train	18	18

Profile 20 — **Stage 2**

	Geol	Engr
Mgr	12	6
Tech	20	8
Train	22	10

Profile 21 — **Stage 3**

	Geol	Engr
Mgr	16	2
Tech	22	5
Train	26	5

200 to 400

Profile 22 — **Stage 1**

	Geol	Engr
Mgr	11	10
Tech	18	20
Train	21	22

Profile 23 — **Stage 2**

	Geol	Engr
Mgr	13	7
Tech	23	9
Train	27	11

Profile 24 — **Stage 3**

	Geol	Engr
Mgr	18	3
Tech	26	6
Train	32	6

>400

Profile 25 — **Stage 1**

	Geol	Engr
Mgr	12	10
Tech	19	22
Train	22	26

Profile 26 — **Stage 2**

	Geol	Engr
Mgr	15	7
Tech	24	11
Train	28	14

Profile 27 — **Stage 3**

	Geol	Engr
Mgr	20	3
Tech	28	7
Train	34	8

Figure 5-12. Solution to Staffing Profiles Problem

First, we need to find the staffing profile that corresponds to each of the seven projects to be completed (i.e., the proper combination of project type, size, and stage).

Exploration Project 1: Size = 200–400, Stage = 1 (Profile 4)
Exploration Project 2: Size = <200, Stage = 2 (Profile 2)
Exploration Project 3: Size = >400, Stage = 3 (Profile 9)
Production Project 1: Onshore, Size = 200–400, Stage = 3 (Profile 15)
Production Project 2: Offshore, Size = <200, Stage = 2 (Profile 20)
Production Project 3: Onshore, Size = 200–400, Stage = 1 (Profile 13)
Production Project 4: Offshore, Size = >400, Stage = 2 (Profile 26)

Next, add up the staffing requirements for the seven projects (three exploration and four production) in each of the six job categories:

Position	Geology		Engineering	
Manager	Exploration Project 1:	10	Exploration Project 1:	9
	Exploration Project 2:	8	Exploration Project 2:	10
	Exploration Project 3:	3	Exploration Project 3:	18
	Production Project 1:	16	Production Project 1:	3
	Production Project 2:	12	Production Project 2:	6
	Production Project 3:	9	Production Project 3:	12
	Production Project 4:	15	Production Project 4:	7
	Total:	**73**	**Total:**	**65**
Technician	Exploration Project 1:	22	Exploration Project 1:	16
	Exploration Project 2:	10	Exploration Project 2:	18
	Exploration Project 3:	7	Exploration Project 3:	26
	Production Project 1:	24	Production Project 1:	6
	Production Project 2:	20	Production Project 2:	8
	Production Project 3:	16	Production Project 3:	22
	Production Project 4:	24	Production Project 4:	11
	Total:	**123**	**Total:**	**107**
Trainee	Exploration Project 1:	24	Exploration Project 1:	19
	Exploration Project 2:	12	Exploration Project 2:	20
	Exploration Project 3:	8	Exploration Project 3:	32
	Production Project 1:	30	Production Project 1:	6
	Production Project 2:	22	Production Project 2:	10
	Production Project 3:	19	Production Project 3:	24
	Production Project 4:	28	Production Project 4:	14
	Total:	**143**	**Total:**	**125**

the company defined a series of profiles, one for each unique combination of type, size, and stage. In this example, there are twenty-seven unique combinations (and thus twenty-seven separate staffing profiles).

To use these profiles, the company defines the actual type, size, and stage for each project (or proposed project). Based on these, the company selects the staffing profile for each project that corresponds to that combination of parameters. This profile defines the staffing needed to support that project. The results can then be summed across projects to determine overall staffing requirements.

Case Study: Combining Approaches

As discussed earlier, it is often necessary to combine various approaches for defining demand in order to determine the staffing requirements in a given situation. Here is a simple example that combines several of the approaches for calculating demand that were just described.

A restaurant chain was analyzing its needs for management staffing. Each restaurant requires general managers, assistant managers, and management trainees. Because restaurant capacity and design are standardized, a management staffing profile can be created. Here are some critical assumptions:

- The restaurant is open for business from 11 A.M. to 10 P.M. Monday through Friday, 11 A.M. to 12 A.M. Saturday, and 11 A.M. to 9 P.M. Sunday.
- Prep work and cleanup require two hours before opening and another two hours after closing.
- There must be one general manager on site at all times.
- There must be one assistant manager on the floor and a second in the kitchen at all times for a restaurant that seats 200 people.
- On average, general managers and assistant managers each work fifty-three hours per week.
- Three management trainees can be accommodated in a restaurant of this size.

How many managers and trainees are needed to support ten restaurants?

The solution to this case requires both staffing ratios and staffing profiles. First, create the staffing profile for each restaurant. Calculate the total amount of time that the restaurant is open (including prep and cleanup time):

Monday–Friday:	15 hours/day
+ Saturday:	17 hours/day
+ Sunday:	14 hours/day
	106 hours/week

Given that there must be a general manager on duty at all times, the required number of general managers for each restaurant is 2 (106 hours/week divided by 53 hours/week/general manager). Because there must be one assistant manager in the kitchen and another on the floor at all times, there must be four assistant managers per restaurant (106 hours/week divided by 53 hours/week/assistant manager for the kitchen and an identical number for the floor). The number of management trainees is set according to restaurant capacity and is 3. Thus the standard management staffing profile for the restaurant would be:

Job Type	Number Required
General manager	2
Assistant manager	4
Management trainee	3

Given this profile, 10 new restaurants would require 20 additional general managers, 40 additional assistant managers, and 30 more management trainees.

Up until now, this restaurant chain has operated only inside upscale shopping malls. To build business and increase visibility, the chain is planning to build new, stand-alone facilities in mall parking lots. Because rents are much cheaper in the lots, the chain plans to double the seating capacity of these restaurants (to 400 diners). What will the staffing profile be for each new facility?

First, we need to determine the impact of increased capacity on staffing. Because the required number of general managers did not depend on restaurant size, the required number per restaurant remains the same. We also still need one assistant manager for the kitchen. The number of assistant managers on the floor will be different, however. If one assistant manager could handle 200 diners (e.g., visiting each table, each party, each visit), two will be needed to provide that same level of service to 400 diners (the new capacity of the larger restaurant). The number of management trainees will also change. If a restaurant that seats 200 can support three trainees, a facility that seats 400 can support six. Thus, the new staffing profile for the parking lot–type restaurant will be:

Job Type	Number Required
General manager	2
Assistant manager	6
Management trainee	6

How many assistant managers will now be needed to support ten new facilities? This is really a trick question. If all 10 facilities are of the large, parking lot type, then 60 will be needed (6 assistant managers per location times 10 locations). If all are small, inside-mall locations, then only 40 will be needed (4 assistant managers per location times 10 locations). If there will be 5 large restaurants and 5 small ones opened, then 50 will be needed (5 times 6 for the large plus 5 times 4 for the small).

Summary

The definition of staffing requirements is a critical component of the strategic staffing process. There are many ways in which staffing requirements (both capabilities and staffing levels) can be determined, several of which are described in this chapter. In many cases, you will need to mix and match approaches; rarely will a single approach be appropriate for all job categories in your model.

But what do you do if staffing requirements are not well defined? Chapter 6 describes how staffing requirements can be determined even where business plans are uncertain.

CHAPTER 6

Defining Staffing Requirements Where Plans Are Uncertain

Sometimes we need to create staffing strategies in situations for which we lack perfect, complete information regarding business strategies and plans. In some cases, business strategies may be unclear or may describe only strategic objectives. In other cases, business plans may describe several possible outcomes or approaches, but do not specifically define which ones will be implemented. Sometimes the business plans are clear, but information on the staffing levels and capabilities needed to implement those plans is sketchy at best.

If the missing data can be uncovered and documented within a realistic time frame by expending a reasonable amount of effort, by all means go get those data. But what do you do if that full set of data doesn't exist or is just too difficult to gather? The answer in these cases is not to try to get those missing data or (worse yet) to wait around until the data become available. Instead, you should forge ahead with your strategic staffing efforts and do the most you can with what you have. In virtually every case, you will find that you know more than you think you do about staffing requirements, and in most cases, there will be plenty of data that you can use to create some helpful staffing plans. Remember, a complete solution to part of a problem is better than no solution at all.

This chapter describes various approaches that can be used to develop staffing strategies and plans that maximize the value of the information that *is* available.

Alternatives to Perfect Data

Even when you don't have all the information you think you need in order to develop a staffing strategy, you probably have access to at least some good information. The objective here is to create staffing plans that are helpful and that maximize the value of the information that is available. Here are some specific examples of approaches you might take to create helpful staffing strategies, even if business plans seem unclear or incomplete.

Fully Solve Part of the Problem

Often, you won't have all the information for all the units or job categories in your plan, but you will have most of the data for some of the units. In these cases, create staffing strategies and plans for those units for which you have sufficient data. Don't be concerned that you are excluding parts of the organization. Don't do nothing for anyone just because you can't do everything for everyone.

Similarly, you may have all of the data for some of the jobs in your units. In these cases, create staffing plans for the jobs for which the data are available. Don't hold up work in those areas for which you do have data just because there are other areas for which you have insufficient data.

Here are some examples of how you might solve part, but not all, of a staffing problem. In most organizations, there are really two kinds of jobs: core jobs (i.e., foundation-type jobs that are probably needed regardless of the level of business volume or activity) and incremental jobs (those jobs that depend on business volume). Usually, quite a lot is known (or can easily be determined) about the core jobs, including the staffing levels and capabilities that will be required in the future. Because these jobs are usually more stable and are not volume-dependent, it is easier to forecast the number and types of individuals that will be needed to fill these jobs in the future. Thus, you can create specific staffing plans to ensure that the right talent is available for these critical positions. Even if no information is available for the incremental jobs, it is still better to create the strategies needed to fully address the core positions than to do nothing until information on the incremental jobs becomes available.

In other cases, you may have very specific business plans for some parts of your organization, but not for others. If this happens, you should create specific staffing plans for those units for which information is available. Don't do nothing just because full information is not available for all units. Suppose you are sure of 20 percent of what your organization is going to accomplish. Create complete staffing strategies for that 20 percent. Don't think in terms of the missing 80 percent; instead, think that you will be better off if you fully address the 20 percent than if you do nothing for the 100 percent.

Conduct Scenario Planning

Some organizations incorporate various scenarios into their business plans. Each scenario probably has different staffing implications. One approach to creating a staffing strategy would be to try to determine which scenario will actually occur and then define staffing plans for that scenario. Not only is this difficult to do, but there could be significant problems if you choose incorrectly and staff for one scenario, and instead another occurs. Instead, define the staffing requirements for each of the most likely scenarios and look for staffing requirements that are common to all (or at least most) of those scenarios.

Suppose that there are three possible scenarios for expansion of a business unit. In case 1 (perhaps the least optimistic scenario), forty new sales associates will be needed. In the second case (possibly your "most likely" scenario), fifty will be needed. The third case calls for "mega" growth; one hundred new sales associates will be required. Rather than choosing one of these scenarios and defining the staffing requirements only for that scenario, create and implement a strategy for attracting the minimum number of associates. No matter which scenario occurs, you are likely to need at least forty new sales associates, so create a staffing plan to obtain those forty sales associates. Create separate contingency plans for hiring any associates that are needed above this number (or create more specific plans if and when more specific data become available). Think through what you might do to hire ten more sales associates (i.e., if scenario 2 occurs) or sixty more sales associates (to support scenario 3). You probably won't have to go out and hire those people, but you will have a better understanding of what you will do if that need actually arises. While obtaining the minimum number of required staff will not solve all your problems, you will certainly be better off than if you have to scramble to hire the right number on short notice once the actual scenario is determined.

Scenario planning can also be helpful when no business strategies exist. In such a case, it may be possible for you to develop a small number of likely business scenarios on which your staffing strategies and plans can be based. Remember to validate your scenarios with line managers (and incorporate any changes that they think are necessary) before completing your staffing plans.

Here is an example of how scenario planning might be used to support staff planning. Two insurance companies were merging. Obviously, mergers can create a host of staffing issues, some more critical than others. One of the areas that was affected most significantly was claims administration. The company needed to create a staffing strategy that focused on the combined claims function. Prior to the merger, the claims functions of the two companies had been managed and staffed quite differently. One company was organized by (and staffing ratios were developed for) functions (e.g., verification and disbursement). The other was managed by (and staffing ratios were developed for) impairment category (e.g., long-term physical disabilities and psychological disabilities). A longer-term, succinct, focused staffing plan to integrate the two workforces was needed. Two separate scenarios were developed, one that assumed that the combined claims function would be managed by function and a second that assumed that the unit would be managed by impairment category. The staffing implications of both scenarios were defined and a staffing plan was created to meet the minimum needs that would arise regardless of the approach chosen.

Prepare "What If" Plans

Some plans are even less certain than the scenarios described above. With scenarios, specific options are defined; the uncertainty involves which scenario will actually occur. Some organizations have plans that are less well defined than scenarios. They may be debating among several general approaches or trying to better define alternatives. In these cases, the organization discusses potential business strategies and plans, but the implementation of these strategies and plans remains uncertain. Given the high level of uncertainty, it is not possible to select specific scenarios that may be implemented.

Even in these situations, strategic staffing is possible and can add value. True, it is not possible to select (and create staffing strategies and plans to support) just one business option. Neither does it make sense to staff up for each possibility so that all bets can be covered. However, despite the degree of uncertainty, some strategic staffing is possible.

It is usually possible to discuss, in this "what if" sense, the staffing implications of the various business plan alternatives (e.g., "If we were to implement that strategy, we would need 200 additional network administrators"). These "what if" discussions and analyses usually address such questions as:

- What skills would be required?
- How many people with those skills are out there?
- How many of these people could we attract?
- At what rate of pay?
- Where would we look?

In some cases, staffing trends or minimum staffing requirements emerge that are valid no matter which "what if" scenario is studied. In these cases, it may be possible to define some specific staffing plans that are consistent with the trends or that support the minimum standards.

In other cases, it may be appropriate to use the "what if" approach to define contingency plans. With this technique, it is possible to identify possible scenarios, define the staffing implications of each, and identify the staffing strategies and plans that best address staffing needs. The difference is that these plans are not meant to be implemented per se. Instead, their value is in allowing you to "prethink" what you would do to meet staffing requirements if any of those scenarios were to actually occur. Since you have already identified issues and defined plans in advance of need, you will be better able to react to one of these scenarios if it really does occur. Sometimes it is even possible to take some preliminary steps based on contingency plans, such as identifying and having preliminary discussions with agencies that might later be called upon to provide specific talent in a very short time frame.

Here is an example of how "what if" planning can work. A company had a large technical workforce with unique skills. The company estimated that most new hires needed eighteen months to two years to fully master their jobs. To account for this in its planning models, the organization defined a concept that it called "proficiency." Human resource staff adjusted its new hire data to reflect the learning curve of new employees. For example, a new hire was assumed to be only 50 percent productive in the first quarter on the job. Productivity was assumed to increase at a given rate until the individual was deemed fully proficient (e.g., after four full quarters on the job). This assumption had significant effects on required staffing levels. Conceptually, each time a fully proficient employee left the organization, that employee would have to be replaced by two new hires (since each was only 50 percent productive). To better understand the impact of these proficiency and productivity assumptions, the organization created a series of "what if" plans, each one reflecting a given set of proficiency assumptions (e.g., what if we can accelerate learning through targeted development and get people to be proficient in one year, not two? What impact would that have on required staffing levels?). Though no changes in staffing or training practices were made right away, this analysis gave the organization a better idea of the specific actions that would be required later on.

There is another version of "what if" planning that can also be quite helpful: sensitivity analysis. Organizations that use this technique try to define the impact that a known change in staffing drivers will have on required staffing. They then use the results of the analysis to help them choose from among the alternatives tested. The merging insurance companies used this technique when combining their claims functions. One claims group had a 40-hour workweek, the other a 37.5-hour workweek. The company used sensitivity analysis to define the losses in productivity that could be expected if all staff adopted the shorter workweek and the gains that could be expected if all staff worked a 40-hour week. The decision on which alternative to select was not based solely on this analysis (e.g., the impact on morale was also considered), but the information represented an important input to a critical management decision.

Creating Specific Plans in an Uncertain Environment: An Example

Here is an example of what one medical center did to create a staffing strategy for patient care staff in the face of great uncertainty. It was relatively easy for the center to calculate a staffing ratio that specified the number of patient care staff (e.g., registered nurses) required per patient in a given unit. That was not the problem. The problem was that the center had very little idea of how many patients could be expected in any given unit at any given time. While the number of patients in each unit was not random, it fluctuated greatly on a daily basis. The center had attempted to predict the number of patients in each unit on given days, but these efforts had proved fruitless. Consequently, staff planning seemed impossible, since there was no clear number of patients to which the known staffing ratio could be applied. Schematically, the situation in one unit looked like the graph in Figure 6-1.

This graph indicates that the number of patients fluctuated significantly over the course of a year, following no particular pattern or cycle. However, the medical center realized that no matter how random the number of patients seemed, there were at least three

Figure 6-1. Number of Patients Over Time

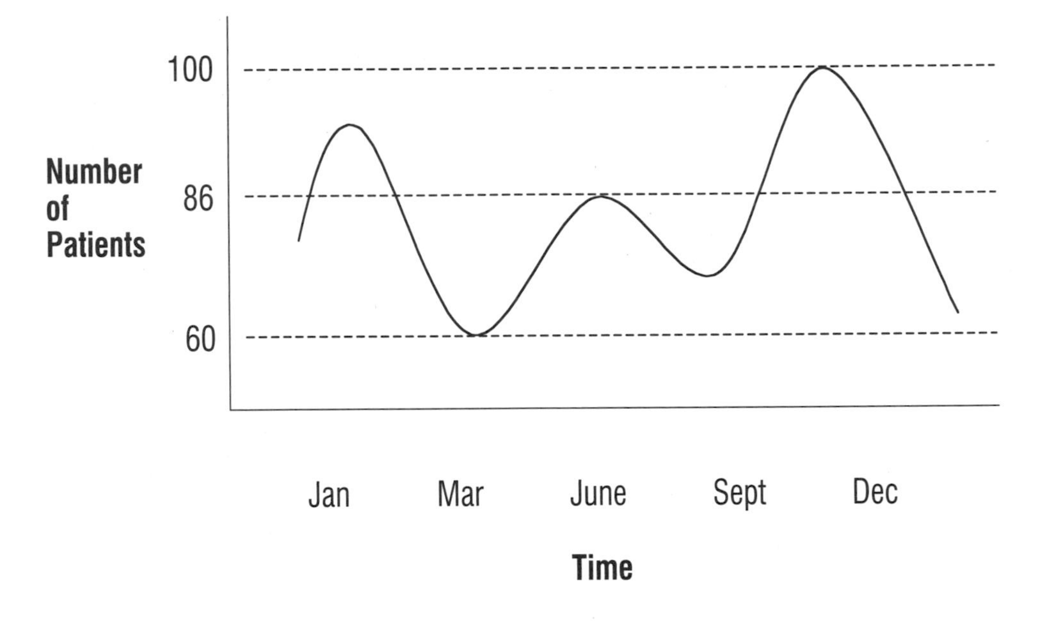

pieces of critical information that were known for sure. First, historically the number of patients in this unit had never been less than 60. Similarly, the number had never exceeded 100. Finally, the overall mode (i.e., the number of patients most often observed) was 86 patients. As stated previously, the medical center had already established specific staffing ratios for each patient care staff position. If we assume (for example) a 2:1 patient/nurse ratio, we can determine that the minimum number of full-time equivalents (FTEs) required for this unit is 30 (i.e., 60 patients/2 patients per nurse), the maximum is 50 (i.e., 100/2), and the mode is 43 (i.e., 86/2). What staffing level was appropriate?

One alternative was to calculate and staff to the maximum, but this would be inefficient, and the cost would be prohibitive. Another option would be to staff to an average number of patients, but this would mean that half the time the unit would be overstaffed (creating expense that could not be tolerated) and half the time the unit would be understaffed (with dire impact on patient care and satisfaction). A third option would be to staff to the minimum, but then what would be done on those days when there were more than a minimum number of patients?

The staffing strategy that the medical center actually devised had three parts. Each unit would be staffed with the hospital's full-time staff up to the minimum required number (in this case, a base staffing of 30 full-time staff). Whenever the number of patients exceeded the minimum but was less than the mode, the hospital's own part-time staff would be used. For the unit in the example, that meant that up to 13 FTE nurses would be required from the center's part-time pool, where 13 equals the difference in staff needed to support the mode (43) and the minimum (30). Any staffing above the mode would be obtained from an external registry. In this case, required staffing levels could range from 0 to 7 FTEs, where 7 equals the difference in staff needed to support the maximum (50) and the mode (43).

This approach allowed the hospital to create very specific staffing plans, even though there was great uncertainty regarding the number of patients that were expected on any given day. Because full-time staffing was based on a minimum that did not change, staffing plans for full-time staff could be developed completely, and in great detail. There were always thirty full-time staff required, no matter how many patients there were.

There was some uncertainty regarding the number of part-time staff needed, but this approach allowed the hospital to define the size of the part-time pool (i.e., none when patient count was at the minimum up to a maximum of thirteen FTEs when patient count was at the mode or above). In fact, the hospital realized further efficiencies (and reduced uncertainty) by creating common pools of part-time staff for units that had similar needs (e.g., one pool for medical-surgical units, another for the cardiac care unit and the intensive care unit, a third for the emergency department). Because it was unlikely that all the units served by a given pool would require minimum (or maximum) staff at the same time, the number of staff in the pool could be modulated. In effect, there would always be a need for some staff, and there would never be a need for maximum staffing in all units.

There was even more uncertainty regarding the external pool (i.e., half the time none would be needed; the rest of the time as many as seven FTEs might be needed), but this uncertainty was, in effect, absorbed by the external contractor. Because the hospital could provide the contractor with fairly specific parameters regarding its potential need (e.g., the maximum size of the pool, the skills required, and the turnaround time expected), the contractor knew what was expected and could price the contract accordingly.

In the end, the hospital was able to develop and implement a very specific staffing plan even though it had no idea how many patients to expect on any given day.

Reducing Uncertainty: A Second Example

A state agency assumed that it could not do any strategic staffing because it perceived that the services it provided were subject to the whim of the legislature and could change at any time. In fact, however, only a portion of the agency's services were in that category. Other services were well defined, and still others were at least predictable. In fact, staffing plans could be prepared for a large part of the agency.

The agency provided basic services to a segment of the state's population. These services were to be provided (and were not subject to legislative control) for the foreseeable future. Thus, very specific staffing plans could be prepared to ensure that these services would be delivered on an ongoing basis. A second set of services was to be transferred from federal control to the state level. This transfer was communicated well in advance, so the agency was able to define the staffing impacts of this increased activity and plan accordingly. Only a small portion of what the agency did was truly at the whim of the legislature; no staffing plans were developed for these services. While the agency did not develop complete staffing plans for all services, it was certainly better off having created plans that supported the services that it could define.

Considering Project Probabilities

In some cases, it may be helpful to consider probabilities when determining staffing requirements in a project-based environment. In such an environment, it is usually possible to determine the staffing requirements for any given project. That's not the problem. What is unknown is which of the projects will actually be implemented.

On the one hand, it is not feasible to staff up to meet the requirements of all the possible projects. That would lead to significant overstaffing if any of the projects that were being considered were not implemented. On the other hand, it may not be realistic or possible to wait until project plans are certain, because that might leave insufficient time to identify, recruit, and deploy the number of qualified employees needed to implement those projects successfully. Applying a Monte Carlo approach can give the organization a head start on meeting its staffing needs while minimizing the probability of its taking on too many staff.

In order to apply this technique, you need to know two things: the staffing that would be required to implement each project fully, and the probability that each project will actually be implemented. Conceptually, the technique includes just three steps:

1. For each project, define the number of staff of each type that would be required if that project were to proceed.
2. Determine the probability that each project will occur and multiply this probability times the number of staff required in each category for that project.
3. Sum the required staff in each category across all projects.

The result of this analysis will be the number of staff that "should" be available prior to project initiation, across all projects. The analysis will not tell you how many staff are needed for each project (as you still don't know which projects will be implemented), but it will tell you the most likely staffing levels that you can use as a foundation (across all projects).

Here are two examples of how this technique might be applied.

Example 1: Staffing Strategies for an Oil Company

An oil company needed to prepare staffing strategies and plans to recruit the geologists and geophysicists that were required in order to support the company's exploration and production business. Staffing plans were needed on a quarterly basis. Defining the staffing needs of each exploration project was fairly easy; similarly, straightforward staffing plans could be prepared for each producing project that was underway. The problem was that it was not possible to determine in advance exactly which of the exploration projects would become producing projects. If the go-ahead was given and an exploration project became a producing project, work would continue and staffing would be required. If an exploration project did not prove commercially viable (and thus did not become a producing project), work would stop and no staff would be needed.

Given the uncertainty of these project transitions, it might seem that it would be difficult for the company to create meaningful staffing plans and strategies. Waiting for plans to become more definite (so that more accurate staffing plans could be developed), however, was not an option. Competition for the geologists and geophysicists that were needed was intense. In order to identify and attract a sufficient number of qualified staff, commitments from recent graduates had to be received well in advance of need. Clearly, some kind of staffing plans and strategies were required.

Remember that earlier in this chapter I suggested that you do the most you can with what you have. At a minimum, the company could determine its staffing needs for all exploration projects and all producing projects in each quarter, because these needs were well defined. It did not do nothing just because it could not create definite plans for all jobs. Even if the company had stopped here, it would have been better off than if it had done no staff planning at all. But the company did not stop here.

The final component of the staffing plan addressed the staffing needs of those projects that would make the transition from exploration projects to producing projects during the planning period in question. As mentioned previously, the company could accurately forecast its staffing needs for each such project, but it did not know which specific exploration projects would become producing projects (with staffing needs) and which would not (and thus would have no staffing needs). Given all the data that were gathered during the exploration phase, it was possible to define the probability that any given exploration project would become a producing project. This probability was called P_s (pronounced "P sub S")—shorthand for "probability of success." Each project had its own unique P_s. To

Figure 6-2. The Monte Carlo Method: An Oil Company

Project	P_s	Geologists Required (if Project Proceeds)	Geologists × P_s	Geophysicists Required (if Project Proceeds)	Geophysicists × P_s
1	0.20	40	8	30	6
2	0.10	20	2	10	1
3	0.10	30	3	20	2
4	0.15	60	9	40	6
Total		150	22	100	15

complete this component of the plan, the company applied the Monte Carlo method. First, for each exploration project that might become a fully operational producing project during the quarter, it defined the staffing needs should that project make the transition. Next, it multiplied the staffing requirements for each such project by the P_s for that particular project. Finally, it summed the results across all projects to define its best guess regarding the number of staff that would be needed for the projects that made this transition. Figure 6-2 is a simplified example of what that analysis might look like.

Given these data, the company should recruit twenty-two geologists and fifteen geophysicists to support the projects that would make the transition from exploration to producing during the quarter. Each of these numbers was significantly smaller than the total number of geologists and geophysicists that would be required for all four projects, but the probability of all four projects becoming viable was quite small (actually, it was just 0.0003!). At worst, hiring the twenty-two geologists and fifteen geophysicists created a foundation; if additional staff were needed, they could be found and recruited later on.

Example 2: Staffing Strategies for a Technical Consulting Firm

A technical consulting firm had five large proposals outstanding. Each project required data "miners" and senior data analysts. Unfortunately, the firm did not know which of these proposals (if any) would be accepted. Still, the firm needed to recruit a pool of qualified staff in advance, because work on each project would have to begin as soon as the proposal was accepted by the client. Given the short time between proposal acceptance and project initiation, it was not possible to wait until plans became fixed to recruit the required staff.

Like the oil company in the previous example, the consulting firm defined the probability that each proposal would be accepted. Next, it defined the number of data miners and senior data analysts that would be needed for each project if that project were to be initiated. Finally, the firm multiplied the staffing requirements for each project by the probability that the proposal would be accepted and summed the results across all proposals. The result showed the firm how large the staff pool needed to be. Figure 6-3 shows an example of what that analysis might have looked like.

The consulting firm's staffing pool ought to include forty-seven data miners and seventy data analysts. This should be considered a best guess or the most likely outcome. Note that the number needed is much closer to the overall total for each job category (i.e., 77 versus 47 and 120 versus 70) than it was for the oil company example. This is because the probabilities of getting these assignments are much higher than the P_s for the oil exploration projects. In fact, the probability of the consulting firm's getting all five projects is

Figure 6-3. The Monte Carlo Method: A Consulting Firm

Project	Probability of Proposal Acceptance	Data Miners Required (if Proposal Is Accepted)	Data Miners Required × Probability of Acceptance	Senior Data Analysts Required (if Proposal Is Accepted)	Senior Data Analysts Required × Probability of Acceptance
1	0.50	10	5	20	10
2	0.30	20	6	30	9
3	0.75	12	9	20	15
4	0.60	15	9	30	18
5	0.90	20	18	20	18
Total		77	47	120	70

0.06075—not high, but much higher than the 0.0003 probability that all of the oil company's exploration projects will become viable.

Summary

When you create a staffing strategy, you don't need perfect data. Do the most you can with the data you do have. Plan fully for those parts of the organization where you have a good idea of future plans. Create scenarios when you have some idea of future plans but are not certain. Prepare "what if" plans when you are unsure so that you will be better prepared to act when you become more sure. You will always be better off doing something about the part you can define and ignoring the part you can't define than you will be if you wait for those missing data to be developed. You may be waiting a long time!

CHAPTER 7

A Staffing Model Example

As described earlier, strategic staffing/workforce planning is, at its simplest, a form of gap analysis that defines the required skills and staffing levels, projects staff availability, calculates staffing gaps and surpluses, and defines the specific staffing actions that are needed in order to close gaps and eliminate (or at least reduce) surpluses.

This chapter provides a specific example of a process for creating a staffing plan. The process described here is fully consistent with the context and approaches described in detail throughout this book.

The first seven steps describe how to define staffing gaps and surpluses; the next six steps walk you through the process of defining the staffing actions that will be needed to eliminate these gaps and surpluses. Figure 7-1 provides an overview of the process that is used in this example. To make it easier to follow, this example is also included on the CD-ROM that accompanies this book. (You will need to copy the file to your hard drive in order to be able to edit it). Steps 1 through 7 are already filled in on the CD-ROM; you can complete the remaining steps yourself as you go through the example.

You may wish to use this model as a template for your own process. Of course, remember that this is just an example. The process will need to be tailored to reflect the staffing issues you are facing.

Part 1: Defining Staffing Gaps and Surpluses

First, identify the issue to be addressed or the job categories on which your model will focus. For this example, let's assume that we

Figure 7-1. The Strategic Staffing Process As It Appears in the Example

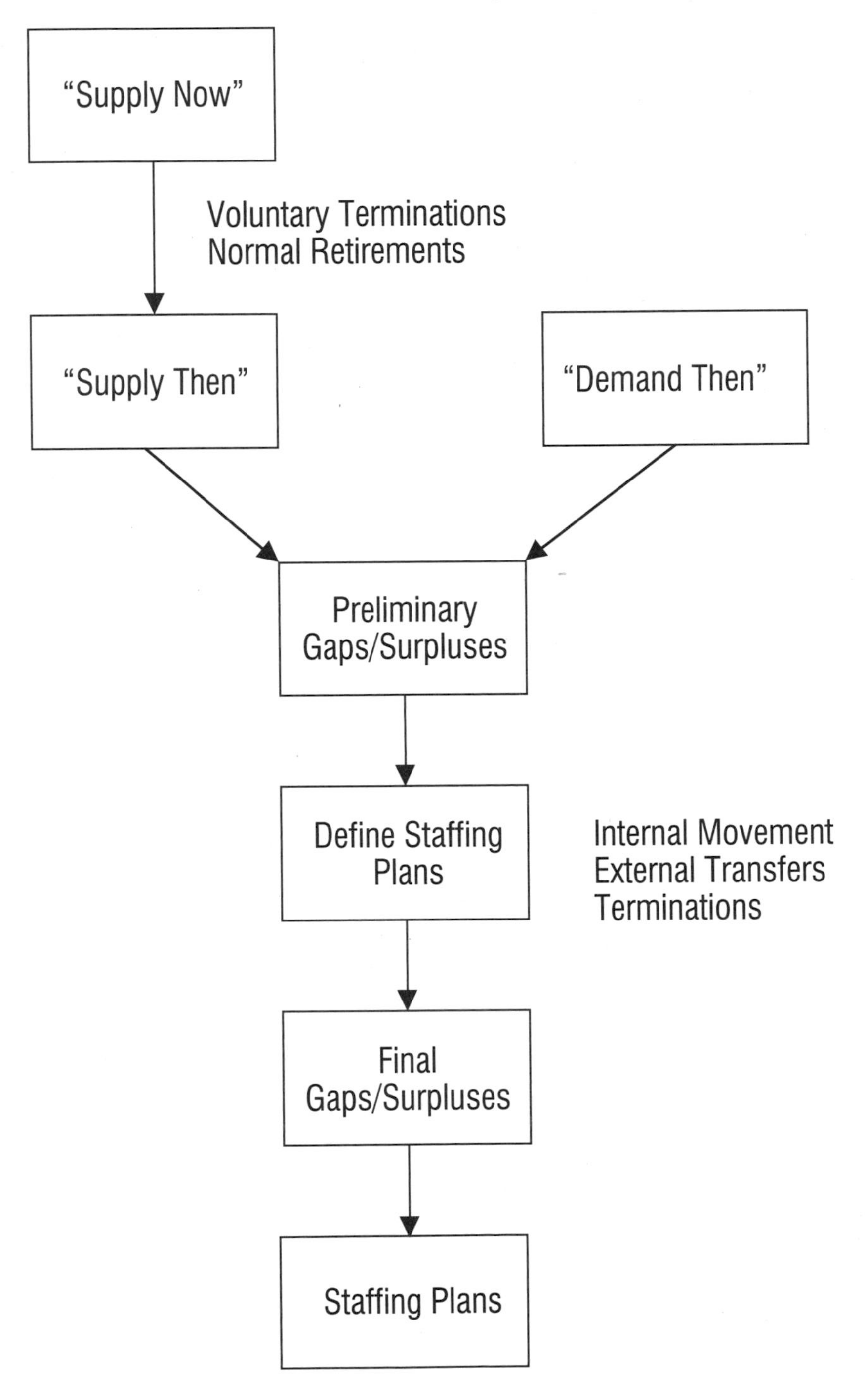

are going to define our specific needs for software engineers and object-oriented programmers because the demand for individuals with these "hot skills" far exceeds the supply. Our model will focus on and include only the positions that require these particular skills. If other positions are also critical, they will be defined in a separate model.

Step 1: Define the Model Parameters

Define the three planning parameters that you will use to structure your model: population to be included, planning horizon, and matrix structure.

Population. Define the existing positions in your unit that fall into the two job categories we are focusing on. We will include incumbents of these positions in our model. In an actual model, we would want to also include in the model any other positions that might require these critical skills and any positions that might be able to use these skills. To keep this example simple, however, we will assume that there are no other jobs that might be sources of or uses for these skills.

Planning Horizon. Now define your planning horizon. This has two components:

1. *Define the end point.* If you are creating a one-year model, this will probably be the end of the year. If you are creating a staffing plan to support a five-year strategy, it might be five years. In an area that is growing and changing rapidly, it might be six months. Because technology is changing so rapidly, we will assume for this example that our long-term planning horizon is one year.

2. *Define the period of your model.* For example, a strategic workforce plan might have a five-year end point, but the model would define staffing needs for each of those five years separately. In an annual budget, it may be sufficient to consider just one period. If an objective is a quarterly staffing plan, however, that one year would

need to be broken into quarters (with a model run for each quarter). In this example, our period will, in fact, be one quarter.

In our example, we would probably run a model for each of the four quarters of our one-year planning horizon (although the plan for only one of those quarters is shown here). This would allow us to create and update staffing plans on a quarterly basis—a time frame that is appropriate for the kind of staffing decisions we will be using the model to support. A longer time frame (e.g., one year) would prevent us from addressing seasonal staffing issues; a shorter time frame (e.g., one month) would provide a level of detail that just isn't needed.

Model Structure. Next, we need to define what rows and column headings to use to structure our model. Figure 7-2 shows the suggested structure for this example. Columns usually denote areas of expertise, organization units, or locations (depending on the issue you are addressing). There is a balance that has to be struck here between the need to differentiate and the need to keep the model simple. A single column for "programmers" would create a simple model, but would eliminate the possibility of differentiating among various areas of programming expertise (and we will probably need to consider those differences when we create recruiting and staffing plans for this unit). In our example, we will have two columns, one for software engineers and a second for object-oriented programmers.

Figure 7-2.

	Software Engineers	Object-Oriented Programmers	Total
Project manager			
Lead			
Individual contributor			
Entry level			
Total			

Next, define the row headings. In almost every case, rows depict increasing levels of capability or responsibility (i.e., entry level is at the bottom and lead practitioners or more senior managers are at the top). In our example, we have four levels, entry level, individual contributor, lead, and project manager. Since we are focusing on "hot" technical skills, there is no need to include any positions above project manager in our example, as this is the highest-level position for which some technical skills are still required.

Step 2: Define Demand ("Demand Then")

Normally, this matrix contains staffing requirements (both capabilities and staffing levels). These demand estimates may come from plans, budgets, or interviews with managers. On a separate sheet, document the required capabilities that you have assumed for each job category. Here are some hints to keep in mind:

- **Identify a small number of really important capabilities.** Don't try to define all the capabilities for each job category. Instead, focus on those that are most critical. You should ideally identify less than ten, and you may find it possible to define as few as five. Try to identify those few capabilities that are needed to win the game, not just play it.
- **Identify capabilities that differentiate one job category from another.** When you build your model, you will probably assume that there are significant differences between cells in different rows of a given column or different columns of a given row. Try to define these differences in specific terms. For example, if the difference between one level/row and another is the addition of management skills, define just those additional skills. Similarly, if the difference between one column and another is a different technical discipline, define only the skills that are different.
- **Define capabilities in behavioral terms.** It is often helpful to define capabilities in terms of behaviors that can be observed. Instead of defining a particular skill, knowledge, or understanding, define what happens when that skill, knowledge, or understanding is applied to accomplish something particular.

Once the required capabilities have been identified, the required staffing levels can be defined. There are many common methods that can be used to define demand (several of these are described in Chapter 5). In this example, we have assumed that demand for staff in each category will simply increase by 15 percent. This means, for example, that for software engineers/lead, twenty-five would be needed (i.e., $22 \times 1.15 = 25.3$). Once you have determined the number of people that will be required, enter that number in the appropriate cell. For our example, assume that a detailed analysis produced the "Demand Then" matrix shown in Figure 7-3.

Figure 7-3. "Demand Then"

	Software Engineers	Object-Oriented Programmers	Total
Project manager	12	9	21
Lead	25	21	46
Individual contributor	62	52	114
Entry level	83	77	160
Total	182	159	341

Step 3: Determine Existing Staff Level ("Supply Now")

Enter the number of people you currently have in each category into the appropriate cell of the "supply now" component of your model (e.g., enter the number of entry-level software engineers currently on staff in the software engineers/entry level cell). Enter only the number of people that are actually in place. Usually these numbers can be extracted from a human resource information system. Alternatively, it is sometimes possible to actually count the number of individuals in each category and enter those numbers.

On a separate sheet, document the critical skills that the employees in each of these cells now have. Remember to focus on a small number of really important capabilities.

For our example, we will assume the starting population shown in Figure 7-4.

Figure 7-4. Existing Staff Level/"Supply Now"

	Software Engineers	Object-Oriented Programmers	Total
Project manager	10	17	27
Lead	22	18	40
Individual contributor	54	45	99
Entry level	72	67	139
Total	158	147	305

Step 4: Define Voluntary Turnover

Voluntary turnover between "now" and "then" will reduce the number of people available to you. Estimate the voluntary turnover rate for each category and enter it in the appropriate cell. If you have historical data, consider what the turnover for this group has been, but make sure that you project what you think it will be. Will it be at that level in the coming period? Will changing economic conditions make it higher? Will they make it lower? Enter in the model the turnover rate that you think will apply in the period you are modeling. Remember to adjust the rate so that it is consistent with your model period. For example, if your annual turnover rate is expected to be 4 percent, enter 0.04 if your period is one year and 0.01 (i.e., 0.04 divided by 4) if your period is one quarter.

Your model should allow for a different turnover rate for each category, but this level of differentiation may not be necessary. Here are some simplifying assumptions:

- Turnover usually varies by length of service. People who have been with your company for a longer time are less likely to leave than those with less tenure. Consequently, the turnover rate may vary by row, with the lower rows having a higher rate than the higher rows. Estimate a rate for each row and use it for all columns.

- Turnover varies by area of expertise. In areas where there are hot skills, turnover will be particularly high. In these cases, use a rate for those columns that is different from the one used for all the other columns.

- Turnover varies by organization. If you are unsure of how turnover might vary, use the same rate for each cell.

Once turnover rates have been entered, calculate the expected number of voluntary quits for each category. Multiply the voluntary turnover rate for each cell times the number of people in that cell at the beginning of the period (as defined in the existing staff level/"supply now" matrix) and enter that number in the voluntary turnover matrix. In step 6 you will deduct this number from the corresponding number in the existing staff level/"supply now" matrix.

For our example, we have assumed a voluntary turnover rate of 15 percent for software engineers and 11 percent for object-oriented programmers (Figure 7-5).

Figure 7-5. Voluntary Turnover Rate

	Software Engineers	Object-Oriented Programmers
Project manager	0.15	0.11
Lead	0.15	0.11
Individual contributor	0.15	0.11
Entry level	0.15	0.11

Figure 7-6. Voluntary Turnover

	Software Engineers	Object-Oriented Programmers	Total
Project manager	2	2	4
Lead	3	2	5
Individual contributor	8	5	13
Entry level	11	7	18
Total	24	16	40

For each cell, multiply these rates times the starting headcounts (i.e., ''supply now'') to estimate the number of people that will leave each category voluntarily. The losses that would be expected are shown in Figure 7-6.

These numbers will be deducted from the corresponding numbers in the existing staff level/''supply now'' matrix in step 6.

Step 5: Estimate Retirements

Retirements should also be factored into your analysis. Review your workforce and identify those employees that will become eligible for retirement during your planning period (e.g., those that will reach normal retirement age or meet standard retirement criteria). Usually, it is a good idea to assume that all these people will retire (those who don't are usually offset by those who retire early). If you are expecting retirements from any of the jobs included in the model, simply enter the number of retirements in the appropriate cell(s). Again, you will need to subtract these retirements from your existing staff level/''supply now'' matrix in step 6. Figure 7-7 shows the retirements we assumed.

Figure 7-7. Retirements

	Software Engineers	Object-Oriented Programmers	Total
Project manager	1	2	3
Lead	1	0	1
Individual contributor	0	0	0
Entry level	0	0	0
Total	2	2	4

Step 6: Forecast Available Resources ("Supply Then")

This section of the model displays the number of people in each category that will remain at the end of your planning period, taking into account the losses you have assumed.

Let's look at the software engineers/lead cell in our example. The calculation for that cell would be as follows:

Starting headcount	22
Less voluntary turnover	−3
Less retirement	−1
Available resources	18

Applying this logic to the entire example produces the available resources matrix depicted in Figure 7-8.

This is the population that you expect to have if all of your turnover and retirement assumptions are correct (and actually occur). A more detailed model would probably include additional uncontrollable staffing assumptions.

Figure 7-8. Available Resources/"Supply Then"

	Software Engineers	Object-Oriented Programmers	Total
Project manager	7	13	20
Lead	18	16	34
Individual contributor	46	40	86
Entry level	61	60	121
Total	132	129	261

Step 7: Calculate Preliminary Gaps and Surpluses

Next, compare the "supply then" that you have calculated with the "demand then" that you have entered on a cell-by-cell basis. The results of this comparison (i.e., staffing gaps and surpluses) are displayed in a separate matrix (sometimes referred to as a net needs matrix). Subtracting demand from supply gives us a negative result when demand exceeds supply; therefore negative numbers represent deficits or gaps, and positive numbers represent surpluses. This is the convention we will use.

In our example, in the software engineers/lead category, our net need is a deficit of seven people (i.e., eighteen people will be available and twenty-five will be needed). Applying this logic to our example yields the matrix shown in Figure 7-9.

Figure 7-9. Preliminary Gaps/Surpluses

	Software Engineers	Object-Oriented Programmers
Project manager	−5	+4
Lead	−7	−5
Individual contributor	−16	−12
Entry level	−22	−17

Note that we don't calculate totals. That's because totals really don't make sense, and may actually be misleading. For example, there is a deficit of five project managers in software engineering and a surplus of four in object-oriented programming. Therefore, a total for that row would show an overall deficit of one project manager. This number, however, really isn't helpful. We created separate columns for software engineering and object-oriented programming in the first place because the capabilities required for those two areas were significantly different. From a staffing perspective, we probably would not be able to redeploy the project managers from object-oriented programming to software engineering because of these capability differences. Consequently, we would have to define one set of actions to reduce the deficit of five project managers in software engineering and another set to alleviate the surplus of four project managers in object-oriented programming. If we simply looked at the row total, we might have been led to believe that all we needed to do was to hire one project manager, but clearly this would not be sufficient.

In an actual example, we would need to define staffing gaps and surpluses for all our planning periods before we defined staffing strategies and plans for any period. Since this example includes only one planning period, we can move ahead to action planning.

Part 2: Defining Required Staffing Actions

Once preliminary gaps and surpluses have been calculated, it is possible to define the specific staffing actions that are needed to eliminate those gaps and surpluses. Usually, your staffing strategies define a pecking order: Certain kinds of staffing actions are preferred and take precedence over others. For example, we will assume that our staffing strategy dictates that we fill as many jobs as possible internally (e.g., through promotion or redeployment) before we hire from the outside. The order in which you define required staffing actions should reflect the staffing strategies and preferences of your organization.

In this example, we have defined the required staffing actions only for software engineers. A similar process would be used to define the staffing plans for object-oriented programmers.

Step 8: Define Internal Movement

The next two sections of the model (internal transfers out and internal transfers in) are illustrated in Figures 7-10 and 7-11. They allow you to define the internal transfers (including lateral moves, rede-

Figure 7-10.

Internal Transfers Out

	Software Engineers	Object-Oriented Programmers	Total
Project manager			
Lead	5		5
Individual contributor			
Entry level			
Total	5		5

Internal Transfers In

	Software Engineers	Object-Oriented Programmers	Total
Project manager	5		5
Lead			
Individual contributor			
Entry level			
Total	5		5

Figure 7-11.

Internal Transfers Out

	Software Engineers	Object-Oriented Programmers	Total
Project manager			
Lead	5		5
Individual contributor	12		12
Entry level	16		16
Total	33		33

Internal Transfers In

	Software Engineers	Object-Oriented Programmers	Total
Project manager	5		5
Lead	12		12
Individual contributor	16		16
Entry level			
Total	33		33

ployments, and promotions) that you think are necessary to address the gaps and surpluses that you have identified. Note that for the purposes of this model, *internal movement* is defined as someone moving from one job in your model to another job in your model. Here is how these matrices should be used.

Assume that you wish to eliminate a gap of five in one job category by promoting qualified individuals from the category just beneath it. This action should be recorded by placing a 5 in the cell from which the people will be coming on the internal transfers out matrix and a corresponding entry of +5 in the cell on the internal transfers in matrix that corresponds to the job these people are being promoted to. Remember that each move you want to include must be documented on both of the internal movement matrices (it's almost like double-entry bookkeeping).

In some cases, internal transfers (whether lateral or promotional) are feasible only if additional training is provided. If this is the case, make a note of the skills that will need to be strengthened and include a reference to this required training in your staffing plan.

In our example, we are going to address a gap of five at the software engineers/project manager level by promoting five individuals from the lead category of that group. Figure 7-10 shows how that particular staffing action would be recorded.

Of course, promoting these five people will increase the deficit at the lead level from the original seven to twelve. This deficit will probably be dealt with by promoting twelve individual contributors, but this action will increase the deficit at that level from sixteen to twenty-eight. In our example, we have determined that only sixteen of those slots can be filled by promoting staff from the entry level. The remaining openings will be filled through outside hires. By definition, none of the openings at entry level can be filled by promotions.

Our final internal transfer matrices for software engineers would look like the ones in Figure 7-11.

Step 9: Define External Transfers

The next two sections of the model (external transfers out and external transfers in) address movements of people from jobs in your model to other units in your company or into jobs in your model from other units in your company. Because in these cases you are interested only in movement into and out of your unit/model, no double entries are required. For example, if you plan to eliminate a surplus by redeploying ten individuals to another unit (i.e., one not covered by your model), simply enter a 10 in the cell on the external transfers out matrix from which the individuals will come. Similarly, if you want to address a gap in a job category by accepting fifteen people from another unit, simply enter 15 in the appropriate cell of the external transfers in matrix. Of course, corresponding entries would be made in models that were being developed for those other units (if such models are indeed being prepared separately).

We have assumed no external transfers in our example.

Step 10: Determine New Hires

Enter the number of new hires you expect to make in each category. Just to be clear, the model assumes that these people are being hired from outside the company (a "new hire" from another unit of your company should be considered an external transfer, not a new hire).

In our example, we assumed that sixteen of the twenty-eight openings at the individual contributor level in software engineering will be filled through promotion. The remaining twelve will be filled by new hires. At the entry level, we now have thirty-eight openings (the original deficit of twenty-two plus the deficit of sixteen that we created by promoting these individuals to the individual contributor level). All of these openings will be filled through new hires. These staffing actions would be recorded in the new hires matrix as shown in Figure 7-12.

Figure 7-12. New Hires

	Software Engineers	Object-Oriented Programmers	Total
Project manager			
Lead			
Individual contributor	12		12
Entry level	38		38
Total	50		50

Step 11: Define Involuntary Terminations (If Any)

If you plan on reducing surpluses through early retirement, reductions in force, or any other method beyond normal retirement and attrition, that information should be entered in this section of the model. Simply create another matrix with the same format, and remember to subtract these numbers from your supply when calculating gaps and surpluses. If no involuntary terminations are needed, no entries should be made in this section.

Step 12: Calculate Final Gaps and Surpluses

This section of the model should display the gaps and surpluses that still exist after all the staffing actions you have included in your model (i.e., those from steps 8 through 11) have been taken into account. In most cases, your objective is to define the staffing actions that will make this matrix contain nothing but zeros. If you still have gaps or surpluses, you should go back to steps 8 through 11 and make additional (or different) assumptions regarding staffing actions (e.g., increase hiring if gaps still exist; institute reductions in force if there are still surpluses).

Step 13: Create Staffing Plans

Once you are satisfied with the results of your model (i.e., when all cells of the final gap matrix include zeros or some other acceptable numbers), you will need to create staffing plans. This entails documenting the staffing assumptions you have made along the way, including each kind of move that you have assumed will take place.

Figure 7-13 provides a suggested structure.

Figure 7-14 depicts what a final staffing plan for our model for software engineering might look like.

Figure 7-13. Suggested Staffing Plan Structure

Step/Type of Action	Information to Be Documented
Voluntary turnover	Rates that were assumed
Retirements	Number of retirements for each cell
Internal transfers (both in and out)	For each type of transfer, document the number of people moving, the job category they are coming from, and the job category they are moving to (noting any training or development needed to support the move)
External transfers in	For each type of transfer, document the number of people moving, the unit they are coming from, and the job category they are moving into
External transfers out	For each type of transfer, document the number of people moving, the job category they are coming from, and the unit they are moving to
New hires	Number of hires for each job category
Involuntary terminations (all types)	Number of terminations per job category by type

Figure 7-14. Staffing Plan for the Example

Type	Staffing Action(s)
Promotions	5 from software engineers/lead to software engineers/project manager 12 from software engineers/individual contributor to software engineers/lead 16 from software engineers/entry level to software engineers/individual contributor
New hires	12 into software engineers/individual contributor 38 into software engineers/entry level

Don't forget that in a real case, you would also need to define the staffing actions required to address issues for object-oriented programmers.

Follow-on actions should also be documented (e.g., any training that may be needed to support the assumed promotions). You may also choose to document any gaps and surpluses that you have not addressed (and your rationale for not addressing them).

CHAPTER

8

Effective Strategic Staffing: Case Studies and Examples

This chapter describes two specific case studies in which strategic staffing had a major impact on the organization implementing the process. It also includes several shorter, less detailed summaries of successful strategic staffing projects. In each case, the company used the various processes described in this book.

Case 1: A Pharmaceutical Company

Introduction

This case study describes a project that was completed for a large pharmaceutical company. The organization chose not to follow the traditional one-size-fits-all process (i.e., expecting every unit of the organization to create staffing plans at the same time, at the same level of detail, using the same planning horizons, using the same templates). Instead, this company developed a targeted staffing strategy that focused on a particular unit within the information technology (IT) organization that was about to undergo significant growth. This case study identifies the issues that had to be faced and describes the planning approach that was taken. It also highlights the results of the project—both longer-term, broad staffing strategies and shorter-term, specific staffing plans and actions.

The Strategic Context

The staffing strategy described here was developed for the technical support group within the IT function. The technical support group provides critical services to the business units of the firm, such as local and/or wide area network (LAN/WAN) setup, cabling, server configuration, operating system installation, and telecommunications support. In the near future, the company as a whole was expected to grow significantly; consequently, demand for the services that the technical support group was expected to provide was expected to grow significantly as well. At the start of the project, full-time employees of the technical support group were handling the majority of the work, but it had become clear that the existing staff would be unable to support all the projects that would result from the planned growth. The technical support group manager wanted to develop a staffing strategy that would ensure that his unit had a sufficient number of qualified staff available to provide these services when they were needed.

The Strategic Staffing Model

As a first step, staffing needs were defined. A strategic staffing model was developed to support this analysis. The basic format of that model is described below.

Model Structure. The core of the model was a two-dimensional matrix. Each row of the matrix combined two concepts: the particular technical area of expertise (e.g., WAN, LAN, voice, desktop, or messaging) and the role that was to be played. There were two roles defined for each technical area:

1. *Oversight*, which included defining the work to be done, setting objectives, preparing work plans, providing technical guidance, and supervising the work of others
2. *Staff*, which included those actually doing the work in the hands-on sense

Each row of the model described a pairing of technical expertise and role (e.g., Wide Area Network (WAN) oversight, WAN staff, voice oversight, voice staff). Each of the three columns of the model denoted a particular level of expertise:

1. *Senior:* Individuals that had a deep knowledge or understanding of a particular technical area (e.g., a platform or set of software) as it was applied within the company's business context
2. *Individual contributor:* Individuals that had the technical skills, experience, and understanding of the company's technology, systems, platforms, and business practices needed to contribute to projects without constant supervision
3. *Foundation:* Individuals with basic capabilities and aptitudes but no in-depth understanding of the company's technology, systems, platforms, or business practices

Conceptually, each job (i.e., each cell of the matrix) could be described as a particular combination of technical area, role, and level of expertise (e.g., WAN oversight at the senior level, voice staff at the individual contributor level). Figure 8-1 shows a portion of the model framework.

Time Frame. The overall planning horizon for the model was one year; staffing plans were developed for each of the four quarters within

Figure 8-1. Case Study Model Framework—Technical Support Staffing Model

Job Category	Senior	Individual Contributor	Foundation
LAN oversight			
LAN staff			
WAN oversight			
WAN staff			
Voice oversight			
Voice staff			
Etc.			

that year. The plan was to be updated on a rolling basis (i.e., each of the four quarters included in the plan would be updated on a quarterly basis).

The Modeling Process. The model itself was a fairly traditional, spreadsheet-based supply/demand model.

- Overall staffing requirements were calculated by defining the staffing requirements of each project to be supported and then summing the staffing requirements across all projects on a job-by-job, quarter-by-quarter basis.
- The initial supply was defined to be the existing pool of full-time technical support group employees (i.e., those who were already employed full time at the beginning of the planning period).
- For each period, the model compared demand to supply and calculated gaps and surpluses for each job category (i.e., each cell of the matrix).

Managers in the technical support group first reviewed staffing gaps and surpluses for the first quarter and determined the staffing actions that would best eliminate those gaps and surpluses for that quarter (e.g., reallocating the time of existing employees among projects, contracting work out, or hiring). Once these staffing actions were entered in the spreadsheets, the model then determined the numbers and types of employees and contractors that would be available at the start of the second quarter (assuming that all the first-quarter staffing actions were implemented as planned). It also compared that supply to the requirements for the second quarter, and recalculated the gaps and surpluses. Again, the technical support group managers determined how best to eliminate the staffing gaps and surpluses for that quarter and entered those data into the spreadsheets. This process was repeated for all four quarters of the one-year planning period.

The Staffing Strategies and Plans That Emerged

Once specific staffing needs had been defined, the overall staffing strategies that would most effectively meet those needs were developed. The first strategies that were developed clearly defined what the oversight and staff roles would be in the future and (ideally) how openings in each role should be filled. When the managers looked at technical areas and roles (i.e., the rows of the model), they reached the following general conclusions:

- **Oversight roles would primarily be filled by full-time technical support group employees.** Oversight roles were especially critical to the mission of the technical support group. The individuals that served in these roles should bring a depth of technical expertise and an overall understanding of the company's business context that was especially valuable. These roles were thought of as core in that they directly supported the implementation of company strategies and provided distinct competitive advantage. Because of the strategic value of these roles, it was determined they should be staffed by the company's own full-time employees.
- **Staff roles should be filled by contractors on a short-term, as-needed basis.** The individuals in staff roles provided critical services, but those services were not unique to the company and provided no particular competitive advantage. In most cases they involved skills that could be learned outside the company's business context. The services could be thought of as commodities that were readily available outside the organization. As a result, it was decided that contractors should be used to staff these roles.

When they looked at the various levels of expertise (as denoted by the columns of the model), they drew the following conclusions:

- In addition to all of the oversight roles, some senior- and individual contributor–level staff jobs were also considered core. This was especially the case in technical areas that were deemed critical or proprietary in nature (e.g., systems development and architecture).

- None of the roles included in the foundation column of the model were considered core.

Once core roles had been identified, the company decided (at a strategic level) to focus its recruiting, training, and development efforts on providing and strengthening core roles and capabilities. Few resources, if any, would be spent on recruiting and training in noncore areas. This strengthening would be focused on two areas in particular:

1. **The oversight capabilities of technical support group employees.** For current employees, development efforts would be aimed at enhancing oversight capabilities (e.g., planning, supervising, and managing performance), not technical skills.
2. **Capabilities relating to and supporting the development and implementation of proprietary technologies.** Where necessary, specific individuals would be developed in technical areas that were also identified as core.

It was also decided that changes in core roles had to be implemented over time, not all at once. Initially, oversight capabilities (such as planning and supervising) would be positioned as additions to the technical capabilities that were already developed and demonstrated by individuals at these levels. Over time, however, the development and utilization of oversight capabilities would be emphasized and development of new technical skills would be de-emphasized.

Additional Short-Term Actions

Within the context of these staffing strategies, several more specific, short-term staffing actions were also defined.

A Logic for Eliminating the Staffing Gaps and Surpluses Defined by the Model Was Developed. Managers created a rationale or set of priorities that could be used to eliminate staffing gaps and surpluses in each quarter. If a need for a core role was defined, managers would first try to meet that need by reallocating surplus time from a current technical support group employee. If that was not possible, a new employee would be hired (if the need was ongoing) or a contractor would be retained and developed (if the need was short-term). If a need for a noncore role was identified, managers would still try to reallocate surplus time from a current technical support group employee. If that was not possible, a contractor would be retained.

Specific Training Plans Were Developed. If the staffing plans that emerged from the strategic staffing model were implemented as designed, the work being done by several full-time technical support group employees would change significantly. For example, one individual would move from having no responsibilities in the messaging area in the first quarter to working solely in that area in the fourth quarter. The individuals whose responsibilities would change so significantly would probably require additional (concentrated) training in order to perform satisfactorily in these new technical areas. Targeted development plans were developed for these individuals so that during the second and third quarters they could acquire the skills they would need in the fourth quarter.

Plans for Increasing the Effectiveness of Contractor Relationships Were Developed. The staffing strategy clearly identified the areas in which contractors would be needed over the coming year. In some cases, actions had to be taken in advance of need to ensure that a reliable source of qualified contractors would be available when needed. These actions might include:

- Reviewing staffing needs with those companies that are already providing talent to ensure that those companies will continue to provide contractors with the needed skills and capabilities.
- Identifying new sources of talent if current suppliers are unable to provide sufficient numbers of properly skilled talent.
- Identifying new sources of qualified talent in areas where contractors have not been used previously. This might include

identifying suppliers, discussing staffing requirements with those suppliers in advance of need, and gathering information regarding what would have to be done if that supplier were to be called upon to provide talent (e.g., what the lead times and contract terms/provisions might be).

Other Key Findings

In addition to the strategic and short-term staffing initiatives just described, there were two additional findings:

1. Deferring projects would not alleviate any staffing issues. Prior to the analysis, managers had assumed that since many projects were front-loaded into the early quarters of the planning period, there would be staffing shortages in those quarters and staffing surpluses in later quarters (when fewer projects were planned). If this were true, staffing gaps and surpluses might be balanced by simply deferring some projects to later quarters. The results of the analysis did not support this conclusion.

2. It had been thought that there might be some cases in which it might be less expensive to add, as full-time staff, individuals with noncore skills (as opposed to using contractors) if those skills were needed on an ongoing basis. The staffing strategy showed that this was not the case within the technical support group. There was no set of noncore skills that was needed throughout the planning period; consequently, there was no need to add full-time employees to provide noncore skills.

Conclusions

Taking a more strategic approach to staffing had a significant impact on this organization's staffing actions. By developing a longer-term staffing strategy and using that strategy as a context for near-term decision making, the company was able to define the staffing actions that would allow it to best meet its needs for talent. Without that strategy, it is likely that the technical support group would have implemented staffing actions that were less effective and more costly than those that were implemented as a result of using this process.

Case 2: An International Bank

Introduction

In this case, a staffing strategy was to be developed for a development unit of an international bank. Each of the bank's development units supports lending operations by providing borrowers (primarily developing countries) with the technical and functional expertise they need if they are to implement the projects for which bank funds were being loaned. Initially, strategies and plans had been developed to revitalize this particular development unit, and the bank's board of directors had approved a sizable budget increase to support these efforts. Work had begun on a staffing strategy that would support these revitalization efforts. Then, rather unexpectedly, the political climate both inside and outside the bank changed—the expertise offered by this development unit was suddenly on everyone's agenda. The revitalization effort took on new importance, and staffing that effort became even more important.

The Strategic Context

Traditionally, this development unit of the bank had directly supported education-related lending. It provided both technical and operations support. Developing countries turned to the bank for the capital, expertise (both economic and educational), and project management needed to build schools, conduct teacher training, obtain and create textbooks, develop curricula, and provide other infrastructure. The unit's efforts (both lending and development) focused on all aspects of learning, from preschool through adult education.

As the bank's business environment changed, so did the role of this development unit. In many cases, education efforts became a part of larger projects (e.g., a program to reduce a significant health risk) rather than stand-alone efforts (as had been the case previously). In addition, the bank began to move toward program-based lending. Instead of providing capital and expertise that focused on particular projects (as it had traditionally done), it provided capital to countries in need as long as they achieved certain policy goals and milestones (e.g., improving literacy rates). The sudden emphasis on education also meant that this development unit would have to provide additional services and support both to its traditional lending and to emerging programmatic loans. The board of directors also called on the unit to define specific progress measures (including one addressing staffing) and to report progress against those measures on a quarterly basis.

The bank was organized by region. Within each region, there were individuals with expertise in education. There also was a centralized unit that provided staff, some level of expertise, and administrative support to the education professionals located in the regions. Some staff were functional experts; however, most spent a large part of their time managing projects and tasks.

It was in this environment of growth and change that a strategic staffing process was to be implemented. Initially, the bank began to implement the approaches described in this book. As the project progressed, however, some significant differences emerged.

Critical Business Issues

As described earlier in this book, the strategic staffing process normally begins with the definition of the staffing implications of business strategies and plans. In this case, however, as the strategic staffing project began, several larger business issues were identified. Among the senior managers, there was some difference of opinion regarding what this development unit was to accomplish during the planning period. First, there was a lack of consensus regarding the overall mission of the bank in general and of the education unit in particular. Some felt that the bank's main role was to have a significant positive impact on the countries being served (e.g., to maximize the impact that the bank's capital would have on learning). Others felt that the bank should concentrate more on lending operations and less on development. Some managers felt that the new program-based lending was appropriate in most cases; others felt it should be implemented only on a selected basis. Complicating this situation was the fact that the performance evaluation of most country managers was based largely on the size and performance of their lending portfolios. The impact of their development efforts carried much less weight. Obviously, all these differences in business objectives, strategies, and approaches were significant. The staffing needed to implement some of these alternatives varied widely.

Initiating the Strategic Staffing Process

Once the basic parameters of the model had been defined (e.g., population, planning horizon, and model structure), efforts to define the staffing requirements began.

The bulk of the staff within the development unit fell into three job categories: economics, education, and operations. Each of these streams included three levels of jobs: individual contributor, senior level, and lead level. In addition, there were research analysts and operations analysts. Traditionally, the bank hired younger professionals (including many Ph.D.s) who had a particular expertise in educational economics or in some education specialty.

A staffing model was built to support the development of staffing strategies and plans. The model included all staff that directly supported the lending activities of the development unit. It focused on staff within the existing three job streams (i.e., economics, education, and operations) in the regions and the corporate unit. It also included the operations and research analysts; it excluded the small number of managers.

The columns of the model denoted organization unit (e.g., region or corporate, headquarters or field locations). Jobs in each region were divided into three categories on the basis of location (i.e., corporate headquarters, corporate positions in the field, and local office positions). The rows of the model denoted job stream and level. While the qualitative portion of the project looked ahead three years, the quantitative model focused on the coming fiscal year. The model structure is shown in Figure 8-2.

The actual model included all regions, not just the two shown in the example. It captured current staff levels, forecast future staff availability, defined staffing requirements, and calculated staffing gaps and surpluses.

Strategic Staffing Issues

Even given the uncertainty surrounding the business, several well-defined staffing issues were identified. One staffing issue emerged

Figure 8-2. Sample Staffing Model Structure

Job	Region 1 HQ	Region 1 HQ–Field	Region 1 Local	Region 2 HQ	Region 2 HQ–Field	Region 2 Local	Corporate
Lead economist							
Senior economist							
Economist							
Lead education specialist							
Senior education specialist							
Education specialist							
Lead operations officer							
Senior operations officer							
Operations officer							
Operations analyst							
Research analyst							

early in the project. The three job streams (i.e., economist, education specialist, and operations officer) had been designed to be quite different. However, a review of existing job profiles, internal postings, external ads, and other documents showed that staff in all three streams were primarily playing the same role—that of project manager, not that of technical expert. The capabilities required in the three streams were more alike than different. Although many of the individuals in the sector had been hired because of their technical expertise, most of this specific expertise was not being applied; instead, they were working as generic task managers. The more these individuals focused on project management, the more rusty and outdated their technical expertise became. Many of these people had become disheartened and disillusioned—they had been hired by the bank to apply their expertise, but they were unable to use it. This lack of differentiation would be less of a problem if the bank were to focus on lending, but it was a critical problem if the bank were to focus on development.

A second staffing issue was related to organization structure. While each region required some education expertise, not all were large enough to afford full-time education staff. Since they could not afford individual experts, many of these smaller regions had created positions that spanned or combined functional areas (e.g., education, health, and social programs). These regions then chose to employ staff with some expertise in these multiple functions rather than take on experts in each area. While most of the people playing these combined roles met the minimum qualifications for each functional area, few of them were experts in all the areas in which they worked. As a result, there was a general lowering of the bar regarding technical expertise. This was a particular problem in countries and situations where particularly deep expertise was required. This lack of deep expertise would only get worse where the bank was called on to provide development assistance in addition to capital.

A third staffing issue was related to the move to program-based lending. To support this approach, the bank would need staff that was experienced in creating and developing the high-level policies and strategic objectives that served as the standards by which country performance was measured. Program-based lending required staff with experience in meeting with high-level government officials and conducting meaningful policy-level dialogue. The bank did not have a large enough pool of staff with this expertise to support a significant number of program-based loans.

A fourth staffing issue dealt with the inappropriate use of consultants. In a move designed to reduce fixed costs and provide additional flexibility, the bank had mandated that most staffing needs in all units (including the education unit) should be met by a blend of full-time, "core" staff and short-term consultants. In fact, it set a specific ratio of core staff to consultants that could not be exceeded. For many units, this mandate reduced the number of "core" staff and increased the number of short-term consultants that were working. However, in many cases, there was more "value-add" work required than could be handled by the number of core staff that remained. As a result, core staff tended to be "overprogrammed" and less experienced contingent staff and short-term consultants were doing much of the "real" work that might be completed more effectively by core staff. This approach was inefficient in the near term and also created significant problems in the longer term. Critical expertise that the development unit would need in the future was being developed in short-term consultants, not core staff. Consequently, this needed expertise could be lost as contracts expire and these short-term consultants leave the bank.

The final staffing issue related to management depth. There was an insufficient number of qualified managers available to fill vacancies that were expected in the near future. This lack of qualified candidates would probably force the development unit to replace those that retire with external hires. Given that the bank's prior experience with placing external candidates in senior-level positions was tenuous at best, an overreliance on external hires could create significant performance and staffing problems in the next few years.

There were also several issues regarding the bank's staffing processes and practices. Most staffing programs were reactive in nature; staffing efforts began only after specific openings were identified. Other programs were not specifically needs-based. In many cases, "promotions" were position upgrades based on performance and credentials, not staffing actions that were implemented to meet particular needs. A batch hiring process brought skilled individuals to the bank, but these individuals were normally not recruited or selected to fill particular openings.

Finally, the bank tended to have a one-size-fits-all approach to staffing processes. New processes tended to be implemented across the board. Relatively few targeted solutions were developed and implemented to address specific staffing issues.

The Staffing Strategies and Plans That Emerged

As a result of this project, several staffing strategies were proposed to address the staffing issues that were identified:

- **Differentiate job streams to support needed specialization.** Job profiles, accountabilities, and definitions of required skills would be changed to allow technical specialists to develop and apply the deep expertise needed to support the bank's mission. Education economists would focus on economics, education specialists would focus on their particular area of expertise, and operations officers would focus on project and task management.

- **Position and develop the corporate unit as a "center of excellence."** Rather than being purely administrative, the corporate unit would now provide the regions with the specific expertise that they currently could not afford. Individuals with deep economic and education expertise would be part of the corporate unit, but would be allocated to the regions on an as-needed basis. This would allow a region that had a need for a third of a full-time equivalent in education to apply the needed expertise. The region would no longer have to compromise by using a less experienced generalist who happened to be available.

- **Recruit and develop high-level policy development expertise.** Since the bank lacked individuals with this expertise, it would actively recruit from the outside to fill the positions needed to support the move to program-based lending. These recruits would be provided with accelerated development so that they could get up to speed on the bank's procedures and operations.

- **Redefine the role of short-term consultants.** The unit would identify and designate as "core" those jobs that are absolutely critical to implementing plans and strategies, require specific technical or functional expertise on an ongoing basis, provide significant "competitive advantage", and require a full, in-depth knowledge of bank or development unit policies, procedures, and systems. Wherever feasible, these core positions would be filled by full time, core staff. Further, all of the unit's recruiting and development efforts would focus on these core positions. All positions that do not meet one of the four criteria described above would be filled using consultants. Short-term consultants should also provide any expertise that is needed for a short term, at a particular point in time.

- **Develop management candidates in advance of need.** The development unit would work to develop a "pool" of candidates for critical senior management positions in advance of need. This will ensure that there are qualified internal candidates that can be considered and selected to fill senior management openings that arise (whether due to retirements, transfers, or voluntary turnover). Effective management succession and development processes are quite proactive. They usually include the definition of specific management requirements and identification and development of candidates (in advance of need). The objective of a process should not be to identify the specific individual that will be placed in the position when a particular incumbent leaves.

Needless to say, these staffing strategies could not be finalized or implemented until the business issues (as described above) were addressed. The managers in the development unit were not in a position to dictate this resolution. Instead, they needed to develop contingency plans and compromises that would allow the sector to move forward with its revitalization as solutions to the business issues were developed.

The Role of Quantitative Analysis in This Project

In most strategic staffing projects, a staffing model is developed and used to define specific staffing plans and actions that are needed to eliminate (or at least reduce) critical staffing gaps and shortages that are expected in each planning period. While gaps and surpluses were defined as part of this project, specific staffing plans and actions were not. Managers were willing to talk about qualitative staffing issues and strategies, but they were reluctant to discuss those staffing issues in quantitative terms. Some did not see the value of being so specific. Others had participated in quantitative workforce planning efforts in the past that had proven to be primarily "number crunching exercises" that were of little value. Still others had done some quantitative staffing analyses of their own areas and saw little benefit in doing a similar thing for the unit as a whole. Most managers seemed to think that it would be very difficult to implement the specific, quantitative staff planning approach that had been proposed, given some of the bank's current practices regarding headcount planning and control. Some of these impediments included:

- **Inflexible budgeting processes:** Staff planning was part of the annual budgeting cycle. This made it difficult to adjust staffing requirements and staffing plans as changes emerged during the year. Further, since managers had to rejustify staffing needs before even previously approved positions could be filled, proactive staff planning and action was difficult at best.
- **Staff cost ratios:** The fixed/variable staffing ratios that had been set limit management flexibility regarding staffing decisions. The ratios were not fully based on need and were set at somewhat arbitrary levels. In some units, effective staffing might require a higher percentage of "core" staff than is allowed by the ratio. In other units, it might be possible to perform the work adequately with a higher percentage of consultants. The "fixed" nature of the ratios eliminated the possibility of this needed variation.
- **Unclear accountability for staffing decisions:** Within the bank's matrix structure, accountability for staffing was not well defined. Managers preferred to have staff report directly to them and were not comfortable in using staff (no matter how highly skilled) that reported to another manager. In concept, functional managers were to play critical roles in staffing regional positions, but in reality regional managers were the ones making the "final" staffing decisions. Because staffing accountability was not fully defined, some managers were able to "work around" the system (e.g., not communicating openings until preferred candidates were identified and hiring talented individuals that did not necessarily meet predefined position

requirements). Many of these "work around" practices were counter to the open, proactive nature of strategic staffing.

- **Strict policies and procedures regarding staff reductions make it difficult to add appropriately skilled staff.** The bank's policies and procedures regarding staff reductions were quite strict. Because of this high standard, managers were unwilling to take the difficult steps necessary to remove staff—even those whose performance was inadequate or whose skills had become obsolete. Given that headcounts and budgets were strictly limited, new recruits that had newly required skills could only be hired if other employees left to make room for them. Yet the bank's strict reduction policies made it hard for managers to remove poor performers in order to make room for these needed recruits. Again, these practices made it difficult to be proactive regarding staffing and implement staffing practices that meet the unit's needs.

In order to implement strategic staffing effectively, including its quantitative components, the bank would need to change some of these practices. To the extent that the impediments remained, the bank would be unable to plan strategically to meet its staffing needs and would be forced instead to react on a tactical, short-term basis.

Because of these concerns, the quantitative staffing analysis and planning proceeded no further. While the lack of a well-developed quantitative staffing model may not prove to be an issue in the near term, the lack of quantitative staffing information may become more of a problem in the future because:

- **Staff losses were not considered.** Even in its preliminary format, the model indicated that the numbers of staff that should be added during the planning horizon were higher than management estimates for that same period. The primary cause of these differences was staff losses. In some cases, managers were thinking incrementally (i.e., determining how many "more" than the current headcount would be needed) and were not considering the fact that staff would be leaving (e.g., as a result of contracts with individuals expiring, voluntary turnover, and probable retirements). For example, a manager might estimate that three staff should be hired to support planned growth (thinking in terms of a net increase). In fact, six staff may be required (the increase of three plus three more to replace other staff that will be leaving the bank during the planning period). The more detailed, quantitative analysis would have more precisely identified the actual number of openings that could be expected. Staffing plans that did not consider the need to replace individuals that leave would be ineffective and incomplete.

- **Progress measures could not be created and applied.** As stated earlier, the bank's board not only charged the education unit with meeting its business and staffing objectives, but also asked for regular progress reports that addressed staffing needs. The lack of quantitative data would make it difficult for the unit to report what its needs are, the particular staffing actions that were taken, the impact these actions had, and what needs remain.

- **Plans would be difficult to implement.** It is always extremely difficult to implement qualitative plans effectively and efficiently. By definition, qualitative plans can only be directional in nature; they cannot and do not describe scope measures in any way. Such plans may be able to determine that "more" staff with policy-making expertise will be needed, for example, but they cannot describe how many more such staff will be needed and when those people should be placed. If the organization hires ten more people, is that the right number? Might there be a need for more than just those ten? Might fewer be needed? Staffing plans just can't be developed or implemented effectively unless they contain some quantitative measures.

Conclusions and Recommendations

This project did a good job of raising and crystallizing critical staffing issues. The strategic staffing process provided a good forum for discussing these issues and proposing and evaluating staffing strategies. For the most part, the strategies that were proposed were a direct result of these discussions and had not been considered before. However, the reluctance to analyze the quantitative data in detail may prove problematic later on as managers find it increasingly difficult to implement purely "directional" plans and measure progress against generic objectives.

Even though bank policies and procedures may have inhibited the effectiveness of the strategic staffing process, they in no way prevented its implementation. Based on the findings drawn and the conclusions that were reached during this project, it was recommended that the education unit take the following steps:

- Complete the quantitative staff planning work that was suspended, developing staffing plans for all regions and increasing the planning horizon from one year to three years.
- Implement each of the staffing strategies described above.
- Analyze each of the impediments to effective strategic staffing that are described above and identify which might be modified or eliminated, creating plans for making those modifications and working within those that cannot change.

Additional Examples

Here are several more examples of companies that have successfully implemented strategic staffing processes. For each example, I have summarized the strategic context in which the strategy was developed, described the components of the strategic staffing process that was used, and highlighted the outcomes and benefits that were realized.

Telecommunications Company

Strategic Context. This company was about to implement a new, radically different technology for voice transmission. The change was to be installed nationwide, on an office-by-office basis, over a four-year period. The company anticipated that the change in technology would affect required capabilities and staffing levels in both technical (e.g., local facility troubleshooting and repair) and ''soft'' (e.g., customer service) skills areas. Complicating this situation, many individuals in the current workforce were nearing retirement.

Strategic Staffing Approach. Initially, staff planning efforts focused on technical jobs (separate models for customer service positions were completed later on). For planning purposes, the company created the new role of central office technician, a category that encompassed several existing jobs and titles. First, the company defined the skills and capabilities that would be required in this new position to fully support the implementation of the new technology. Next, it defined how many such technicians would be required, in which locations, during which planning periods (following the rollout plan that had been prepared). Several staffing models and supply/demand scenarios were developed, including some that analyzed the impact of several different retirement scenarios.

Outcomes/Benefits. After a review of the various scenarios, the company decided that most of its needs could, in fact, be met through redeployment of its current employees. It created specific redeployment plans for each planning period and defined the specific training and development that would be needed to support those moves. The company also developed plans for selective hiring and targeted staff reductions (e.g., eliminating staff with obsolete skills who were unwilling or unable to develop new skills) in cases where needs could not be met through redeployment.

Insurance Company

Strategic Context. As a result of a strong economy, this company expected to grow the consumer component of its business quite rapidly over the coming five-year period. Unfortunately, the strong economy also meant that opportunities abounded; an increased number of managers was expected to leave the company to take jobs elsewhere. This business growth and increased turnover would create a large number of openings for branch managers that would need to be filled in the coming years. The traditional career path for branch managers (through underwriting) would be unable to provide a sufficient number of qualified branch manager candidates, so alternative sources of talent had to be identified.

Strategic Staffing Approach. The company created a staffing model that focused on branch manager positions and the career paths that fed these positions. The model defined how many candidates could reasonably be expected to move along the traditional career path through underwriting into branch manager slots and how many additional openings would have to be filled through external hiring and increased internal placements. Two scenarios were generated. The first assumed that the development and promotion of candidates would proceed normally and that all additional openings would be filled through external recruitment. The second assumed that accelerated development and movement would be used to increase the number of internal candidates that would be available during the planning horizon, with recruitment used only as a last resort.

Outcomes/Benefits. By analyzing the two scenarios simultaneously, the company was able to determine the optimum blend of accelerated promotions and external recruiting that was needed to fill the branch manager openings that were anticipated. The model allowed the company to plan for the development effort that would be needed in terms of scope (how many individuals needed to be trained), objectives (what capabilities needed to be developed), and timing (when training needed to begin). The model also let the company determine how many external candidates would be needed, and when.

Aerospace Company

Strategic Context. This government contractor always worked on several major projects simultaneously. To facilitate accounting, the company chose to create a separate organization unit for each project, with each such unit operating relatively autonomously. Given the nature of the work that was being done, there was a great need for engineering talent in all project units. In the past, each project and organization had created its own staffing plan to meet the needs of its particular project, hiring engineers as the project geared up and laying them off when the project geared down (or was cancelled). Because the projects were run separately (and there was no real coordination of staffing among projects), it was not unusual for one unit to be laying off engineers while another was looking for external candidates with those very same skills. Needless to say, this uncoordinated approach was costly, created much confusion, and had a negative impact on continuity and morale.

Strategic Staffing Approach. The company decided that it needed to coordinate engineering staffing among projects. It created a single staffing model that analyzed engineering requirements and availability by discipline, across projects. This allowed the company to manage its critical engineering talent as a pool, allocating engineers to and from projects as required.

Outcomes/Benefits. Obviously, there was an immediate and significant reduction in simultaneous hiring and firing, and a major reduction in related staffing transaction costs. The change in staffing practices also brought about improved utilization of engineering talent and experience and more efficient placement of engineering staff.

Medical Center

Strategic Context. A major chain of hospitals decided to open a new medical center in a geographic area that it did not currently serve. The size and scope of the facility was determined after a rigorous analysis of the demographics of that new area.

Staffing the facility with the right talent was critical. Some positions would be filled using local talent; experienced staff that was transferred from existing facilities would fill other jobs. A key question that emerged was: How could the company staff the new facility with the experienced talent that it needed while minimizing the talent drain on the existing medical centers?

Strategic Staffing Approach. The company created a series of staffing models that included the new medical center and all other existing facilities from which talent might be drawn. The model was segmented by unit (e.g., Medical/Surgical, Intensive Care, Emergency Medicine). Separate models were necessary because different assumptions had to be made regarding the likelihood that individuals with these skills would commute to the new center. For example, intensive care unit staff might be willing to commute long distances (e.g., because job opportunities for individuals with these specialized skills were limited), but medical/surgical staff would not (e.g., because they had many opportunities to work at other medical facilities that were close to their homes). In each case, the staffing model defined specific needs for both the new and the existing medical centers. Where needs in the new center were met by transferring staff from existing facilities, the models and plans defined the staffing actions to be taken to fill the openings that the transfers created.

As part of the strategic staffing process, the company also conducted an economic analysis of the area to be served (to better define the mix of patient care services that would be needed) and a demographic analysis (to identify what skills would be available in the area surrounding the new facility).

Outcomes/Benefits. Several important conclusions were reached. The company discovered that there was a critical shortage of skilled medical technicians in the geographic area surrounding the new medical center. To meet this need in the near term, the company was forced to relocate many more individuals from existing facilities than it had originally thought. The staffing model allowed the company to identify (and develop plans to address) the "back fill" issues that the large number of relocations created. Many of those who were replacing the relocating staff needed specific training so that they could perform in their new assignments.

The company determined that future, longer-term staffing needs for medical technicians in the new facility had to met locally; additional relocation from existing medical centers was not feasible. To this end, the company actively funded external education (e.g., trade schools), built alliances with nearby teaching hospitals, established community college license programs, and implemented a co-op program at local high schools. It also convened a task force to address recruiting issues on an ongoing basis.

SECTION

3

Implementing and Supporting Your Strategic Staffing Process

CHAPTER 9

Implementing Your Process Effectively

Implementing any new methodology, process, or tool can be a daunting task. No matter how well it is designed, a tool can fail miserably if it is not rolled out effectively. Strategic staffing is no exception. This section describes an approach for implementing the strategic staffing process that I have found to be particularly useful. (By the way, while this approach is specifically appropriate for the strategic staffing process, it can also be used equally well whenever a new process or tool is being introduced.) It also summarizes implementation roles and responsibilities and highlights some obstacles that may hinder the effective implementation of your strategic staffing process.

An Effective Implementation Framework

Here is a model that you can use to help you create an effective plan for implementing the strategic staffing process in your organization (see Figure 9-1). Whenever an organization is implementing a new process, it must balance two separate parameters: scope and impact.

- **Scope.** Think of scope as the size of the group to be included in the process. It might be defined in terms of the number of jobs, job levels, locations, functions, or organization units. Sim-

Figure 9-1.

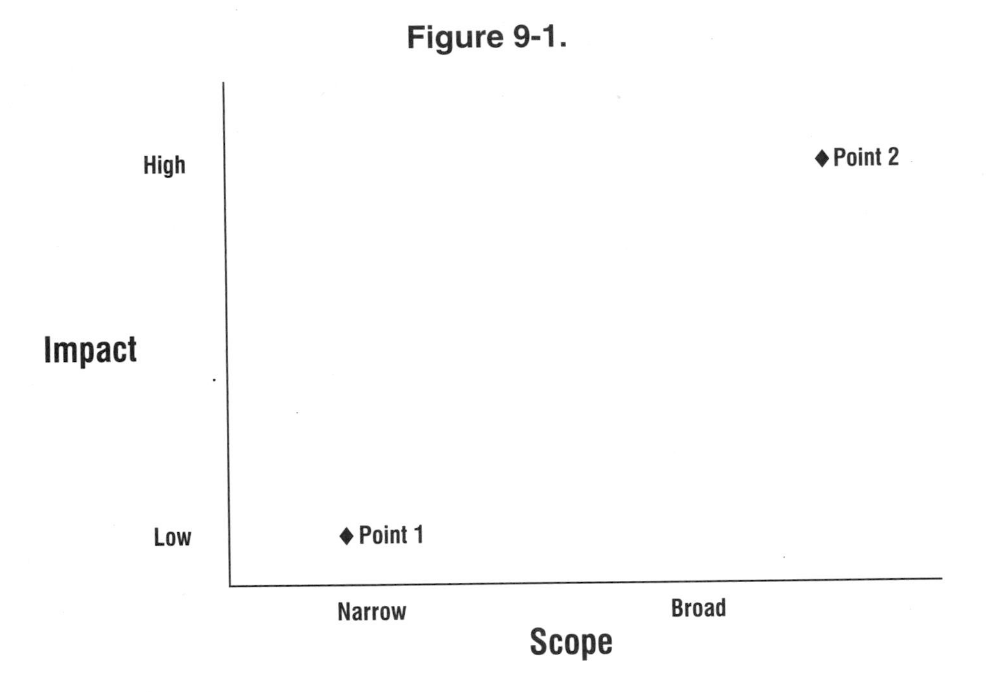

ply defined, you could implement this process for "a few," for "many," or for something in between. In Figure 9-1, scope is shown on the x (horizontal) axis.

- **Impact.** Think of impact as the extent to which the new process is positively affecting the organization. A new process could have an impact that ranges from low to high. In Figure 9-1, impact is shown as the y (vertical) axis.

If this is truly a new process, you are probably starting out at point 1 at the bottom left-hand side of Figure 9-1 (i.e., currently there is no process or the existing process is having little impact over a narrow organization scope). Normally, your objective would be to get to point 2 on the upper right-hand side of Figure 9-1, where your new process will be having a high impact over a broad scope. But how do you get to point 2 from point 1?

Clearly, it would be possible to get to point 2 from point 1 in a single step only if massive resources were available to support implementation. Because staff time, money, and other critical resources are usually limited, it is generally not possible to have a high impact over that broad scope all at once. Some kind of step-by-step approach to implementation is more feasible. There are two basic approaches to consider.

Approach A

Figure 9-2 depicts a horizontal approach—approach A. Your objective is still to have high impact over the whole organization, using a step-by-step approach. The given is that you must initially include in your implementation a broad scope of the organization. With approach A, you complete *each* implementation step (thus having some impact) for a *wide scope* (perhaps even all) of the organization for which the new process is being applied. Once a step is complete for that broad scope, the next step can be taken (again including all the units that are included in this implementation). Following this step-by-step approach will allow you to implement the new process over the entire scope of the organization.

Figure 9-2. Approach A.

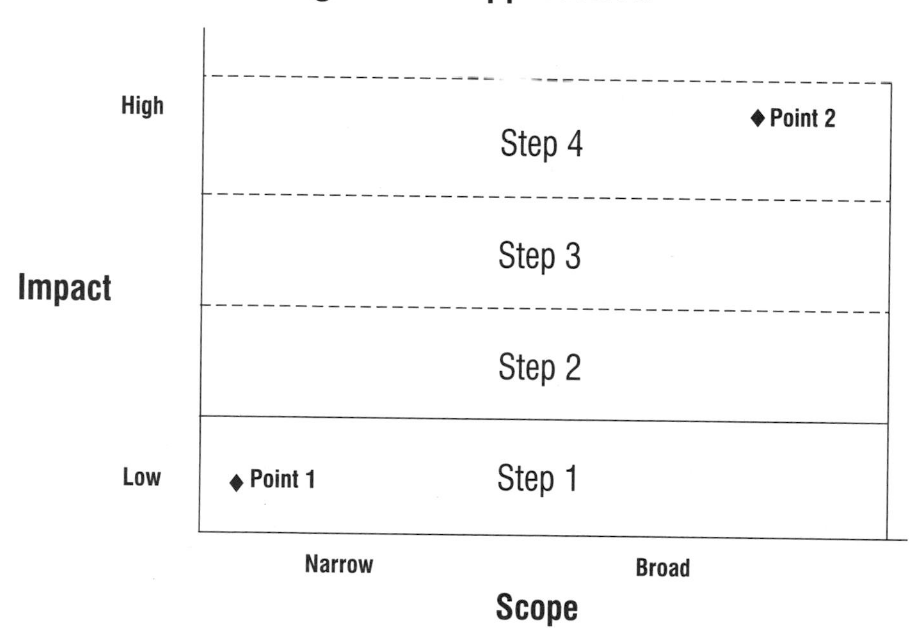

Here is an example of approach A. Suppose that your staffing process included these four basic steps:

Step 1: Understand the longer-term business context.

Step 2: Define staffing requirements and availability.

Step 3: Define required staffing plans and actions.

Step 4: Implement staffing plans.

Suppose further that your objective was to implement this process simultaneously in four organization units. If you were using approach A, you would first develop an understanding of the long-term business context of each of the four units. Once that understanding was developed, you would define staffing requirements and availability for all four units (step 2). Once step 2 was complete, you would create staffing plans for all four units (step 3). Once these staffing plans were complete, you could begin step 4 (implementing those plans) for all units. This would meet your objective of creating and implementing a staffing strategy for each of the four units.

Approach B

Figure 9-3 depicts a vertical approach—approach B. Your overall objective is still to have high impact over the whole organization, and you must still use a step-by-step approach. The given this time is that you must have a high impact right away (as opposed to having some impact over a broad scope). With approach B, you complete *all* implementation steps (thus having high impact) for *one* piece of the organization (thus having a narrow scope) for which the new process is to be applied. Once all steps have been taken for a given piece of the organization, the process can be implemented for a second piece.

The entire process is implemented piece-by-piece until it has been fully implemented. Like approach A, approach B allows you to implement the new process over the entire scope of the organization.

Here is an example of approach B. Suppose that your strategic staffing process includes the same four basic steps described in the example for approach A. Suppose further that your overall objective was to implement this process eventually in four organization units.

Figure 9-3. Approach B.

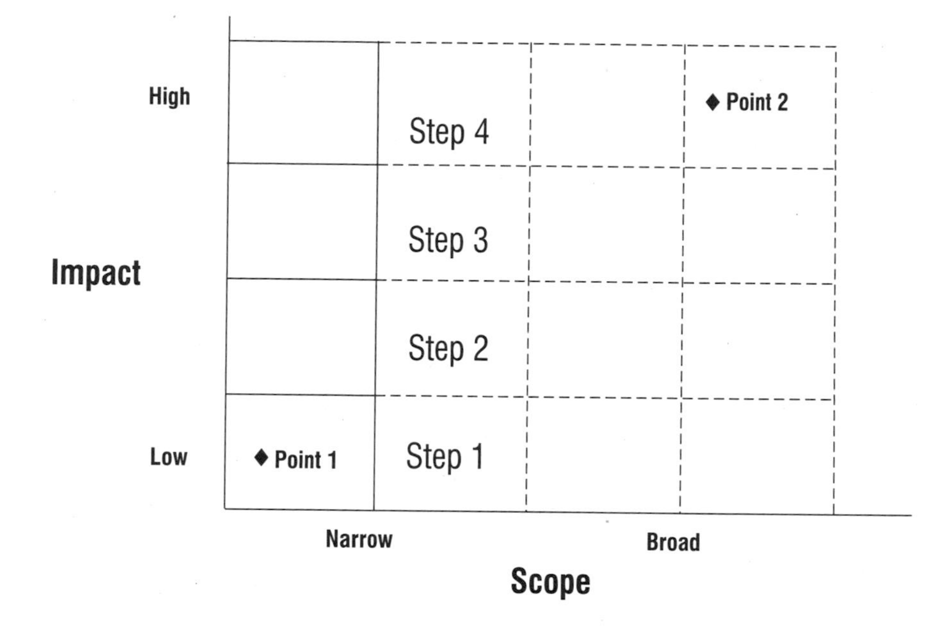

If you were using approach B, you would first develop an understanding of the long-term business context of unit 1, then define the staffing requirements and availability for unit 1, then define staffing plans and actions for unit 1, and finally begin implementing the staffing plans for unit 1. Once the implementation of the unit 1 plans had been initiated, you could begin the process for unit 2. Similarly, once plans for unit 2 were under way, you could begin the process for unit 3, and then for unit 4. This would meet your objective of creating and implementing a staffing strategy for each of the four units.

Which Approach to Use

Which approach is more appropriate? Would you choose approach A or approach B? At first glance, it seems that the correct answer is "sometimes A and sometimes B". In reality, when you are implementing a strategic staffing process (especially for the first time), approach B is almost always the preferred approach. Here are some reasons why I think that this is the case:

- **The impact argument.** Part of the reasoning for choosing Approach B is rooted in a very particular definition of impact. For this model, I always define ''high impact'' as ''fixing a problem'', ''resolving an issue'', or ''answering a question''. In these cases, there just is no benefit to having ''some'' impact. All these definitions all make ''impact'' a binary concept. Either you solve a problem or you don't. Either you resolve an issue or you don't. Consequently, either you have high impact or you have no impact at all. When you set out to implement a new process, you must have high impact, which means that by definition you must narrow the scope of your efforts to ensure that you can fully address a critical staffing issue.

Contrast this approach with Approach A. Remember that I have defined ''impact'' in terms of solving problems. How much of any staffing problem can you address by taking just step 1 (e.g., understanding the unit's business plans), as you would if you were following Approach A? None! That step is necessary, but taking it does not in itself address the problem at all. What about defining staffing requirements and availability? Does that in itself solve any problems? No, it doesn't. What about the creation of staffing plans? Again, this is a necessary step, but it adds no value by itself. Only when the staffing plans are implemented is there any value seen. With Approach B, you begin to add value very quickly, once all steps are taken and the first issue is addressed.

• **The elapsed time argument.** In the very first chapter of this book, I suggest that instead of creating staffing strategies for business units, you create staffing strategies that address specific, critical issues. Approach B is particularly effective in these cases. You should narrow the scope of your initial efforts by focusing on one *issue* at a time, not one unit at a time. In this way, you will have that high impact when you create and implement the staffing strategies that best address that issue.

If you were to use approach A, how long would it take for you to understand the long-term business context of all four units in the example? Probably several months. How long would it then take to define staffing requirements and availability for all those units? Probably several more months. What about defining specific staffing plans for each unit? Yet more time. By the time you get around to implementing plans, you are ''fixing'' the problems that you thought would occur when you began the process a year or more ago—which are not necessarily the issues that managers now consider critical.

- **The credibility argument.** By actually resolving issues sequentially, you will be building credibility for your process and your expertise. You will be building a reputation as a business-oriented problem solver, not just an implementer of processes that may or may not have significant impact. The more problems you solve, the more managers will think positively of you, and the more opportunities you will have to solve critical problems. These satisfied managers will become your best marketers, telling their colleagues of the value that you added.

What impact will the implementation of approach A have on your credibility? How long will managers be willing to wait for you to address their staffing issues? Probably not as long as a full implementation of approach A will require. If, after much time adding no value (as you conduct the first three steps of your process), you finally begin to implement strategies that address the wrong issues, that is not going to improve your credibility.

- **The education argument.** Many organizations that are implementing strategic staffing processes are just not sure what an effective process entails or what form it should take. By fully implementing the process for a given issue, you will be creating a realistic sample that you can use to educate your audience regarding what an effective process includes and entails. Samples like these can also be used to train others in the process and applications.

- **The leverage argument.** One possible drawback to approach B is that it appears that only one issue can be addressed at a time. That is not necessarily the case. Most companies create a task force or work team that is charged with developing and implementing the strategic staffing process. Suppose that there are six members on such a team. The entire team, working together, can develop a staffing strategy that addresses the first issue, perhaps completing their work in a month or two. In so doing, each member of the team learns what strategic staffing entails and how effective strategies are developed. Once the first issue has been addressed, each of the six team members can lead a team (with each team including five new team members), permitting six simultaneous efforts to develop staffing strategies for six more issues. Thus, at the end of a three-month period, seven strategies will have been developed. If the process continues, thirty-six more issues can be addressed in the third wave. Needless to say, this allows a large number of staffing issues to be addressed in a relatively short period of time.

Are you still unconvinced that approach B is usually the better way to proceed? Here is one more example. Suppose that you have been called in to develop a plan to fight a massive wildfire. This huge fire is threatening a thousand square miles of territory that includes populated areas, industrial zones, parks, and wilderness. Suppose further that you have a limited supply of water and flame-retarding chemicals at your disposal. What would you do? I seriously doubt that you would spread the water and chemicals evenly over the entire thousand square miles. In fact, that might be the least effective use of your scarce firefighting resources. There might be some initial benefit, but soon the fires would flare up, and you would then have no resources left to fight them. Instead, you would need to allocate the water and chemicals wisely, in ways that would maximize the effectiveness of their use. It is likely that you would first begin to fight the parts of the fire that were directly threatening the lives and safety of people. Only when those fires had been put out (or at least substantially brought under control) would you move to fight the fires that were threatening property (but not lives). In the meantime, the fires that are burning in the unpopulated wilderness may just have to keep burning. If, after controlling the fires that were threatening life and property, you still have some water left, you might then move on to fight the fires in wilderness. By fighting the fires sequentially, and in order of priority, you would maximize the impact of your limited supply of water and chemicals.

Your organization may be analogous to this wildfire. There may be dozens of fires that seem to require your attention. Many managers will be asking you to help them address their staffing issues. However, your resources (i.e., your time and your budget), just like the water and chemicals, are limited and must be used wisely. Clearly, the least effective approach is to spread your limited resources evenly across all the issues to be addressed (i.e., doing something for everyone). This may bring some initial relief, but no manager's staffing issues will be fully addressed if you do this. Like burning embers that were not fully extinguished, the issues will just flare up later—but by then you will have exhausted your resources and will be in no position to fight further. Just as you need to set priorities in fighting the wildfire, you must set priorities when addressing staffing issues. Just as you did not move on to the fires threatening property until you had brought the fires threatening people under control, you must address one staffing issue before trying to move on to the next. And just as you left the fires in the wilderness burning, you may find it necessary to leave some less critical staffing issues unaddressed.

In summary, approach B (i.e., narrow scope/high impact) is far superior and should be implemented each time a staffing strategy is to be developed. When you are launching strategic staffing for the first time, select a critical issue and work to create and implement a staffing plan that fully addresses that issue. By so doing you will have a positive impact on the organization in the near term (a quick win), you will build your own credibility, and you will clearly demonstrate the value of the process to your organization.

Implementation Roles and Responsibilities

Now that we have set the stage for effective implementation, it's time to define roles and accountabilities. The responsibility for developing and implementing staffing strategies and plans lies with those who define the amount and type of resources needed to implement business strategies and then allocate those resources once they become available. In most companies, line managers play this role.

There is no question but that line managers are expected to manage financial and material resources. I think this also applies to human resources. I strongly believe that, in the long run at least, the primary responsibility for developing and implementing staffing strategies and plans lies with line managers, not human resource (HR) staff. Are you unconvinced? Compare staff planning to the budgeting process.

Budgeting is a clearly defined management responsibility. Managers fully understand this and work accordingly; most organizations even provide training opportunities so that managers can better understand the budgeting process and build their skills in this area. The finance function usually supports the process by providing structure and assistance, but it does not prepare budgets for line managers. Why should staff planning be any different? In some ways, the staff planning process and the budgeting process are really quite similar. Both require planning, definition of required resources, allocation of those resources, measurement of results, and adjustments to allocations if objectives are not met. Are not people just another resource that line managers should manage?

Clearly, then, strategic staffing is not a legacy or the key to long-term job security among HR staff! It is the job of HR to ensure that line managers are doing this well. HR staff must play critical supporting roles if managers are to create and implement effective staffing plans and strategies. In the near term these managers may not even be aware of this responsibility and may very well lack the skills and experience they need in order to develop and apply the strategic staffing process effectively. HR staff can play key internal consulting roles here, supporting the managers that are preparing the staffing plans. Specifically, HR staff should:

- Define why strategic staffing is needed and the value it provides.
- Create and support the strategic staffing process.
- Ensure that managers have the tools and resources that they need in order to define staffing needs and develop realistic staffing plans.
- Act in partnership with managers to identify critical issues and develop effective strategies.

- Train managers in the use of the process.
- Work with managers to resolve difficult staffing issues.
- Serve as conduits for transferring and processing critical staffing information.

Needless to say, it will be necessary to build this line management accountability over time. It won't (and shouldn't) happen overnight. Instead, the approach should be phased in. As an external consultant, I am often called in to "transfer" my knowledge to company staff. To do this, I often suggest to clients that when implementing the strategic staffing process for the first time, I should do it and they should watch. The second time, we do it together. The third time, they do it and I watch, providing insight and guidance where necessary. The fourth time they complete the process on their own; I remain available to answer questions but do not participate in the process directly. That approach will probably work well for you as well, with you serving as an internal consultant and your manager being the client.

In addition to serving as internal consultants, HR staff can identify common needs and integrate staffing strategies and plans across units. They can identify when similar issues are identified in different organizations. Their cross-unit perspective greatly facilitates this role; managers who operate primarily within a given unit cannot be expected to do this.

Obstacles to Effective Implementation

Some organizations may have to overcome significant obstacles in order to develop and implement the strategic staffing process. In some cases, line managers, especially those that do not fully understand strategic staffing, impede the implementation process. In an equal number of cases, however, it is HR staff that hinder effective implementation.

Line Managers

Line managers will never fully embrace a process that they do not understand. Typically, many line managers have a short-term results orientation that seems inconsistent with the longer-term perspective of staffing strategy. Other managers are sometimes unaware of (or unconvinced of) the benefits and value of strategic staffing, especially when those benefits are not measured in specific terms. Still others resist the strategic staffing process itself, viewing it as added work that brings them little reward.

When you implement your process, make sure that managers really understand what will be done. Show them that the process will be tailored to meet their needs—that it is not the one-size-fits-all approach that they may think it is. If they have a short-term perspective, emphasize that the process can help them right now. Explain that one of the main benefits of strategic staffing is that it provides a longer-term context within which they can make better decisions in the near term. As for measuring the impact and benefits of the process, show them that you are indeed measuring and tracking both the effectiveness and the efficiency of the process (more on measurement is included in Chapter 14).

HR Staff

In some cases, one of the most significant obstacles to the effective implementation of the strategic staffing process is HR staff themselves. As I sometimes say in my presentations, "We have met the enemy and it is us." The most difficult bias on the part of HR staff that needs to be overcome is the one that assumes that staffing is by its very nature reactive and tactical. HR staff that believe this find it hard to think of staffing in any strategic way. Some HR staff have an egalitarian perspective that is more consistent with organization-wide, one-size-fits-all approaches than it is with the targeted, issue-focused approach I suggest. Some assume that in order to be fair and meet business needs, the process must be applied to all jobs. Still other staff lack the in-depth understanding of their business plans that is necessary to define critical HR issues. Finally, some HR professionals still think and act primarily within functional silos, where every problem can be fixed by applying processes, practices, and tools from a given function (like training or recruiting).

As a human resources professional, ensure that your strategic staffing process is implemented effectively and really brings value to your organization by making sure that you:

- Understand that staffing should be proactive. Learn that forward-looking staff planning is not only valuable but absolutely required if business strategies are to be implemented as planned. Your staffing processes will never be fully effective as long as they remain reactive.
- Understand that staffing can often be strategic in nature, and that long-term staffing strategies may be required if significant, critical staffing issues are to be addressed. Make short-term staffing decisions only within the context of long-term staffing strategies.
- Develop a full understanding of your business, including its mission, objectives, strategies, and tactics. This understanding is needed in order to function as a business partner in general, but it is absolutely critical when developing and implementing the strategic staffing process.
- Create and support processes that are tailored to meet the needs of your managers. Don't expect or force them to use a common process and identical planning parameters where that just isn't necessary.
- Develop staffing strategies and plans that integrate aspects of various traditional HR functions. If the staffing issues that you have identified are truly strategic, it is unlikely that they will be fully addressed by applying processes and tools from just one HR functional area. Pull together teams that utilize staff from all those HR functions that will contribute to the solution to each issue.

Above all, position yourself with your line managers as a helpful, realistic business problem solver with a particular expertise in staffing. If you do this, you will surely be successful.

Summary

No matter how well defined it is, the strategic staffing process is helpful only when it is implemented effectively. Always follow the focused approach B. Carefully define the roles and responsibilities of line managers and HR staff, both for the initial implementation and on an ongoing basis. Work and communicate with line managers to avoid implementation obstacles. And finally, make sure that you don't end up impeding your own implementation by approaching strategic staffing from the wrong perspective.

CHAPTER 10

Placing Strategic Staffing Within Your Business Context

By now you know that strategic staffing is the process of identifying and addressing the staffing implications of business strategies and plans. Clearly, then, any strategic staffing process must be fully consistent with the organization's overall business planning processes. What separates truly effective planning processes from those that are not is the nature of the relationship between strategic staffing and business planning.

This chapter describes how the two processes can be related. It also includes a simple diagnostic that you can use to evaluate your own planning context and identify ways to improve the effectiveness of your planning processes.

Integrate, Don't Align

It is not sufficient to simply align or link the business planning process and the strategic staffing process—after all, two components can be aligned or linked only if they are in fact separate to begin with. To be fully effective, strategic staffing must be seamlessly integrated into the fabric of business planning on an ongoing basis.

To gain the maximum benefit from strategic staffing, you must ensure that:

- **Your business planning and staffing processes include the right components to begin with.** For example, a well-developed planning process includes both long-term business strategies and shorter-term operating plans. Similarly, you should be developing both long-term staffing strategies and short-term staffing plans. It is unlikely that your planning processes can be effective if any of these major components are missing.

• **The major components of your planning processes mesh fully.** All the components of your planning process need to fit together like the proverbial well-oiled machine. Even if each component is developed masterfully, the planning processes will fail if the linkages between the components are not strong and dynamic. For example, there need to be strong relationships (and information flows) between long-term business planning and staffing strategies. If these relationships are weak (or, worse yet, nonexistent), the planning process will be incomplete and ineffective.

• **All of the various pieces and processes within each component of your planning process are fully integrated.** Each major component of the planning process includes various pieces that must fit together and build on one another. For example, strategic objectives usually define what is to be accomplished during the planning horizon. Strategies then define specifically what is to be done to achieve those objectives. When these two pieces are well integrated, all the objectives will be achieved if the stated strategy is implemented as designed. When they are not well integrated, strategy implementation may leave some key objectives unmet.

Those well-managed companies that we all hear about typically have well-defined business plans that cover both the long and the short term. Similarly, these companies often produce and implement both longer-term staffing strategies and shorter-term staffing plans that fully support the implementation of their business plans. In your organization, however, it is possible that some of these planning processes need to be improved, better integrated, or created from scratch. In fact, you may be using this book specifically to create a strategic staffing process in an organization where one does not currently exist. How can you quickly assess your business planning situation and determine where strategic staffing fits in best?

A Simple Diagnostic

In some organizations, there are many different planning processes and components that are used to varying degrees to guide actions and resource allocations. Understanding the objectives of these components, and how they fit together, is an important precursor to implementing any strategic staffing process. The diagnostic in Figure 10-1 can be used as a framework to help you identify and evaluate the components of your planning processes and assess the relationships among those various components. The diagnostic should be used in two ways:

1. It can help you to best develop the components of the strategic staffing process and integrate them into ongoing planning efforts *as they apply to your company specifically*. This analysis will allow you to define the context in which your strategic staffing process will be implemented. It will help you to identify what you have to work with and to define the business and staff planning components that you can build on. You will be able to identify missing pieces, bad fits, and other impediments to effective business planning and strategic staffing. Armed with the results of your analysis, you can then focus and prioritize your strategic staffing efforts, adding those needed components and processes.

Figure 10-1. The Diagnostic Framework

	Business Planning	Staff Planning
Long Term		
Short Term		

2. The diagnostic may also help you to identify specific opportunities for improving the effectiveness of your current business and staff planning processes. By using this diagnostic, you can identify key elements of the planning process that may be missing, opportunities to better integrate the pieces within various components of the planning process, and ways of better meshing the components themselves.

This tool should be applied at the organizational level for which the staffing strategy is being developed. Apply the diagnostic at an overall corporate level (e.g., defining corporate business strategy) if a corporate staffing strategy is to be developed. Apply it at a business unit level (e.g., defining business unit strategy) if the staffing strategy is to be developed for a business unit. Avoid mixing levels, though (e.g., defining business planning at a corporate level and staff planning at a business unit level). If you are trying to define a unit staffing strategy, but there is no specific unit business strategy, try to define what the unit will need to do to accomplish its part of the overall corporate strategy. On the other hand, if corporate values apply at the business unit level as well, feel free to include them.

Each of the four steps of the diagnostic process is described in detail. To help you further, there is a diagnostic worksheet at the end of this chapter that you can use to document your analysis, findings, and recommendations. A blank copy of the worksheet is also included on the CD-ROM that comes with this book. (You will need to copy the file from the CD-ROM to your hard drive in order to be able to edit it.) You can then print and use a copy of that form if you don't want to write in the book itself.

The simple two-by-two grid shown in Figure 10-1 forms the basis of the diagnostic. The columns address the two major elements of your planning process:

- **Business planning.** The business planning column will be used to capture any or all aspects or components that can help your business to define and allocate required resources other than people. Typically, this includes all aspects of your strategic planning and budgeting processes.
- **Staff planning.** Include in the staff planning column any processes or components that can help you to define your needs for

and allocate staffing resources in particular. This will include all aspects of your staff planning and staffing processes.

The rows of the diagnostic address your particular planning horizon:

- **Long-term.** The top row includes all long-term planning, however you define long term for your particular organization or unit. In many cases, "long term" is defined by the planning horizon of your strategic planning process (e.g., three to five years). For some units, however (such as information technology), "long term" may be defined as a much shorter period—perhaps just twelve to eighteen months.
- **Short-term.** The bottom row addresses the short term, again as you define it. For many companies, this is often defined as the time frame for the annual budget or operating plan. In other cases, it may be defined as a single quarter.

Thus, the diagnostic defines the four major components of your business planning process: long-term business planning, long-term staff planning, short-term business planning, and short-term staff planning.

Step 1: Take an Inventory of Your Current Pieces

Next, identify what your company is actually doing in each of the four cells and document that in the matrix itself. Include (and specifically document) each process in each cell. Don't just think about the elements; actually write the name of each piece in the appropriate cell of your matrix. If you are simply using this tool to analyze the effectiveness of your current processes, it is probably sufficient to simply identify each piece. If you are using this tool as a guide for creating a staffing strategy, however, actually gather, study, and understand each piece (e.g., actually obtain and read a copy of the business strategy). If there are multiple versions of the same pieces (e.g., if there are different vision statements for the business unit you are analyzing and for the company as a whole), obtain copies of all versions.

Here are some examples of what you might find and document in each cell/component of your planning process:

- **Long term/business planning.** List in this cell any efforts that help your organization to identify requirements for or allocate resources over the long term. This might include your company's mission statement, vision statement, values, strategic objectives, and business strategy.
- **Short term/business planning.** List in this cell any efforts that help your organization to identify requirements for or allocate resources over the short term. This usually includes your operational plan or budget.
- **Long term/staff planning.** List in this cell any efforts that help your organization to identify requirements for or allocate staff over the long term. This would include your human resource (HR) and staffing strategies (if they exist). Be discriminating here. Include only those pieces that are truly long term. Exclude those pieces that appear to have some long-term context, but are really implemented on a short-term basis. For example, include your succession planning and development process here if it is truly viewed and applied as a strategic tool, but place it in the short term/staff planning cell if it is primarily an annual process that drives short-term decisions regarding selection, placement, and/or development.
- **Short term/staff planning.** List in this cell any efforts that help your organization to identify requirements for or allocate staff over the short term. This includes staffing and staffing-related processes that are implemented within your organization that support short-term decisions (e.g., all recruiting and staffing and staffing decisions that are made to meet immediate needs). In many organizations, the vast majority of staff planning and actions occurs in the short term and should thus be included in this cell. You may also wish to include processes that directly

support the staffing processes (such as training and development).

When conducting your inventory, be as complete and thorough as you can be, but keep your analysis at a big-picture level. It is not necessary to capture every variance and nuance. Figure 10-2 shows what a typical diagnostic looks like once all processes and components have been identified and recorded in the appropriate cell.

Figure 10-2. A Typical Result

	Business Planning	Staff Planning
Long Term	Mission Vission Values Objectives Strategies	HR strategies Staffing strategies
Short Term	Operating plans Budgets	Recruiting Movement Career planning Succession planning Development Training

Step 2: Review Each Cell

Once you have completed your inventory, the real diagnosis can begin. Begin your analysis by reviewing the content of each of the four cells, answering the following questions.

Is There Anything That Is Missing?

Are there any key pieces that you think are missing from any of the components? For example, in the long term/business planning cell, there might be a well-defined business strategy, but no clear objectives. Does a business strategy exist? In some cases, the long term/staff planning cell may be empty—for example, when neither a comprehensive HR strategy nor a long-term staffing strategy currently exists.

If you do identify missing pieces, determine whether they are absolutely necessary or simply nice to have. If they are absolutely necessary, develop plans for communicating these needs to those that should be developing those pieces (e.g., line managers, planners, or HR business partners). You may wish to take on the work of developing these missing pieces, but you probably would not do that under the umbrella of strategic staffing.

Are Any of the Pieces Ineffective?

It may be that a component includes all the right pieces, but the pieces are not as effective as they should be. Does your business strategy really describe *how* objectives will be met, or does it just restate business objectives (e.g., it states that you are to become a low-cost producer or a "top five" player in your market, but it does not say what will be done to accomplish this)? Are your short-term staffing practices adequately proactive or primarily reactive?

If you identify opportunities to improve the effectiveness of any of the pieces within a business planning component, separate those pieces that you can fix from those that you cannot. Where improvements are outside your area of accountability, make sure that you document the improvements that are possible and pass that information on to those who can implement the needed changes.

Is There Anything That Is Redundant or Unnecessary?

Are there any pieces of the planning process that exist, but that should be ignored? In some cases, there are pieces that exist, but that really have no impact on the business. Does each piece directly support decision making? Are any of the pieces redundant? If the pieces are in fact critical to the business planning process, consider them when you create your staffing strategy, but if they are not critical, ignore them. Here are some common examples of pieces that might be ignored:

- Many organizations have mission statements. For some, these statements are a valuable component of the business planning process, perhaps even defining why the organization is in business. For others, however, while the statement exists, it does not affect decision making in any appreciable way. One organization that I'm familiar with has a mission statement that was created by a team of senior managers (probably at a facilitated, off-site session). It incorporates glowing language and all the right buzzwords. The problem is that this mission statement does not really affect decisions or resource allocations at all.

If your mission statement is valuable (and used), then factor it into your strategic staffing efforts. If it isn't, then don't.

• Company values are often defined but not integrated into the business. I know of an organization that developed, documented, and disseminated a set of corporate values. As a way of communicating these values, the organization printed posters that were hung in every conference room and elevator lobby. Similarly, the values were printed on laminated cards that could be included in every employee's day planner. The problem was, however, that in this organization, those value statements didn't influence individual behavior in any significant way. The words never got beyond the slogan stage. There was no piece of the performance management process that allowed managers to assess the extent to which subordinates put these values into practice on a day-to-day basis.

If company values exist and drive decision making in your company, incorporate them into your strategic staffing process. If they don't, consider ignoring them.

Are the Components Well Integrated?

Look at the processes and pieces *within* each cell of the diagnostic and assess the extent to which they are working together as a well-oiled machine to implement your plans and achieve your objectives. Are they pieces of a puzzle that fit together well, or are they somewhat separate, disjointed initiatives that compete for management time, attention, and resources? Pay particular attention to the long term/business planning and short term/staff planning cells.

Long Term/Business Planning. Each piece should be fully consistent with the piece before and the piece after. For example, consider "mission" to be your reason for being in business. "Vision" should be a description of what you want your organization to look like—the place your company wants to get to over time. "Objectives" are the signposts you pass along the way on your journey from where you are to that place described in your vision. "Strategies" should be the plans that describe how you will move from signpost to signpost (i.e., from objective to objective).

When these pieces are not well integrated, each of them tends to stand alone. For example, as described earlier, there may be a mission statement that is disconnected from the other pieces of the resource allocation process. In some cases, organizations have created vision statements that are virtually indistinguishable from their mission statements. Some organizations have several unintegrated vision statements that were created by separate groups at separate times. Perhaps worst of all, some organizations have developed strategies that, when implemented, will not allow them to achieve their stated objectives.

If the efforts in your long term/business planning cell are well integrated, make sure that your strategic staffing efforts are consistent with that integrated approach. If the pieces do not fit so well with each other, determine which efforts are actually driving decision making and ensure that staffing strategies are consistent with those efforts in particular.

Short Term/Staff Planning. To what extent are your short-term staffing processes integrated? Have you developed cross-functional plans that, when taken together, will ensure that you have the right people in the right place at the right time? Indeed, staffing efforts should be integrated with one another. Yet, this integration may not need to occur at an overall, functional level. If you are taking the issue approach, you may want to integrate recruiting, staffing, internal movement, and development in ways that most effectively address a particular issue. As an example, you might bring together particular individuals (with particular expertise) from these functions and charge that team with addressing an issue of insufficient management depth. Don't assume that you need to bring together the entire recruiting, staffing, and development functions to create an integrated solution.

Do you think that the various functional components of your short-term staffing processes are well integrated? Here are three tests to see if they are:

1. Are representatives of each function present and are they active participants when staffing decisions are being made? If they are, it is likely that your processes are integrated. If they are not all present, if they develop separate functional plans, and/or if integration is left to communication outside such a session, then integration is unlikely.
2. Do you have separate plans for each HR function? For example, do you have separate recruiting and development strategies? This approach, while common, is difficult to implement well. In some cases, it creates competition for resources among functions that actually impedes required action.
3. Think about your development planning processes. Some organizations create separate development plans as part of their performance appraisal, career planning, succession/development, and high-potential programs. If these plans are created at different times, using different criteria and standards, and result in different/separate plans, it is unlikely that your HR/staffing functions are sufficiently integrated.

Step 3: Examine the Relationships Between Cells

Once you have completed your analysis of each cell, look at the relationships between cells. Draw arrows to show the direction(s) in which information flows. If there is dialogue and two-way communication, show an arrow in each direction. Use the thickness of the arrow to show the quality of that information flow (e.g., solid for good flow, dotted for partial flow). Remember that there probably cannot be any relationship at all between a well-developed component and a poorly developed one (e.g., an empty box on the diagnostic).

Here are some examples of what your analysis might include:

- **Long term/business planning and short term/business planning.** This is the relationship between strategy and budgets/operating plans. When this relationship is effective, the short-term budget is fully consistent with the longer-term strategy. For example, the budget or operating plan may actually be the first year of a three-year business plan that is updated annually. If this is the case, draw a dark arrow from the upper left cell to the lower left cell. When this relationship is ineffective, the budgeting process is not really linked to strategy at all. The binder (or deck of slides) that describes the business strategy may exist, but the business strategy has little or no impact on how the business is managed or how resources are actually allocated; it is really the short-term budget that drives decision making. I sometimes refer to this situation as SPOTS, or *s*trategic *p*lan *o*n *t*op *s*helf. If this is the case, draw a very light arrow from the upper left to the lower left—or perhaps no arrow at all.

- **Long term/business planning and long term/staff planning.** Are staffing issues raised when your business strategies are first proposed and developed? Or are staffing strategies created only after business objectives and strategies have been defined? Might there be staffing strategies that really are not related directly to business plan implementation? If staffing strategies are prepared primarily in response to business plans, then draw a dark arrow from the upper left to the upper right. If the number and type of available staff affect the strategies that are proposed (e.g., you decide to enter a market because of the talent that is available internally), then draw an arrow from the upper right to the upper left. If staffing issues are identified and discussed as part of the business strategy process (and strategies for addressing those issues are developed as part of that process), then perhaps arrows should be drawn in both directions.

- **Long term/staff planning and short term/staff planning.** When the strategic staffing process is implemented effectively, this relationship is usually quite clear. As stated earlier, long-term staffing strategies form the context for short-term staffing decisions.

If short-term staffing decisions are made in this longer-term context, draw a dark arrow from the upper right to the lower right. If short-term staffing decisions are not made in this long-term context, then draw a light arrow (or no arrow at all).

• **Short term/business planning and short term/staff planning.** What is the relationship between budget and staffing actions? Does the budget process really define the amount of resources that are available? Do you then simply translate these available resources into the number of people to be hired, promoted, and trained? If so, draw a thick arrow from the lower left to the lower right. Do you sometimes define the numbers and types of staff that will be required and then build a coherent business case for securing the resources to do this? If so, draw an arrow from the lower right to the lower left.

Note that there are no diagonal relationships or lines of communication defined here. For example, it is impossible to directly link long-term business planning and short-term staff planning. Such relationships are not feasible.

When you have completed this step, look at the direction and relative thickness of the arrows you drew. When your company is operating effectively, you will have dark arrows in both directions in two places: between long term/business planning and long term/staff planning and between short term/business planning and short term/staff planning. You will also have dark arrows (probably pointing down) between long term/business planning and short term/business planning and between long term/staff planning and short term/staff planning.

You may end up with two sets of arrows pointing in both directions: between long term/business planning and long term/staff planning and between short term/business planning and short term/staff planning. This implies that there is meaningful dialogue between business and staff planning in both the long and the short term. This dialogue is essential to developing meaningful, realistic staffing strategies and plans. However, creating arrows that point in both directions in these two rows is actually not your ultimate objective (although, at a minimum, it is the place to start). In the final analysis, you want to remove the line on your model that separates the business planning cells and the staff planning cells. This indicates that business planning and staff planning are fully integrated, not just separate processes that are linked well or aligned effectively.

Opportunities to improve the effectiveness of this part of your processes are usually characterized as adding an arrow that does not exist (i.e., creating a relationship or line of communication) or making a light arrow darker (i.e., strengthening a relationship that already exists). Adding an arrow usually entails the creation of a new mechanism or process that facilitates discussion and data exchange. Darkening an arrow usually means that the effectiveness of an existing mechanism needs to be improved. Here are two examples:

- If you need to add an arrow between long term/business planning and short term/business planning, define the process by which short-term plans should be made within the context of the long-term business strategies that exist.
- If you need to darken the arrow between long term/business planning and long term/ staff planning, consider making discussions of staffing implications a regular part of the development of business strategies.

Figure 10-3 shows what a completed diagnostic might look like for a well-developed process.

Some Final Thoughts

Needless to say, the strategic planning process varies widely from company to company; indeed, it may vary within units of the same company. Consequently, there can be no set way of creating the necessary relationships between your business strategy and strategic staffing processes. You should use this diagnostic as a framework to guide your thoughts and actions, not as a cookbook to be followed line by line.

Figure 10-3. A Well-Developed Planning Process

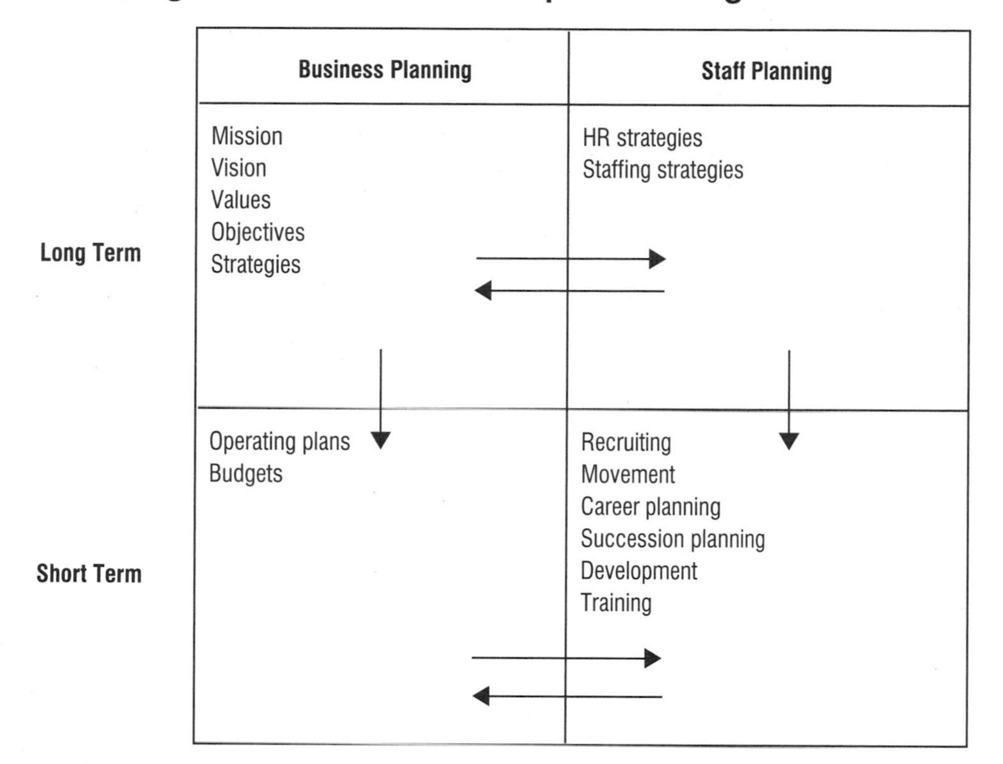

This diagnostic is meant to facilitate action, not prevent it. Consistent with a theme that was raised in Chapter 6, do the most you can with what you have. Even if you find that some pieces or some points of integration don't exist, you can still begin to develop your strategic staffing process. Take full advantage of the processes and information that do exist and create first-generation staffing strategies and plans. Simultaneously, work with others to improve the overall business and staff planning processes, perhaps even using this diagnostic as your framework for discussion.

Here is an example: A multinational oil company wanted to develop a series of staffing strategies for positions that were difficult to fill. Since the company had never developed these strategies before, it used this diagnostic to assess where it was. During the inventory phase, the company determined that a business strategy existed, but during the integration phase it discovered that this strategy consisted primarily of restated business objectives. It lacked the "how" part—it did not describe what was going to be done to achieve those objectives. As stated in Chapter 2, it is not possible to develop a staffing strategy that is based on objectives. Rather than do nothing, the team decided to build its first strategy around a well-crafted vision statement that did in fact provide some of that missing direction. As work on the staffing strategies continued, the team leader worked with the business planning group to create a business strategy that was more descriptive of what would be done, not just what was to be accomplished. During the next planning cycle, this second version of the strategy formed an excellent foundation that was used to create the second-generation staffing strategy.

Defining Your Strategic Context
A Strategic Staffing Worksheet

Step 1: Take an inventory of your current pieces.

What is your organization currently doing in each of these four cells?

	Business Planning	Staff Planning
Long Term		
Short Term		

Step 2: Review each cell.

Are there any pieces missing in any cell?
Are any pieces ineffective?
Are any redundant or unnecessary?

Cell	Findings
Long term/business planning	Missing: Ineffective: Redundant:
Short term/business planning	Missing: Ineffective: Redundant:
Long term/staff planning	Missing: Ineffective: Redundant:
Short term/staff planning	Missing: Ineffective: Redundant:

Step 2: Review each cell (continued).

How consistent are the initiatives in each cell?

Cell	Examples of Integration
Long term/business planning	Effective integration points: Opportunities for improvement:
Short term/business planning	Effective integration points: Opportunities for improvement:
Long term/staff planning	Effective integration points: Opportunities for improvement:
Short term/staff planning	Effective integration points: Opportunities for improvement:

Step 3: Examine the relationships between cells.

How do the cells relate to each other?

Between	And	This Linkage Exists
Long term/business planning	Short term/business planning	Current linkages: Opportunities for strengthening the linkages:
Long term/business planning	Long term/staff planning	Current linkages: Opportunities for strengthening the linkages:
Long term/staff planning	Short term/staff planning	Current linkages: Opportunities for strengthening the linkages:
Short term/business planning	Short term/staff planning	Current linkages: Opportunities for strengthening the linkages:

CHAPTER

11

Assessing Your Current Strategic Staffing Process

The diagnostic represented in Table 11-1 allows you to assess the extent to which your strategic staffing process stacks up against the concepts described in this book. It may also identify opportunities for you to improve the effectiveness of your process. For your convenience, a copy of this form is included in the computer files that accompany this book. (You will need to copy the files from the CD-ROM to your hard drive in order to be able to edit it).

Here is how the assessment tool should be applied:

- Read through all the suggested steps/components in the first column of the form. Make sure that you understand each concept as it is described in this book. If you find a component that you do not understand, go back and read that section of the book before proceeding.
- For each step of the process (i.e., each row of the form), document your current practice. What is it that your organization does? To what extent is that consistent with what is being suggested? Does your process include each component that is listed? If you complete that step, do you do it in the way that is suggested?
- Assess whether your current practices (as you have just described and documented them) are adequate and indicate the result of that assessment in the third column. Are your current

practices meeting your needs? If they are not, why is that? Is something missing? Does something need to be done a different way?

- If you check no in column three of any row, note any opportunities for improvement in column four. Be as specific as you can about what should be done to improve your process—don't just restate the problem. Finally, review the notes that you have made in the fourth column and create a work plan that you can use to implement the changes you have identified.

Table 11-1. Assessing Your Strategic Staffing Process

Suggested Step/Component	Our Current Practice	Is Current Practice Adequate?	Opportunities for Improvement?
Is your process aligned with your business strategy? • Do you have a staffing strategy? • Is it seamless, not a follow-on? • Is it ongoing, not just annual? • Is staffing discussed as each change is considered? • Other: ________		☐ Yes ☐ No	
Does your process focus on strategic staffing issues/gaps? • Are they identified? • Are they defined? • Are they prioritized? • Other: ________		☐ Yes ☐ No	
Have effective staffing strategies been developed? • Do they form a long-term context to guide short-term decisions? • Do they address only critical issues? • Do they adequately or fully address each issue? • Are they long-term? • Are they directional? • Do they define *how* issues will be addressed? • Other: ________		☐ Yes ☐ No	

(continues)

Table 11-1. (Continued)

Suggested Step/Component	Our Current Practice	Is Current Practice Adequate?	Opportunities for Improvement?
Are appropriate staffing plans/models developed? • Do they define appropriate model parameters? • Do they tailor the process to each issue, not assume that one size fits all? • Do they include only relevant jobs? • Do they keep models separate and distinct, not consolidated? • Other: ________		☐ Yes ☐ No	
Are good action plans defined? • Are actions well defined? • Do actions fully support strategy implementation? • Are responsibilities defined? • Is implementation monitored? • Are results measured? • Other: ________		☐ Yes ☐ No	
Are the plans realistic? • Can the plans be implemented? • Do the plans actually drive staffing decisions?		☐ Yes ☐ No	

CHAPTER 12

Involving Managers in the Strategic Staffing Process

Even the most elegant strategic staffing process will be ineffective if senior managers don't understand the underlying concepts and don't buy into the final results. At times, those senior managers will be the only ones who have the information you need to complete your analyses, so their active, enthusiastic participation is critical. This chapter describes the key points regarding the strategic staffing process that you need to make and develop with your line managers and provides some hints regarding what you might do to garner their support. It also provides a very specific outline for a structured interview that you can conduct to gather the information regarding required capabilities and staffing levels that you need. Remember that these are only guidelines. You will need to tailor the message, medium, and approach so that they are fully consistent with the preferences and needs of your management population.

Selling Managers on the Process

Line managers play an important role in the strategic staffing process. Perhaps most importantly, it is their staffing needs that the process is designed to meet. They also provide critical information at key points along the way (such as estimating staffing requirements and evaluating the feasibility of proposed staffing actions). However, if line managers fail to understand the strategic staffing process or lack confidence in the results, it is unlikely that the process will have a positive impact on your organization.

Clearly, then, you will need to ensure that the line managers that you are serving fully understand the strategic staffing process and buy into its results. They need to know what is being done, agree with the information and assumptions you use, understand the expected output, and feel comfortable with the actions that the process suggests. As you work with line managers to develop and implement your strategic staffing process, make sure that they:

- **Understand what is in it for them.** First, make sure that managers understand how implementation of the process will help them to be better managers right now. It's true that strategic staffing can also mitigate future problems, but many managers are just not going to participate fully in a process that does not provide them with direct benefits in the near term. You need to show these managers that by developing longer-term staffing strategies and using those strategies as a context for evaluating shorter term staffing options, they can make staffing decisions that will prove to be effective both now and in the future. Because of this, it is these managers—and not just their successors—who will realize the benefits of the process.

The development and implementation of the strategic staffing process will ensure that managers have the talent they need in order to implement their business plans (and thus meet their performance objectives and bonus targets). In practical, day-to-day terms, this means that the time needed to fill openings with well-qualified talent will be reduced significantly.

- **Understand the objectives and outcomes of the process.** Make sure that managers fully understand the objectives of the process and the expected level of detail of the output. This is especially important when you are implementing the approaches suggested in this book. Some managers will have participated in the past in processes that were burdensome or that produced lackluster results. Make sure that these managers understand how this process will be different from what they have done before. Explain that the process will not use a one-size-fits-all approach and that planning parameters (such as the overall time horizon) will be tailored to reflect their particular needs. Make sure they understand that the analysis will be applied only where necessary (e.g., on critical jobs) and need not be applied to all jobs. Show them that the output (i.e., staffing issues, staffing strategies, and staffing plans and actions) is realistic, specific, and implementable.

- **Are familiar with the process itself.** Managers need to understand how the strategic staffing process will be implemented. They need to understand the various components of the process and how these components fit together. They need to feel confident that the process is robust, yet is flexible enough to reflect change, emerging priorities, and other contingencies.

On the other hand, many managers need this understanding only at an overall, conceptual level. They will not be interested in the details of the process. These managers need to know just enough about the process to allow it to proceed. If there are managers that do want to see and understand the detail, then provide them with as much information as is necessary to secure their support. Just don't give all managers all the detail just because some want or need it.

- **Understand the role that they will play.** Before they will support the strategic staffing process fully, managers usually want to know what their role in the process will be. They want to know how much of their time will be involved. Therefore, you need to clearly describe what their role will be. At a minimum, managers must identify and discuss the staffing issues and implications that they think are most important. Usually, they also provide needed information (especially regarding the capabilities and staffing levels that will be required in the future). Often, they help to develop various planning scenarios and staffing assumptions. Finally, they need to provide input regarding the feasibility of the staffing actions that are the result of the process.

Remember to clearly differentiate the level of effort and management participation that will be needed during the initial implementation of the process from the level that will be needed to maintain the process on an ongoing basis. There is quite a lot of information that managers will need to provide the first time you implement the strategic staffing process. However, when it comes time to update the process, managers can simply modify or revise the information that they provided initially. Clearly, this updating will require far less time and fewer resources than were needed to develop this information from scratch.

Make sure that you strike a proper balance here. Identify the information that managers must provide and make those requirements known. Identify areas in which management input is welcome but is not required, and provide ample opportunity for managers to provide this input as they see fit.

Much of this communication and dialogue with managers can be facilitated if you have a prior example of the process that you can share. Nothing makes some of these points better than seeing what a good example of the process looks like. Rather than describing the benefits in conceptual terms, share the actual benefits that were realized in a prior implementation of the process (e.g., one from another unit or one that addressed a different staffing issue from the one being faced now). Better yet, get a manager who has seen the value of the strategic staffing process share his or her perspective with the managers with whom the process is to be implemented. Instead of showing managers conceptual models, show actual spreadsheets and results. Don't describe what their role could be; share what the actual level of involvement of a prior group of managers was.

When launching a strategic staffing process, it is usually most effective to present the process to a group of managers, then follow up with each manager individually. Included on the CD-ROM that came with this book is a set of slides that can be used for this type of group presentation. In its current form, it highlights the process at an appropriate level of detail, providing a big-picture overview of the process and its implementation. The presentation can be edited if you need to tailor it to meet your own particular needs. Above all, remember to be open to questions at all times and to be readily available for management discussions on an ongoing basis.

Defining Staffing Implications: An Interview Guide

There are times when business plans or strategies simply don't contain the clearly defined, detailed information that is needed to identify staffing issues and implications. Staffing profiles don't exist, and there is no obvious information regarding staffing requirements. In such cases, this needed information can often be gathered quickly and efficiently by interviewing the line managers and planners who were responsible for creating the plans.

This section contains some hints that you can use in preparing for and conducting such interviews. In general terms, you will need to prepare by identifying current staff availability (both skills and staffing levels). During the interview, discuss the manager's business plans and objectives for the coming period, and then discuss the impact that implementing those plans will have on required capabilities and staffing levels. These discussions are also good opportunities to identify staffing issues, propose staffing strategies, and test the viability of staffing plans and actions.

Preparing for the Interview

Prepare for such an interview by learning about the manager's business (if you don't already know). Make sure that you are familiar with:

- Services and products currently offered
- Objectives, strategies, plans, measures (if any), etc.
- Longer-term changes in strategies and objectives

Once you are fully familiar with the nature of the unit's business itself, define current staffing levels for the unit (in broad categories such as job family or management/nonmanagement) and the broad capabilities of each job category. Next, review the business plans for the unit in detail and identify and highlight any changes or aspects of the plan that you think might have staffing implications. You may even want to create a staffing issue crib list (or maybe even a little table) that identifies key business changes and suggests staffing implications for each change. You can also use this list during the interview to make sure that all issues are addressed. Staffing issues/implications might include the following:

- Significant changes in business activity may affect staffing levels (e.g., through growth or contraction).
- Major changes in products offered may imply changes in required capabilities (e.g., new technology may create a need in one area and a surplus of individuals with obsolete skills in another).
- New services may require skills that are unknown or undefined currently.
- Plans may require you to recruit for skills that the company has not needed previously (e.g., it will take time to identify new sources or develop new selection criteria).
- Implementation may require skills that are scarce or for which there is high competition among employers.
- There may be instances in which the obvious or traditional solutions are no longer feasible (e.g., where training and promotion is normal but would now take too long).
- There may be instances in which the indirect impacts are as critical as any of the direct staffing needs that you define (e.g., changes in one job category may affect the number and type of staff needed in another category).

Identify and write down the staffing issues that you think are the most critical. Test each of these with the manager you are interviewing. Don't just focus on these, however. Be prepared to supplement this list with issues that you did not identify prior to the session itself. If you have already identified possible solutions for some of these issues, document your suggestions clearly so that you can discuss them with the manager.

Finally, schedule the interview. Ideally, try to reserve an hour and a half with the manager. Realistically, make full use of whatever time you are offered.

Conducting the Session

During the interview itself, set your sights on identifying critical staffing issues (i.e., gaps or surpluses) and their implications. Initially, focus on problems, not possible solutions. Work to define the right "question" when you are presented with "answers" (e.g., when an interviewee says, "What we need to do is . . . ," get that manager to define the problem for which that approach is the solution). Try to stay focused on future issues and implications, not on the problems that the unit is currently facing (unless, of course, these are critical and can be expected to continue). Where necessary, ask follow-up questions to ensure that you fully understand the issues that are raised. Finally, get at least some input regarding priorities (e.g., by asking if the issue just discussed is more or less important than the one that was discussed previously).

It is often helpful to focus on change—how the business is changing. Change nearly always has staffing implications. Refer to the staffing drivers that are defined in Chapter 4 of this book. Remember that your objective is to define significant changes in required staffing levels, required capabilities, or both. Discuss possible solutions only after you have obtained some level of agreement regarding the issues that are to be faced.

In most cases, it is most effective to conduct these interviews with individual managers following a more general session in which the basic concepts regarding strategic staffing have been presented to a group of managers. In these situations, use the interview to obtain feedback on the process that is being proposed. If, however, the general session is not conducted, make sure that during the interview the manager fully understands the process that is being suggested.

Possible Interview Guide

Here is an outline of a guide that you can use to structure the interview itself.

Introduction/Stage Setting

- Thank the person for taking the time to meet with you.
- Give the person an overview of your project/objective (or ensure that the perspective that the person already has is accurate).

  —Human Resources (HR) has a need for a high-level corporate staffing plan that identifies staffing issues that span business units.

  —The plan will help ensure that the company has the staff it needs in order to implement its overall corporate strategies.

  —This plan will provide a context for creating specific, shorter-term staffing plans.

  —Consider reinforcing this point by showing the person the "upside-down T" diagram (Figure 2-1).

  —Clarify that you are there to talk about staffing issues, gaps, and problems, not answers or solutions.
- Discuss with the manager what the overall process for creating a staffing strategy will look like (or obtain the manager's perceptions of the process if it has already been presented).
- Tell the manager how the information you gather will be used or shared.

Discuss Business Plans/Changes

- Provide a quick overview of your understanding of the unit's current business.

  —Potentially, you could take the lead here, summarizing the business and getting the manager to supplement or clarify your description.

  —"It seems to me that currently your business does this/provides this. . . ."

  —Get the manager to confirm or expand your understanding.
- Review and verify current staffing levels (at a face validity or "looks pretty close" perspective only).

- Get the manager to describe future changes.
  —Ask the manager to talk about what is to be accomplished during the planning period and the ways in which that represents significant change from the current situation.
  —Provide prods or hints and ask clarifying questions (e.g., ''It seems to me that . . .'') based on your knowledge of the business plans (from your homework) to make sure that you really do understand what the business is going to accomplish.

Discuss Staffing Issues/Implications of Future Plans

- Ask the person what staffing issues are foreseen.
- Identify the areas or job families that will be affected:
  —First
  —Most
- Remember to address both skills and staffing levels.
- Identify any major changes in organization or structure (e.g., a change from a product focus to a customer/market orientation, not at the level of who will report to whom).
- If discussion lags, use your potential staffing issue crib list and your definition of current staffing levels to encourage it:
  —''It seems to me that this expansion will mean an increase in staffing levels.''
  —''It seems that this proposed change in technology will have a real impact on required skills in your technical workforce, but not much impact in customer service.''
  —''Right now you have about 100 people in this job family/category—will that go up or down significantly when you implement this change?''
- Clarify any broad statements that the manager makes, but don't be too detailed.
  —If the manager says ''more,'' get her to differentiate between ''a lot'' and ''a few,'' but don't worry about whether the number is 67 or 72.

—If the manager generalizes, get him to identify specific job families.

- Address all the potential issues on your crib sheet.
- Ask the manager if she thinks that any of these issues are being faced by other business units (and thus might be addressed from an integrated perspective).
- Try to assess criticality (i.e., identify the most critical issues).

Obtain Feedback Regarding Proposed Solutions

- Ask the manager for feedback regarding staffing strategies (e.g., "One way of addressing this issue would be to do X. What do you think of that? Would that work here?").
- Ask the manager for feedback regarding staffing plans.

Close the Interview

- "If you could address only one of these issues, which would it be?"
- "What questions didn't I ask that you thought I would?"
- Tell the manager what he can expect from you, if anything.
- Thank the manager for her time and input.

Summary

When implementing strategic staffing, appropriate line management involvement is crucial. Make sure that the line managers fully understand the process and its value. Above all, make sure that they understand how implementation of strategic staffing will make them better managers right now. Finally, when you talk with managers to obtain staffing requirement information, be prepared. Understand their business and define their current staffing availability (both staffing levels and capabilities). Discuss with those managers how their business will be changing, and then (and only then) discuss the impact that these changes will have on future staffing requirements.

CHAPTER 13

Developing a Strategic Staffing Web Site

Clearly, strategic staffing is a powerful tool that can be used to identify and address staffing issues almost anywhere in an organization. Whether those implementing it are managers or primarily human resource (HR) professionals, they need ready access to strategic staffing knowledge, experience, tools, examples, information, and other resources. Needless to say, it doesn't do much good to develop processes that managers don't know about or understand or to develop tools that no one has access to. Nor does it work to hoard the data and support within HR, doling it out carefully on a controlled, need-to-know basis. You should get your strategic staffing capability out there to those who need it as efficiently as possible. A strategic staffing Web site, running on your company's intranet, can meet these needs quickly and inexpensively.

Why Create a Web Site?

Strategic staffing is an ideal Web-based application. Whether it is on the Internet or on your own intranet, a strategic staffing Web site can provide your users with exactly the help they are looking for, exactly when they are looking for it. In different situations, user needs can vary widely, but a Web-based application can offer the kind of flexibility that is required to meet those varying needs both effectively and efficiently. There are many good reasons for developing a Web site, but four of them are particularly important.

Expand the Reach of Your Expertise

It is likely that many managers in your organization will be participating in the strategic staffing process at some level. At some point, each of these individuals will need information or tools in order to develop staffing strategies and plans. Traditional communication channels may provide what is necessary, but these channels are probably going to be ineffective (e.g., they may provide all users with the same information, regardless of need). They may also be inefficient (defined in terms of cost and response time), which means that distribution of the information will be limited (e.g., to minimize costs). Requests may stack up if they are coming in faster than they can be resolved.

A strategic staffing Web site can provide users with immediate and constant access to the specific information and tools that they need in order to develop and implement their staffing strategies. There will be no gatekeepers or bottlenecks that restrict the flow of needed information. Managers will not have to wait for HR staff to become available to answer their questions. Use of a site will allow users to find what they need twenty-four hours a day/seven days a week, an especially critical requirement in a global company that is conducting business around the clock. An ''ask the expert'' section allows users to post, and receive customized answers to, their specific questions without having to track down individual HR staff.

Because all important strategic staffing information and tools are located in a single place, it will also be easier for you to maintain and update this information; this means that users will always be accessing the most current information and tools that are available.

Build Knowledge and Skills

Your users' level of strategic staffing expertise will vary widely. Some experienced users may simply need an answer to a particular question or may need help with a particular part of the process (e.g., defining staffing requirements). Less experienced managers (e.g., those doing it for the first time) may have to learn about strategic staffing from the ground up and may need to be taken by the hand and led through the process of developing, interpreting, and implementing staffing strategies.

A well-designed Web site will meet the learning needs of both of these groups (and everyone in between). By navigating an efficient series of menus, those who understand the process will be able to move quickly to locate the answer they need (or to find someone they can ask). The site can contain a search capability that allows users to pinpoint the exact sections of the site that contain the information and help they need. Those with more comprehensive learning needs can learn about strategic staffing at their own pace by reading the text, following examples, playing with the templates, and interacting with strategic staffing experts. It is also possible to integrate into the site various training modules that provide a more formal, structured approach to learning.

Increase Collaboration

A message board on a strategic staffing Web site can provide users with a forum for discussing strategic staffing issues, identifying common problems and concerns, and sharing best practices (whether internal or external). It can also provide a place to go when a manager needs to ask another manager for guidance ("What should I do?"), advice ("How did you solve this problem in the past?"), or opinions ("What do you think of this proposed solution?"). The site can also be used to identify staffing issues that are common to several business units and solutions that have proved to be particularly effective.

Intranet Web sites can also prove valuable in the data collection process. Through the site, users can exchange information and send in pieces that need to be compiled into a whole (e.g., they can submit staffing requirements for individual projects so that an overall definition of requirements can be developed). The Web site can also serve as a forum for facilitating staffing actions, allowing managers to talk to one another regarding staffing needs and opportunities.

While this kind of communication is obviously available face to face within a limited group, use of the message board will allow managers and other users to cast a wider net. They can initiate and develop contacts with a much larger group of people—many more than they could possibly talk with on a one-on-one basis.

Increase Implementation Efficiency

If you have a specific process in place (or if you are implementing a process for the first time), a strategic staffing Web site can make that process more efficient. The site can be used to describe the context and structure of the process to be implemented. It can provide users with all the forms, instructions, and staffing information that they need in order to complete their staffing strategies and plans. Users can also submit implementation-related questions and obtain answers quickly. The site can also be used as a centralized point for gathering and compiling staffing information from decentralized units and participants.

Designing Your Site

First, create a Web site (or add a series of pages to an existing site) that can be accessed easily and directly by all your proposed users. Make sure that the site is secure, but don't let password protection impede access unnecessarily. If in doubt, err on the side of providing access to more people. Provide hyperlinks to the site from other internal human resource and business planning Web sites and pages.

Organize your site so that the various sections clearly and logically map to the specific needs of your users. Design the menus so that it is easy for users to pinpoint the type of help they need and locate the module, section, or Web page that contains just that help. I often suggest that companies build their sites around the things that need to be shared with users: information, tools, expertise, and resources. Include each of these main points as a clickable option on your site's home page. Similarly, each category might be an option on a subpage. You may want to use a format similar to the one that follows.

Share Information

On this section of the site, post all the information that users need in order to understand your strategic staffing process and how it works.

• **Overall strategic staffing concepts.** Define the objectives of strategic staffing and describe the context in which it works best. Provide diagrams (like the "upside-down T" shown in Figure 2-1) that visually reinforce the points you are trying to make. Where necessary, also say what strategic staffing is not (e.g., describe the less effective, traditional approaches and why they should be avoided).

• **Generic process descriptions.** Describe, in general terms, the processes for developing longer-term staffing strategies and shorter-term staffing plans. Discuss the relationship between the two (i.e., that staffing strategies provide a long-term context within which more effective short-term staffing decisions can be made). Describe process components and how they should be integrated. Provide diagrams to reinforce your descriptions.

• **Company-specific process descriptions.** Describe your actual strategic staffing process. Provide an overview or road map of the process itself. Discuss the various components of your process and how they fit together. Include diagrams that show the relationships among components. Provide specific instructions for completing each step of the process. Describe roles and accountabilities. Talk about timing and describe links to other existing processes (such as business planning, budgeting, succession planning, and job posting).

• **Specific examples.** Provide specific examples of the process. Use actual numbers when describing staffing plans. Provide examples of typical outputs and expected deliverables.

Share Tools

Provide users with direct access to the tools that they need in order to develop their own staffing strategies. Specifically provide versions that practitioners can download, tailor, and use to meet their actual needs. This might include the following tools:

• **Spreadsheet templates.** Create generic versions of supply/demand staffing models that utilize existing, readily available spreadsheet software. Preload each model with all necessary calculation routines, formulas, and linkages so that users can simply adjust the number of rows and columns, load their data, and run their initial models. Don't forget to provide full instructions on how the spreadsheets should be used and updated.

- **Reusable examples.** Provide preformatted examples that users can easily edit (e.g., word processing tables containing draft staffing plans that completely describe required staffing actions). This will ensure that users' work is complete and well organized.

- **Your forms.** If your process requires the completion of forms or templates, provide those in a downloadable, ready-to-use format.

- **Data-gathering procedures.** If your process requires the submission of completed forms, provide users with the ability to submit their data directly through the site (eliminating paper transactions).

- **Suggested communications.** Provide samples of reports, analyses, presentations, and other communications that practitioners can tailor and use to describe the results of their processes to their constituencies.

- **Diagnostics and assessments.** Provide simple diagnostic tools and process assessments that allow your users to evaluate the effectiveness of their existing staffing strategies (including the processes they use to create those strategies) and identify opportunities to improve the effectiveness and efficiency of their strategies. Examples of both diagnostics and assessment tools are described in Chapters 10 and 11 of this book.

Share Expertise

Provide ready access to the strategic staffing knowledge base that has been built within your company. Provide a wide array of options, from canned responses to common questions to real-time, online coaching and consulting. You might do the following:

- **Organize by problem and structure walk-throughs.** In some cases (especially with new users), it will be difficult for people to even know where to begin the strategic staffing process. Use a simple form of expert system to help these individuals, providing a structured approach to identifying and resolving their issues. Here is a suggested process:

—Provide a list of common strategic staffing problems that managers in your organization face (e.g., a shortage of a particular skill or the need to focus attention on a job category that is particularly critical). Have the user click on the problem that is most relevant.

—Have the site prompt the user to define key planning parameters for the selected issue (e.g., time frame, planning horizon, and population to be included).

—Present a series of pointed questions that helps users to define appropriate rows and columns for their staffing models.

—Based on the responses so far, have the site suggest to the user the data that will be needed to build the model that has been designed. Using a generic list, have the site suggest to the user where those needed data might be located.

—Link the user to the spreadsheet templates that are located elsewhere in the site. Describe how those sheets should be modified and loaded to support the analysis.

—Provide a list of possible outcomes (e.g., staffing gaps or staffing surpluses) and a list of staffing actions that might be relevant for each type of outcome.

—Provide a link to the templates (e.g., word processing tables) so that the user can document findings, conclusions, and proposed staffing plans.

- **Provide implementation guidance.** Provide specific advice that supports the effective implementation of the strategic staffing process. Describe what can be done to avoid pitfalls, work around obstacles, and minimize resistance to the implementation of the process. From a more positive perspective, describe what should be done to facilitate implementation. Many of these concepts are described in Chapters 9 and 10.

- **Provide access to an "e-coach."** Allow users to interact with strategic staffing experts, either on a real-time/on-line basis or through e-mail. Identify people with strategic staffing expertise and provide users with direct links to those people. If e-mail links are used, you might even want to create specific Web addresses that allow users to gain expedited access to the experts without having to negotiate normal e-mail channels. Make sure that you measure response time and quality.

- **Provide message boards.** Create a strategic staffing message board that allows users to post questions, ask for advice from other users, or have interactive discussions regarding strategic staffing topics and issues.

- **Address frequently asked questions.** Provide a list of frequently asked questions and the answers to those questions.

Share Resources

Provide direct links to other resources that support the development of staffing strategies.

- Often, there is a great deal of helpful information that already exists within the company. In your strategic staffing Web site, provide direct access to such internal resources as:
  - —**Company data.** Describe relevant company databases and their content. Provide hyperlinks to the search engine of each database.
  - —**Related company systems.** Provide direct links to company systems that are related to, but different from, strategic staffing (e.g., job posting, succession planning).
  - —**Internal experts.** Provide a list of internal staff that can provide help in specific areas or answer particular questions. List the areas of expertise of each individual so that the user can quickly identify the most probable source for the needed information.
  - —**Available training and development.** Provide a list of internal training and development resources that a practitioner might use to gain a better understanding of strategic staffing (e.g., courses, computer/Web-based training).

• There is also a wealth of information available on the Web. Rather than try to provide that information in your own strategic staffing Web site, simply provide hyperlinks to the sites where the needed information resides. That way, you won't need to maintain the information. Check your links frequently; Web addresses change often, and you don't want your users to become frustrated trying to access sites that have moved to new addresses. External resources might include:

—External databases (e.g., federal and state demographic databases, Internet job posting boards)

—Financial and economic forecasts

—Professional societies, both human resource and industry-specific (e.g., Society for Human Resource Management, Human Resource Planning Society)

—Providers of relevant workshops, seminars, and other training (e.g., AMACOM, World at Work, various university executive education programs)

—Online bookstores (e.g., AMACOM, Amazon, Barnes & Noble)

—Web sites of known external experts

You should also provide a search capability so that your users can quickly locate the specific information or assistance that they are looking for.

A Final Note

As you read through this section, you may have noticed that the sections of the Web site that I propose and the sections of this book match quite closely. That is no accident. The information that is provided to you in this book is the information that your users will need to support their strategic staffing efforts. Feel free to include some of the concepts and ideas described in this book as starting points for the various components of this site (although obviously you can't just copy this text!).

SECTION

Beyond Staffing Plans: Analyzing and Applying the Results

CHAPTER 14

Measuring Staffing Effectiveness and Efficiency

The strategic staffing process begins when you review your business strategies and plans and identify your most critical staffing issues. Next, you develop a series of staffing strategies that best address your most critical issues. Finally, you define a specific set of staffing plans and actions—those that best support the implementation of your staffing strategies. Figure 14-1 summarizes this process.

As soon as you begin to implement these staffing plans and actions, you will begin to see results. Some people will be hired and others will leave. Some people will be promoted and others will be transferred. But how will you know if these are indeed the right results? How should you measure the results of the staffing strategies and plans that you implement? How will you know that you are better off for having implemented these actions?

Many organizations track staffing performance using such measures as how many jobs are filled, how long it takes to fill each opening, or what it costs to place a new hire. Such measures can be helpful, but they are by no means sufficient. What tends to be missing from these measures is any indication of quality. The results of your strategic staffing process should be measured using two separate, but related, criteria: effectiveness (i.e., doing the right job) and efficiency (i.e., doing the job right). This chapter describes both of

Figure 14-1. Measuring the Strategic Staffing Process

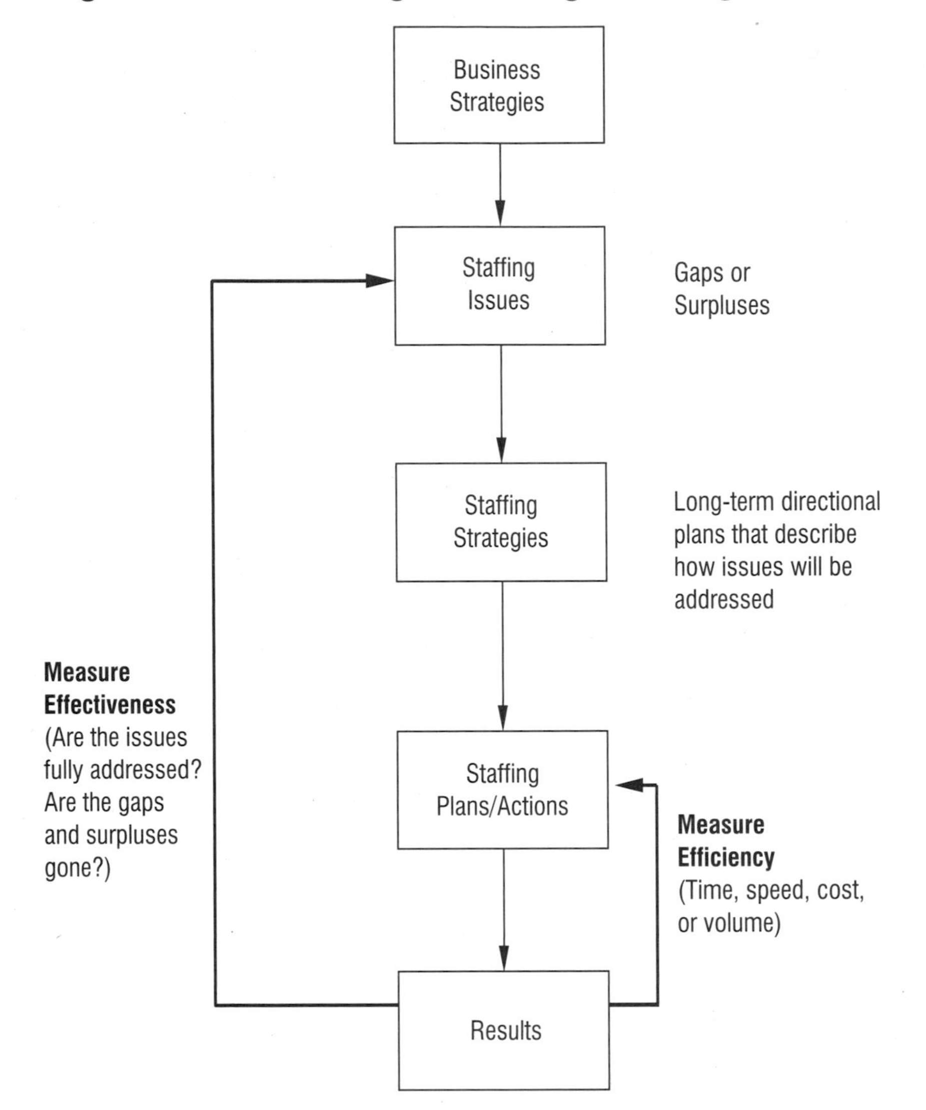

these criteria and proposes measures that can be used to evaluate staffing efficiency and effectiveness.

Measuring Staffing Efficiency

It is fairly easy to measure the efficiency of your staffing processes. Typically, efficiency is measured in terms of time, speed, cost, or volume. Any construct that measures one of these is a measure of efficiency. In staffing terms, the efficiency of your process might be

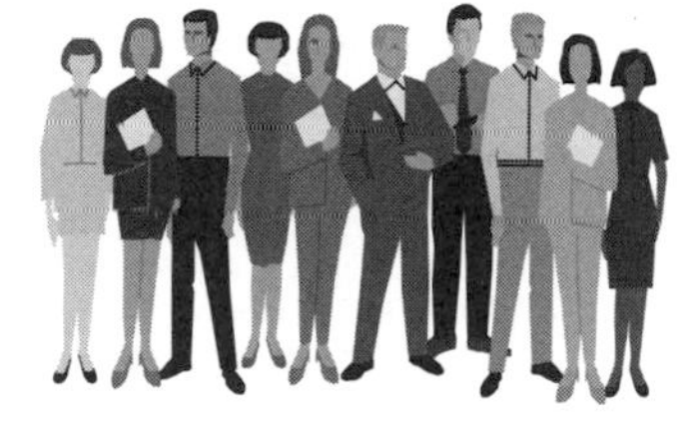

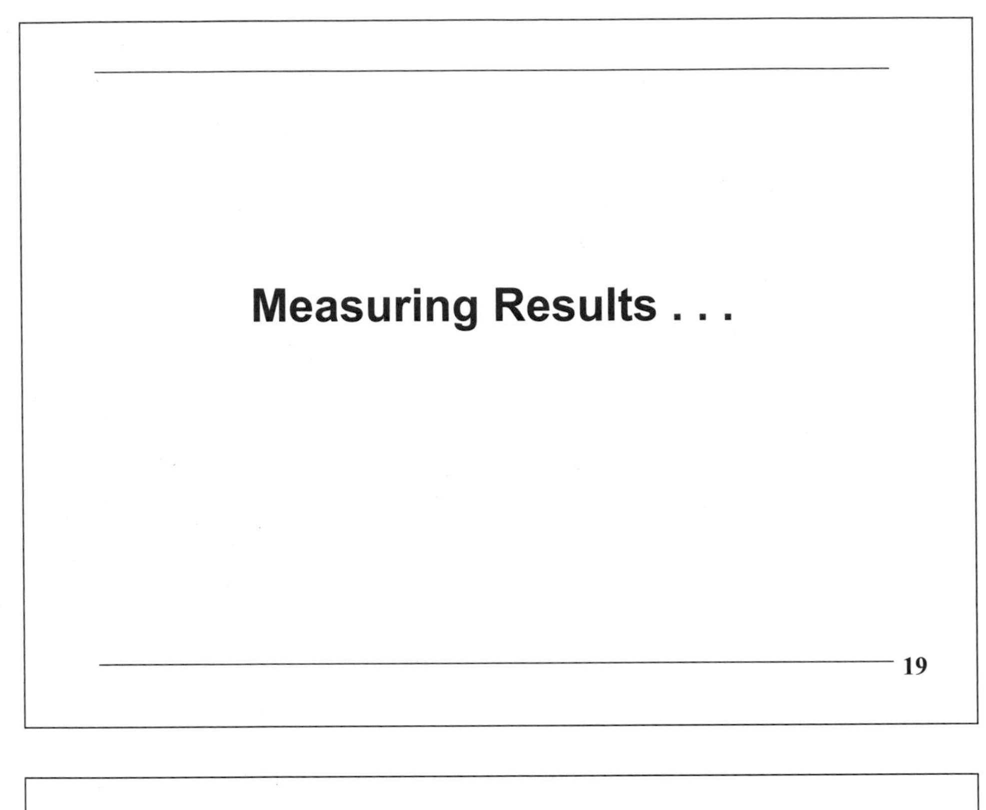

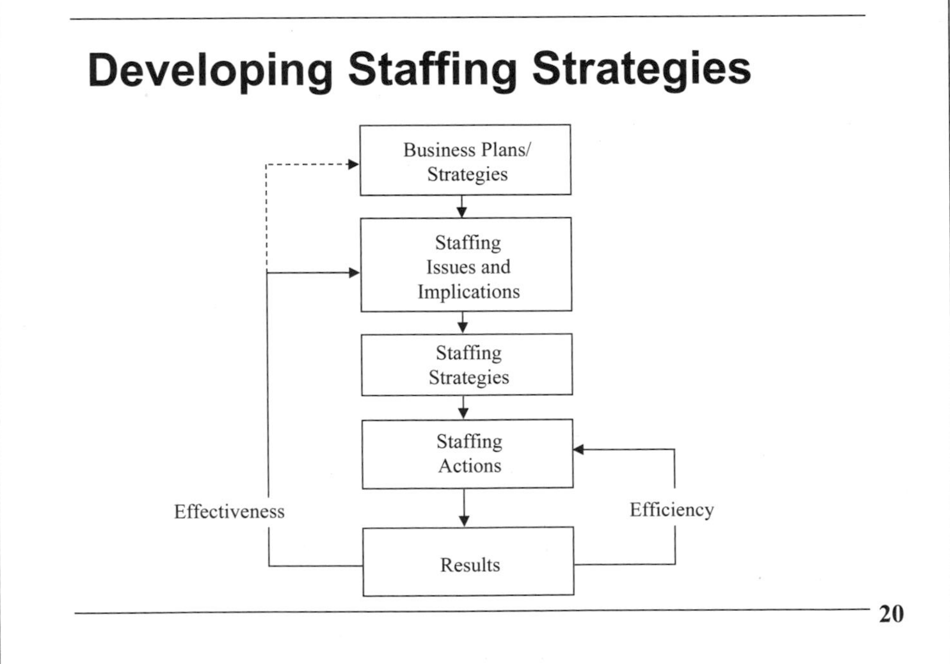

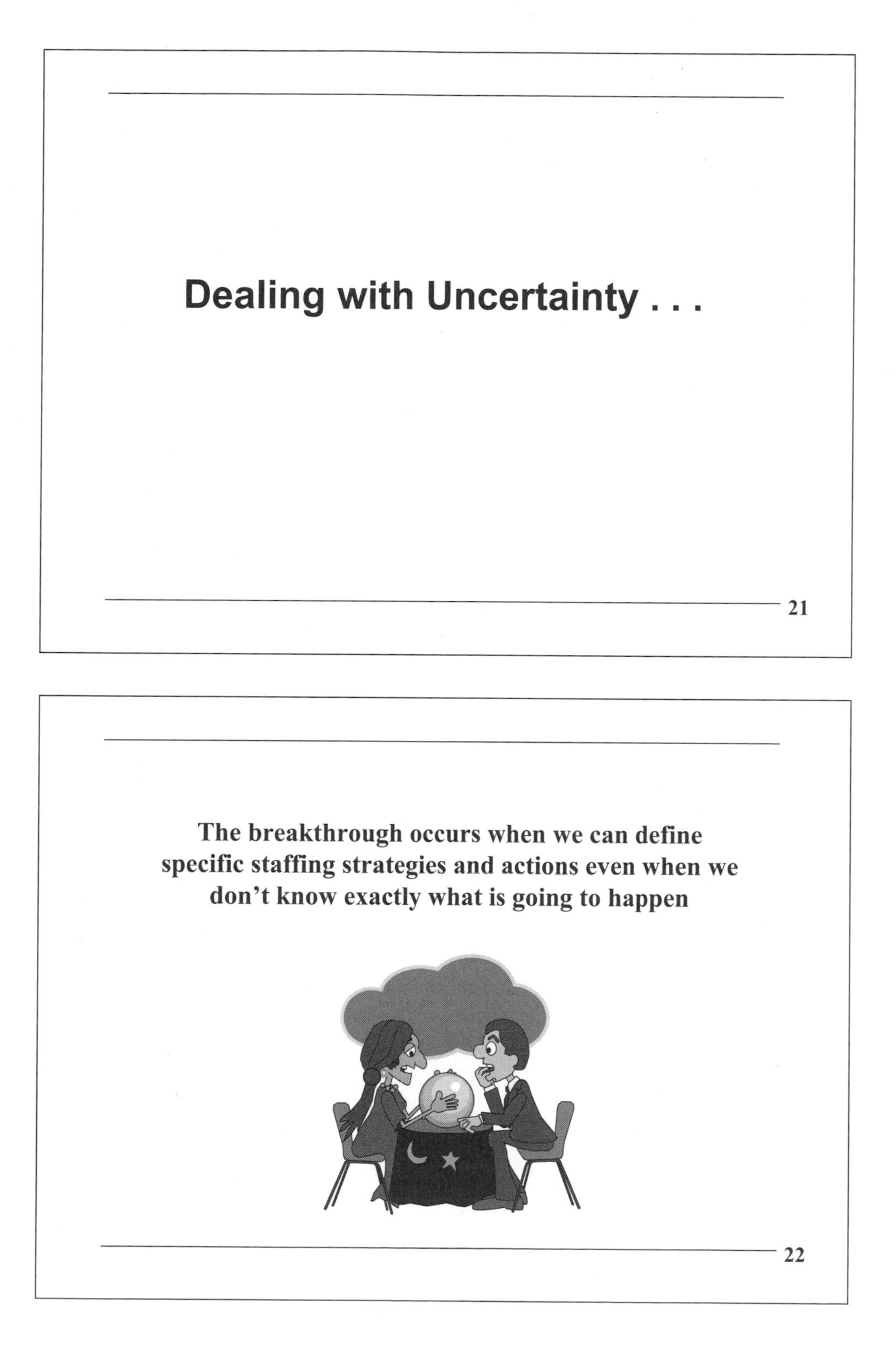

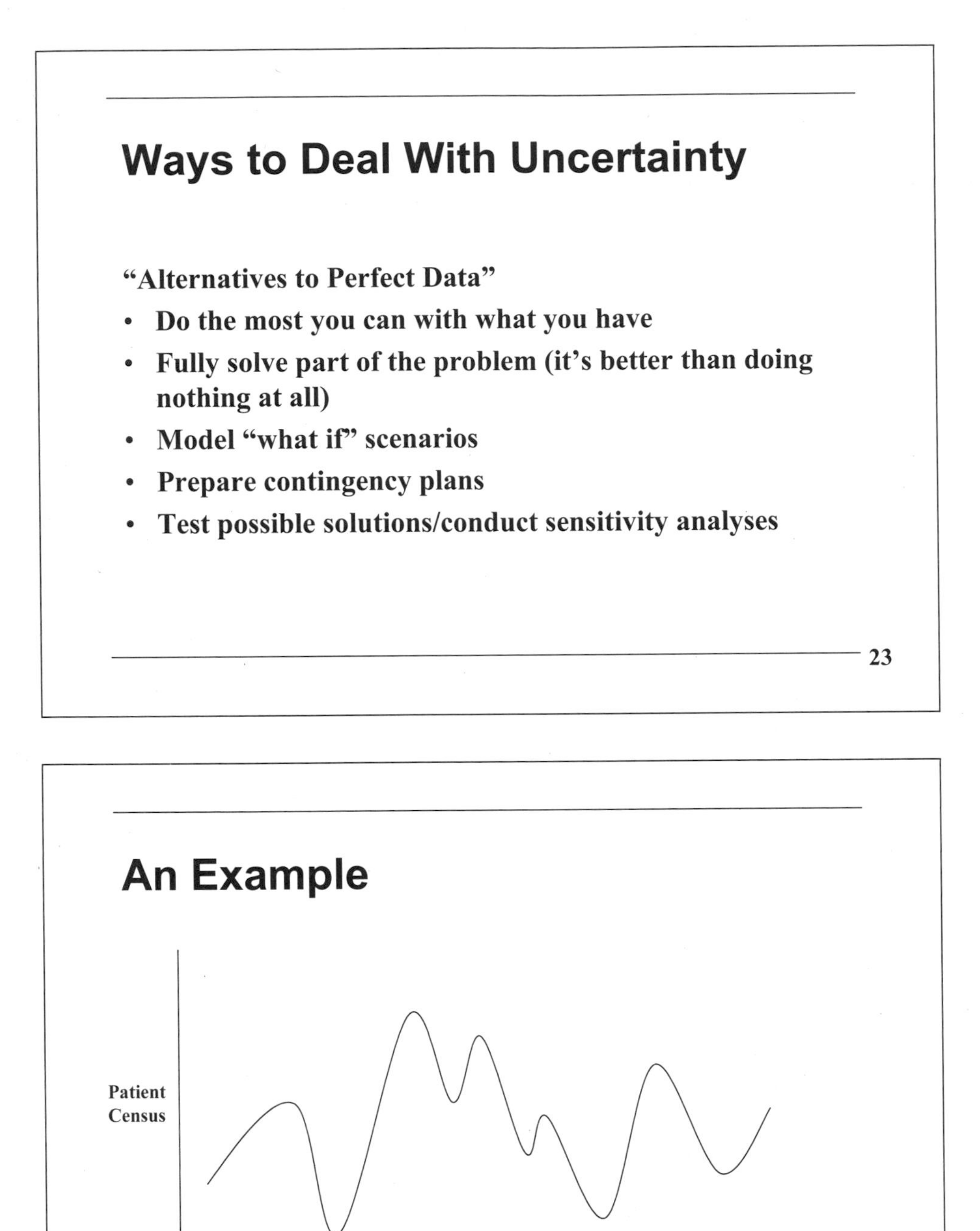

- Adjusts cells up or down to account for internal transfers.
- Subtracts out external transfers out, involuntary termination, and other staff reductions.
- Adds in external transfers in and new hires (recruiting).

Next, the model compares available resources (after staffing actions) to demand and calculates final gaps/surpluses. Ideally, if the staffing actions you entered are correct, every cell of the final gaps/surpluses matrix should be zero (or a gap or surplus that you find acceptable). If this is not the case, it is likely that you will need to modify your staffing plans. Determine what staffing actions need to be added, deleted, or changed. Edit the matrices in step 4 to reflect these changes and again review the final gaps/surpluses matrix.

Step 6: Enter Staffing Data for Subsequent Periods. Once period 1 is final, look at the preliminary gaps and surpluses that have now been created in period 2. These gaps and surpluses will reflect all the staffing actions you entered for period 1. Define the staffing plans that you think best meet these needs in period 2 and enter that information in the appropriate matrices in period 2. When period 2 is final (e.g., when final gaps and surpluses are all zero), repeat the process for period 3. Repeat for all subsequent periods.

Using Template 2

Template 2 (Template 2 (overtime).xls) should be used when overtime should be considered as a staffing resource. In these cases, at least some staffing gaps can be eliminated by asking individuals to work overtime (as opposed to meeting all staffing needs through hiring or transfers). Because of the use of overtime, this template is usually based on FTEs, not "whole people."

The steps for using Template 2 are identical to those described above for Template 1, with one exception. When you are using this version, you may specify that overtime will be used to address staffing gaps that have been identified. Enter in each cell of the overtime (FTEs) matrix how much overtime is planned for that job category. Available resources (after staffing actions) will then include these additional resources. Note that overtime is not "carried over" to a subsequent period. Overtime data must be entered for each period separately.

Using Template 3

Template 3 (Template 3 (contractors).xls) should be used whenever a blend of full-time staff and contingent staff (e.g., contractors or temporary workers) can be used to meet staffing needs. In these cases, at least some staffing gaps can be eliminated by employing contingent workers of some kind (as opposed to meeting all staffing needs through hiring or transfers of permanent employees). If part-time contractors are used, then use FTEs throughout the model, not "whole people." When using this version, the following steps should be taken.

Step 1: Load Initial Data and Run the Model. The following data should be loaded into the appropriate matrix as a first step. You must enter data for existing staff levels for permanent staff and contractors, but all other data are optional.

- *Starting staff levels/employees.* Click on the Period 1 tab at the bottom of the worksheet. Enter into each cell of this matrix the number of permanent staff in each category at the beginning of the planning period ("supply now"). The model can contain "whole people" or FTEs. Make sure that the choice you make is consistent throughout all the matrices in the model (i.e., all are FTEs or all are "whole people").

- *Starting staff levels/contractors.* Enter into each cell of this matrix the number of contractors (use FTEs if part-time contractors are used) in each category at the beginning of the planning period ("supply now").

- *Voluntary turnover rate for employees.* Enter the voluntary turnover rate to be used for each category in each cell. These rates will apply only to permanent staff (contractors that leave are handled in another way), so a rate should be entered for each cell for which there is information in the existing staff levels/employees matrix. Rates can vary for each cell. A 10 percent rate should be entered as

.10. Remember to adjust rates so that they are consistent with the length of your planning period (e.g., use .05 if the annual rate is 10 percent and your planning period is six months, or .01 if your annual rate is expected to be 12 percent and the planning period is one month). The model will calculate voluntary turnover and place the results of the calculation in the subsequent Voluntary Turnover matrix.

• *Retirements among employees.* Enter the number of permanent staff that you expect to retire from each cell during the planning period. There are no retirements allowed for contractors.

• *Planned contractor termination/expiration.* Enter into each cell the number of contractors that are expected or scheduled to leave that job category during the planning period. This would include, but not be limited to, any temporary employees whose contract is slated to expire or be terminated during the planning period.

• *Planned hiring commitment/employees.* Enter the number of hires (commitments) of permanent staff that are expected in each cell during the planning period. Note the reference to commitments. This number should include *only* those individuals to whom offers have already been extended and who are committed to joining the company during this planning period. It should *not* include openings that are authorized but that won't be filled during the period or any additional hires that may be needed to address various staffing gaps the model may identify later on. Once this data has been entered, the model will calculate "supply then" for each cell and place the results of the calculations in the subsequent Available Resources matrix.

• *Demand.* Enter the total number of individuals in each category that will be required in order to implement the company's business plans/strategies. This number should include the total of all positions, whether permanent or contractor. There should *not* be separate demand numbers for permanent employees and contractors. This number can be entered directly or called from another spreadsheet that you may have created to calculate demand based on various assumptions you have made (e.g., calculations based on staffing ratios).

Step 2: Review Preliminary Results for the First Period. Once all preliminary data have been entered, the model will first calculate available resources before staffing actions (employees and contractors) by adjusting existing staff levels for employees and contractors appropriately and summing the result across both categories of workers. The model also calculates preliminary gaps/surpluses for each job category by comparing available resources before staffing actions (employees and contractors) to demand. Review these preliminary results, but do not try to fix any of the gaps or surpluses at this time.

Step 3: Run the Model for Subsequent Periods. The various planning periods included in your model are already linked appropriately. The existing staff level/employees matrix for period 2 is linked to numerous matrices for period 1. It shows the number of permanent employees in each category at the beginning of period 2 (assuming that all the staffing actions planned for period 1 actually take place). The starting staff level/contractors matrix for period 2 is also linked to numerous matrices for period 1. It shows the number of temporary staff in each category at the beginning of period 2 (again assuming that all the staffing actions planned for period 1 actually take place).

For each subsequent period (e.g., periods 2 through 5), however, you will need to enter all information other than these existing staff levels. First, click on the Period 2 tab at the bottom of the worksheet. Next, enter the information that corresponds to the uncontrollable staffing assumptions that you are using, including:

- Voluntary turnover rates
- Retirements
- Planned contractor termination/expiration
- Planned hiring (commitments)

Once these data are entered, staffing gaps and surpluses will be calculated for that period. Enter these data for all periods, one period at a time. If this is the first time that you are going through this process, do not include information for any controllable staffing actions (e.g., internal transfers, external transfers, recruiting, or contractors added or removed). That information will be added later on.

Step 4: Enter Staffing Data for Period 1. As described in this book, the next step of the process is to review staffing gaps and surpluses across all planning periods and define the specific staffing actions that should be taken in each planning period. Enter the staffing plan information that reflects the staffing actions that you think need to take place during period 1 to eliminate the staffing gaps and surpluses shown in the preliminary gaps/surpluses matrix. With this version, the following options are open to you:

- *Internal transfers out and internal transfers in/employees.* These two matrices capture the movement of permanent employees from one cell in your model to another cell in your model (e.g., promotions or lateral moves). They should not be used to capture people who are moving into or out of the model (that comes in the next step).

Determine the number of such moves that are required in order to address staffing needs. Enter the total number of people leaving each cell for all other cells in the internal transfers out matrix. If, for example, you are expecting 2 people *from* a given cell to be promoted and 3 other people *from* that same cell to make lateral moves, enter 5 in that cell (2 + 3).

Enter the total number of people entering a cell from all other cells in the internal transfers in matrix. If, for example, you are expecting 3 people to be promoted *into* that cell and 1 person from another cell to make a lateral move *into* that cell, enter 4 in that cell (3 + 1).

Every individual who moves from one cell in the model to another cell in the model must be deducted from the first cell and added to the second (almost like double-entry bookkeeping). When you have finished defining all internal transfers, verify that the total number of people leaving all cells equals the total number of people entering all cells.

- *External transfers out/employees.* Enter the total number of permanent employees leaving each cell to take jobs in the organization that are not part of the model you are now working with.

• *External transfers in/employees.* Enter the total number of permanent employees joining each cell of the model you are working with from other jobs in the organization that are not included in your model.

• *New hires/employees.* Enter the number of new permanent hires that will be needed in each cell to meet staffing needs *over and above* those already included in the planned hires (commitments) matrix described above.

• *Contractors added (FTEs).* Enter the number of contractors (FTEs) to be added to each cell during the planning period to reduce staffing gaps (over and above any that are already included in the existing staff levels/contractors matrix). This number should also include any contractors included in the planned contractor termination/expiration category whose contact will be renewed.

• *Contractors to be removed (FTEs).* Enter the number of contractors to be removed from the workforce during the planning period to eliminate staffing surpluses. This is over and above those that have already been counted in the planned contractor termination/expiration category described above.

• *Involuntary terminations/employees.* Enter the number of involuntary terminations among permanent staff that are expected for each cell (if any).

• *Other staff reductions/employees.* Enter the number of other reductions (i.e., not voluntary turnover, retirements, or involuntary terminations) among permanent employees that are expected for each cell.

Step 5: Review Results. Once all the above data are entered, the model will first calculate available resources (after staffing actions) for each cell of your model. This calculation starts with available resources before staffing actions (employees and contractors) and:

- Adjusts cells up or down to account for internal transfers.
- Subtracts out external transfers out, involuntary termination, and other staff reductions.

- Adds in external transfers in and new hires (recruiting).
- Adds and deletes contractors as plans define.

Next, the model compares available resources (after staffing actions) to demand and calculates final gaps/surpluses. Ideally, if the staffing actions you entered are correct, every cell of the Final Gaps/Surpluses matrix should be zero (or a gap/surplus you find acceptable). If this is not the case, it is likely that you will need to modify your staffing plans. Determine what staffing actions need to be added, deleted, or changed. Edit the matrices in step 4 to reflect these changes and again review the final gaps/surpluses matrix.

Step 6: Enter Staffing Data for Subsequent Periods. Once period 1 is final, look at the preliminary gaps and surpluses that have now been created in period 2. These gaps and surpluses will reflect all the staffing actions you entered for period 1. Define the staffing plans that you think best meet these needs in period 2 and enter that information in the appropriate matrices in period 2. When period 2 is final (e.g., when final gaps and surpluses are all zero), repeat the process for period 3. Repeat for all subsequent periods.

Using Template 4

Template 4 (Template 4 (overtime + contractors).xls) should be used when both overtime and contractors should be considered as staffing resources. In these cases, at least some staffing gaps can be eliminated by asking individuals to work overtime (as opposed to meeting all staffing needs through hiring or transfers). Because of the use of overtime, this template is usually based on FTEs, not "whole people."

The steps for using Template 4 are identical to those described for Template 3, with one exception: When you use this version, you may specify in the overtime matrix how much overtime (usually expressed as FTEs) will be used in each cell to address staffing gaps that have been identified. Available resources (after staffing actions) will then include these additional resources. Note that overtime is not "carried over" to a subsequent period. Overtime data must be entered for each period separately.

APPENDIX C

Using the Suggested Overheads

Description

The CD-ROM included with this book contains two draft PowerPoint presentations that you may find helpful. Feel free to edit and use these presentations to support the development and implementation of your strategic staffing process. If you do choose to edit the slides, you will need to save a copy of the file(s) on your own hard drive. You cannot edit the files on the CD-ROM itself. This section of the book also contains a hard copy version of the slides that are included in the initial version of each presentation. You may, of course, print the slides (and various handout versions) by using your own PowerPoint software.

These files are meant to provide you with an outline for an effective presentation. While most key points are included on the various slides, the slides should not be used as is or considered as a script to be read. Both presentations need to be supplemented and augmented with the details that are found throughout this book.

In most cases, I present the first set of slides to groups that include both senior managers and the team that is charged with developing the strategic staffing process. I use the second presentation as a teaching tool with the working team only.

The Overview Presentation

The first presentation (Presentation 1.ppt) builds a case for developing and implementing a strategic staffing process. It includes:

- Key definitions of the process and the supporting terminology
- A description of the context in which strategic staffing is best implemented
- An overview or summary of the nontraditional approaches to strategic staffing that I suggest you use
- An overview of the strategic staffing process itself
- Some implementation hints and assistance

This presentation is probably most useful when you need to describe the strategic staffing process to senior managers and convince them that staffing strategies are both necessary and beneficial. It provides a big picture of the process, yet it does not include the level of detail that is required to actually develop and implement the process.

As you give this presentation, make sure that you drive home the following points:

- The definition and objectives of strategic staffing
- The concept that longer-term staffing strategies provide the context that allows effective short-term staffing decisions to be made
- That the alternative approaches to strategic staffing that I propose should at least be considered
- That at its most fundamental level, the strategic staffing process includes identifying issues, calculating staffing gaps and surpluses, developing staffing strategies, and defining staffing plans
- That realistic, helpful staffing strategies and plans can be created even if business plans or staffing requirements seem uncertain (focus on the nursing example and graph in Chapter 6)
- That strategic staffing can indeed fit into your existing business planning context (e.g., using the diagnostic framework I've provided in the book and on the CD-ROM)

- That when implementing the strategic staffing process, approach B should be followed

Of course, each of these key points is discussed in detail in this book.

The Detailed Presentation

The second presentation (Presentation 2.ppt) is much more detailed and in depth. It includes:

- A full description of each step of the strategic staffing process
- A detailed discussion of how staffing gaps and surpluses should be calculated
- A numerical example of a staffing model (including a sample staffing plan)
- A discussion about data requirements and automation
- A word about next steps

This presentation is designed to supplement (not replace) the first, more generic presentation. It is probably most useful in empowering a team or task force to develop an actual staffing strategy.

As you give this presentation, first make sure that the members of your team fully understand the key points and concepts included in the first, more general presentation. The most important part of the second presentation is the detailed description of the process itself. Make sure that your team fully understands each step and actually works through the example that is provided. Finally, work with the team to define specific next steps, including implementation responsibilities and time frames.

Terms of Use

Like the spreadsheet templates, the PowerPoint presentations (and the presentations derived from the templates) may be installed on one PC or server. If additional copies are required, simply purchase additional copies of the book.

Presentation 1: Overview

Strategic Staffing:
Context and Concepts

Prepared for:
ABC Company
Date

Your Name
Title
Telephone Number
E-mail Address

1

Session Objectives

Strategic Staffing

- The strategic staffing process
- Measuring process results
- Dealing with uncertainty
- Key implementation concerns

2

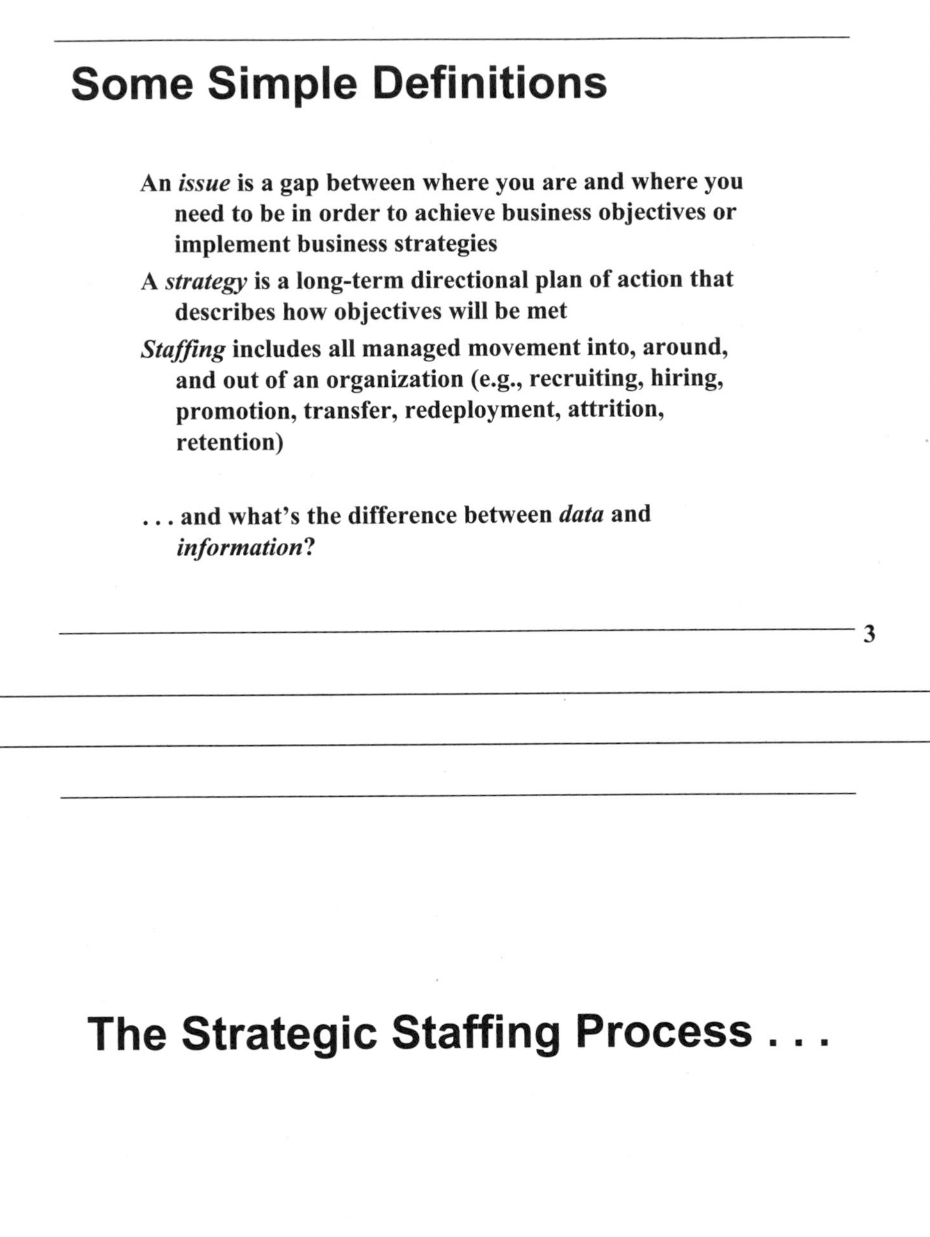
Some Simple Definitions
An *issue* is a gap between where you are and where you need to be in order to achieve business objectives or implement business strategies
A *strategy* is a long-term directional plan of action that describes how objectives will be met
Staffing includes all managed movement into, around, and out of an organization (e.g., recruiting, hiring, promotion, transfer, redeployment, attrition, retention)
. . . and what's the difference between *data* and *information*?
3
The Strategic Staffing Process . . .
4

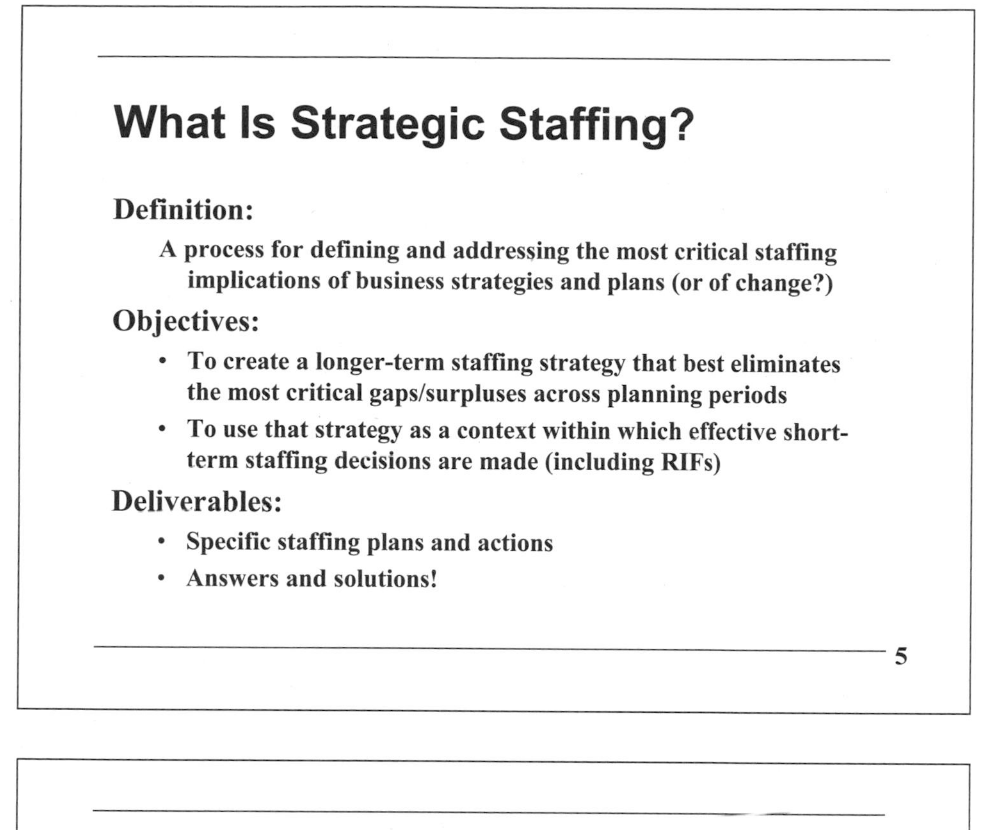
What Is Strategic Staffing?
Definition:
A process for defining and addressing the most critical staffing implications of business strategies and plans (or of change?)
Objectives:
• To create a longer-term staffing strategy that best eliminates the most critical gaps/surpluses across planning periods
• To use that strategy as a context within which effective short-term staffing decisions are made (including RIFs)
Deliverables:
• Specific staffing plans and actions
• Answers and solutions!
5

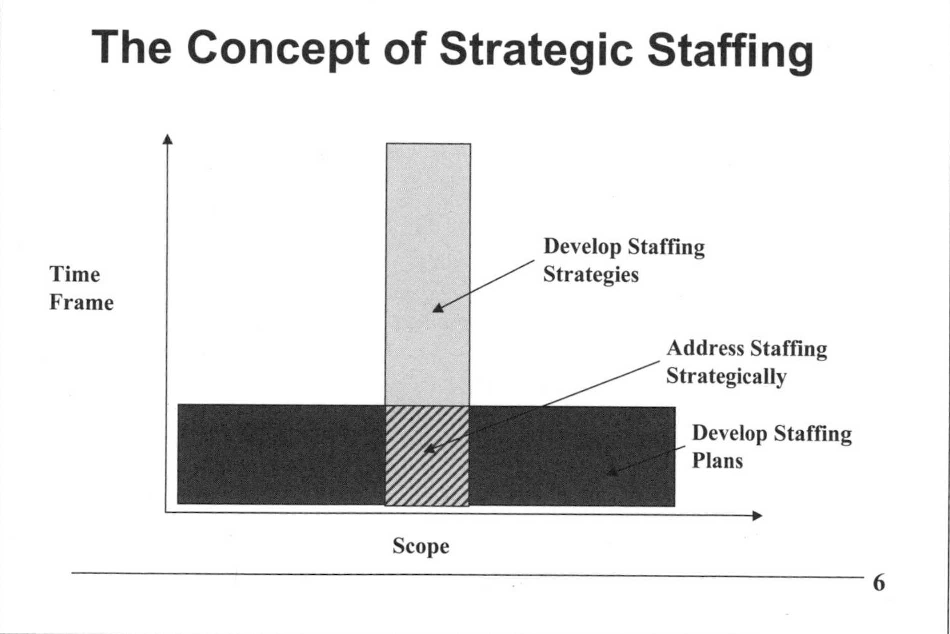
The Concept of Strategic Staffing
Time Frame
Develop Staffing Strategies
Address Staffing Strategically
Develop Staffing Plans
Scope
6

What Does It Usually Entail?

Usually the process includes:

- Defining near- and long-term staffing requirements
- Forecasting staffing availability
- Comparing "demand" to "supply" to define staffing gaps and surpluses
- Developing a long-term staffing strategy
- Defining short-term staffing plans/actions

But in what context should these components be applied?

- All units? All jobs?
- Common process, planning parameters, and templates?
- Compiled results?

7

Alternative Approaches...

Instead of:	*Consider:*
Addressing staffing as an implementation concern	Addressing staffing from a proactive, planning perspective
Focusing on organizations	Focusing on issues
Forcing common planning parameters	Varying parameters by issue
Including all positions	Addressing only "proactive" and "time to respond" cases
Consolidating results	Keeping results separate and detailed
Creating an "event"	Discussing staffing whenever change is considered
Focusing on reports and listings that describe "what was"	Focusing on planning and forecasting "what will be"
Building capability, processes, or tools	Solving problems, addressing issues, and answering questions

8

The Strategic Staffing Process

1. **Define a particularly critical staffing issue**
2. **Define staffing gaps and surpluses**
3. **Develop staffing strategies**
4. **Define specific staffing plans/actions**

9

1. Define a Staffing Issue

Potential staffing issues might include:

- Significant changes in required staffing levels
- Major changes in required capabilities (including positions where required skills may be unknown)
- Positions that will be particularly critical
- Positions that will be hard to fill
- Positions with long learning curves
- Skill sets that you have not needed or looked for previously
- Skill sets for which there is extreme competition externally

Remember to keep strengths strong!

10

1. Define a Staffing Issue (cont.)

When looking for staffing issues, focus on significant changes ("staffing drivers")

- Changes in business focus, objectives, or activity
- Business expansion/contraction
- Changes in markets or customer base
- Capital expenditures/projects
- Changes in technology or manufacturing process
- Changes in product mix
- Productivity improvement/cost containment
- Changes in organization (e.g., structure, acquisition, divestiture)

11

2. Define Staffing Gaps and Surpluses

Create a staffing model framework

- Population to be included
- Time frame/planning horizon
- Model structure (e.g., row and column headings)

Define staffing requirements

- Staffing levels
- Required capabilities

12

2. Define Staffing Gaps and Surpluses (cont.)

Forecast staffing availability

- Define current staff availability
- Estimate losses (e.g., turnover, retirement)
- Factor in planned staffing actions (e.g., promotions, redeployment)
- Consider hiring plans

Compare "demand" to "supply" in each job category

13

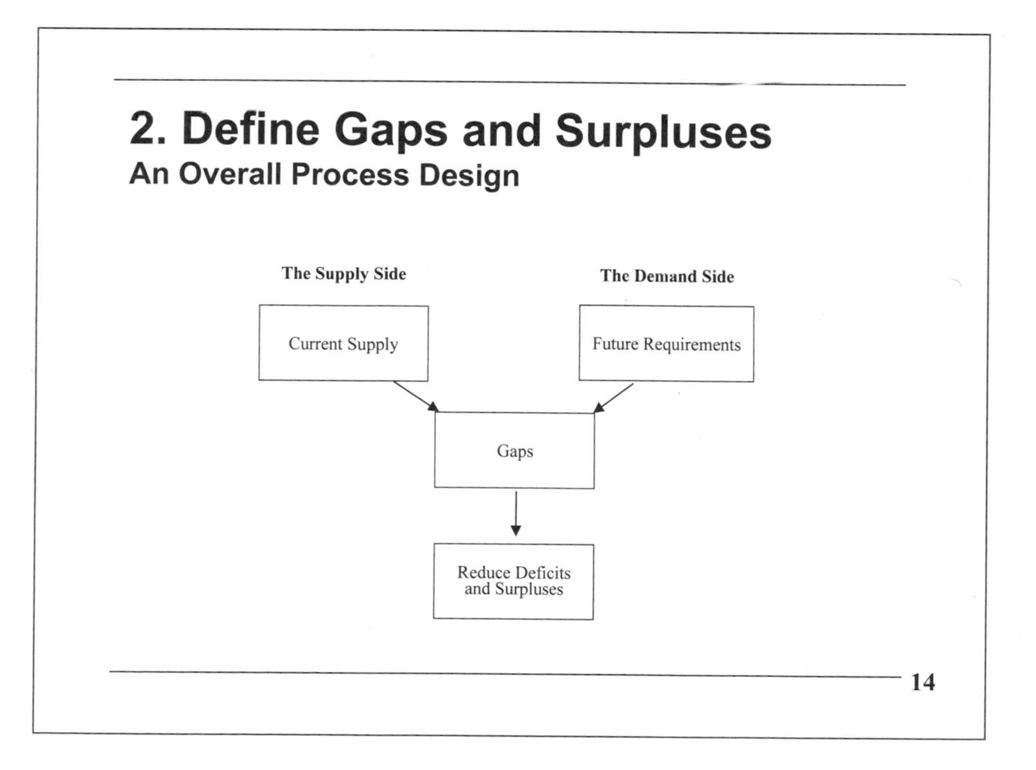

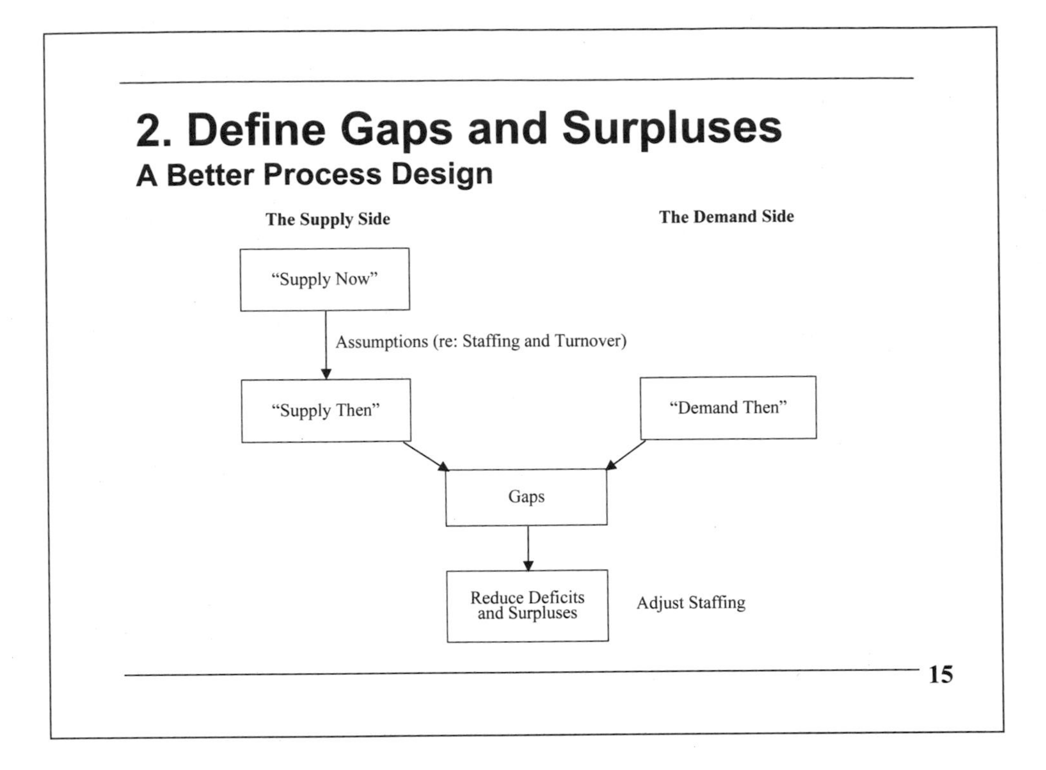
2. Define Gaps and Surpluses
A Better Process Design
The Supply Side
The Demand Side
"Supply Now"
Assumptions (re: Staffing and Turnover)
"Supply Then"
"Demand Then"
Gaps
Reduce Deficits and Surpluses
Adjust Staffing
15

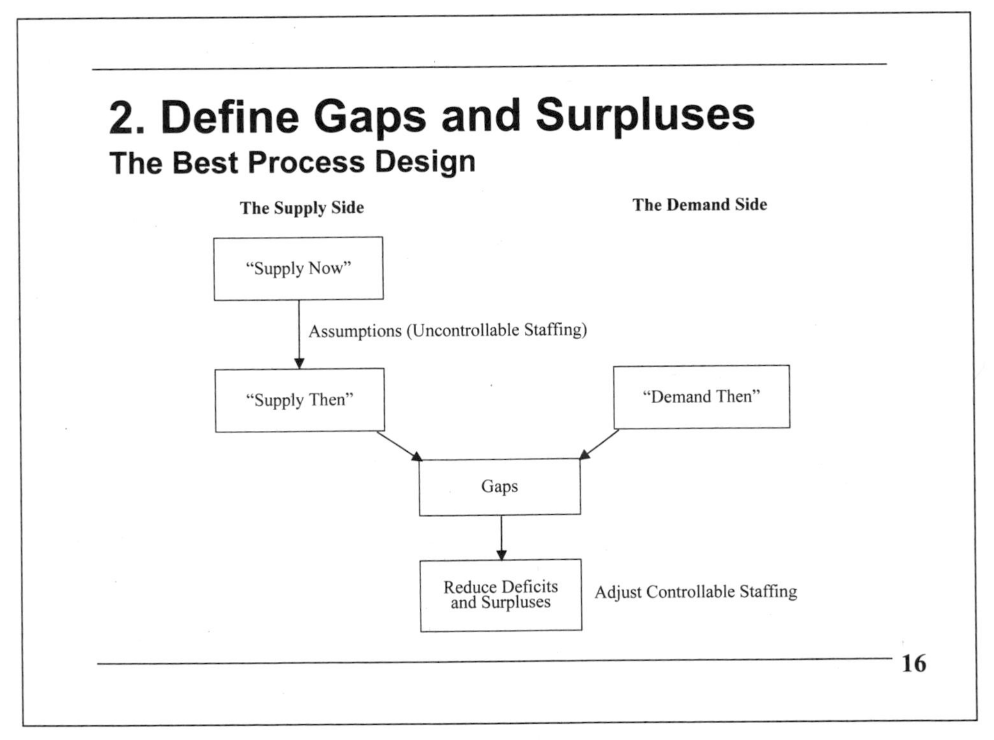
2. Define Gaps and Surpluses
The Best Process Design
The Supply Side
The Demand Side
"Supply Now"
Assumptions (Uncontrollable Staffing)
"Supply Then"
"Demand Then"
Gaps
Reduce Deficits and Surpluses
Adjust Controllable Staffing
16

3. Develop Staffing Strategies

Define what should be done throughout the planning horizon to fully address critical staffing issues

- Review staffing needs and surpluses across planning periods
- Define long-term, directional staffing strategies needed to fully address critical issues
- Ensure that strategies are consistent with how staff/resources will actually be managed
- Use these strategies as a context for defining near-term staffing plans and actions

17

4. Develop Specific Staffing Plans

Define the short-term staffing actions that best eliminate staffing gaps and surpluses

- Retention
- Redeployment/reallocations
- Hiring
- Promotions/transfers
- Training and development
- Reductions

Use the staffing strategy as the context for defining and integrating these short-term staffing actions

18

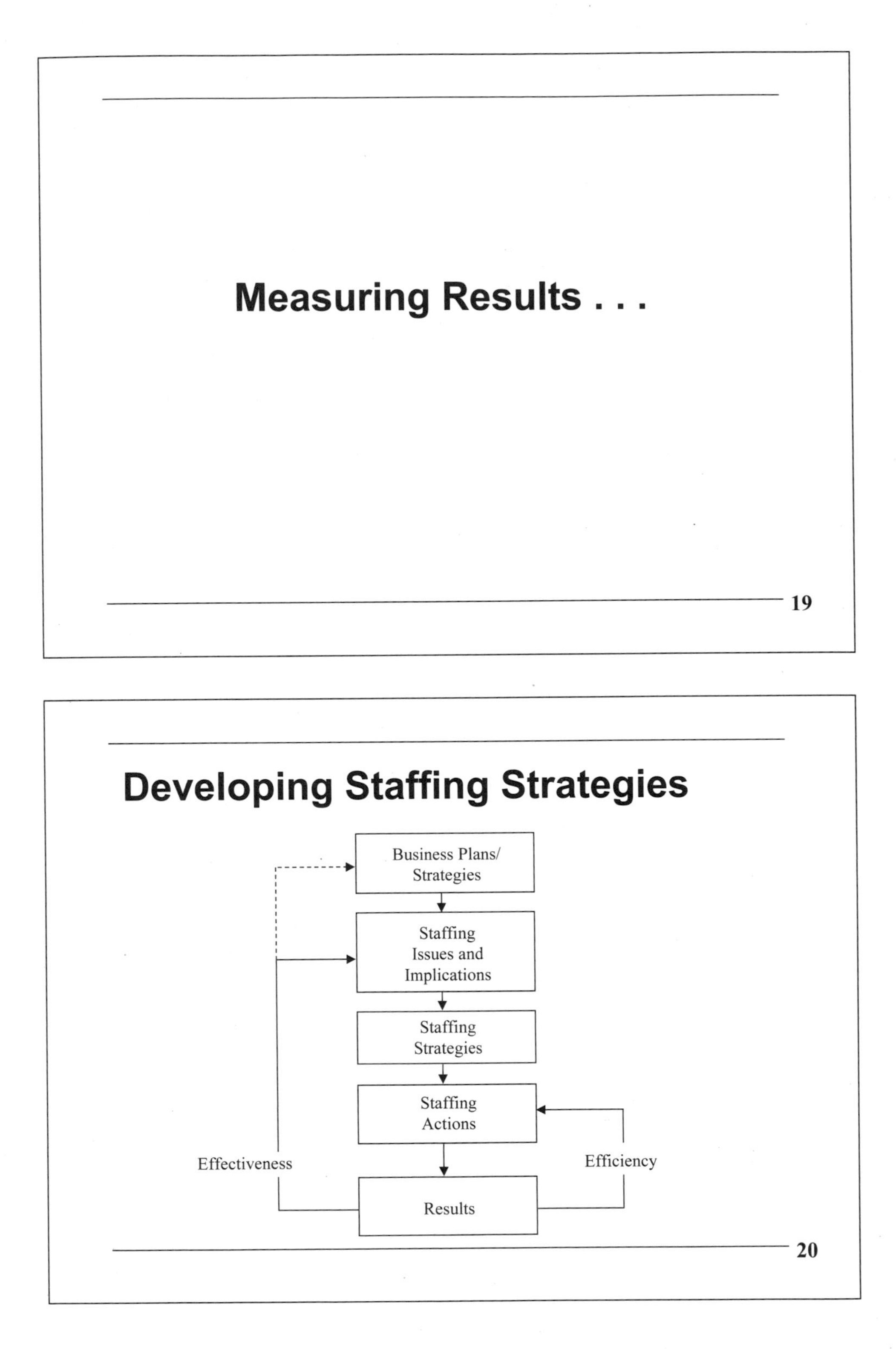
Measuring Results . . .
19
Developing Staffing Strategies
Business Plans/ Strategies
Staffing Issues and Implications
Staffing Strategies
Staffing Actions
Results
Effectiveness
Efficiency
20

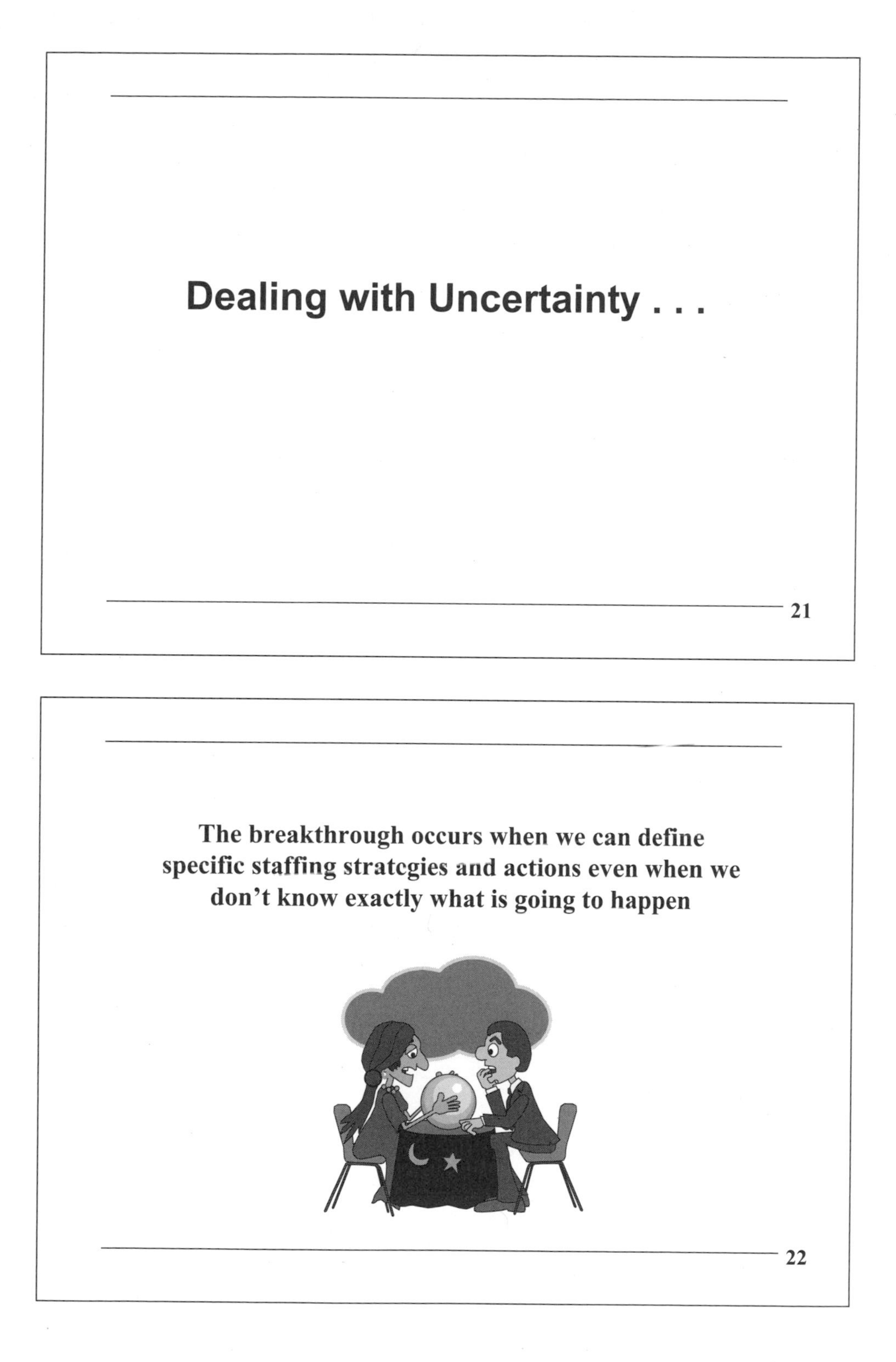
Dealing with Uncertainty . . .
21
The breakthrough occurs when we can define specific staffing strategies and actions even when we don't know exactly what is going to happen
22

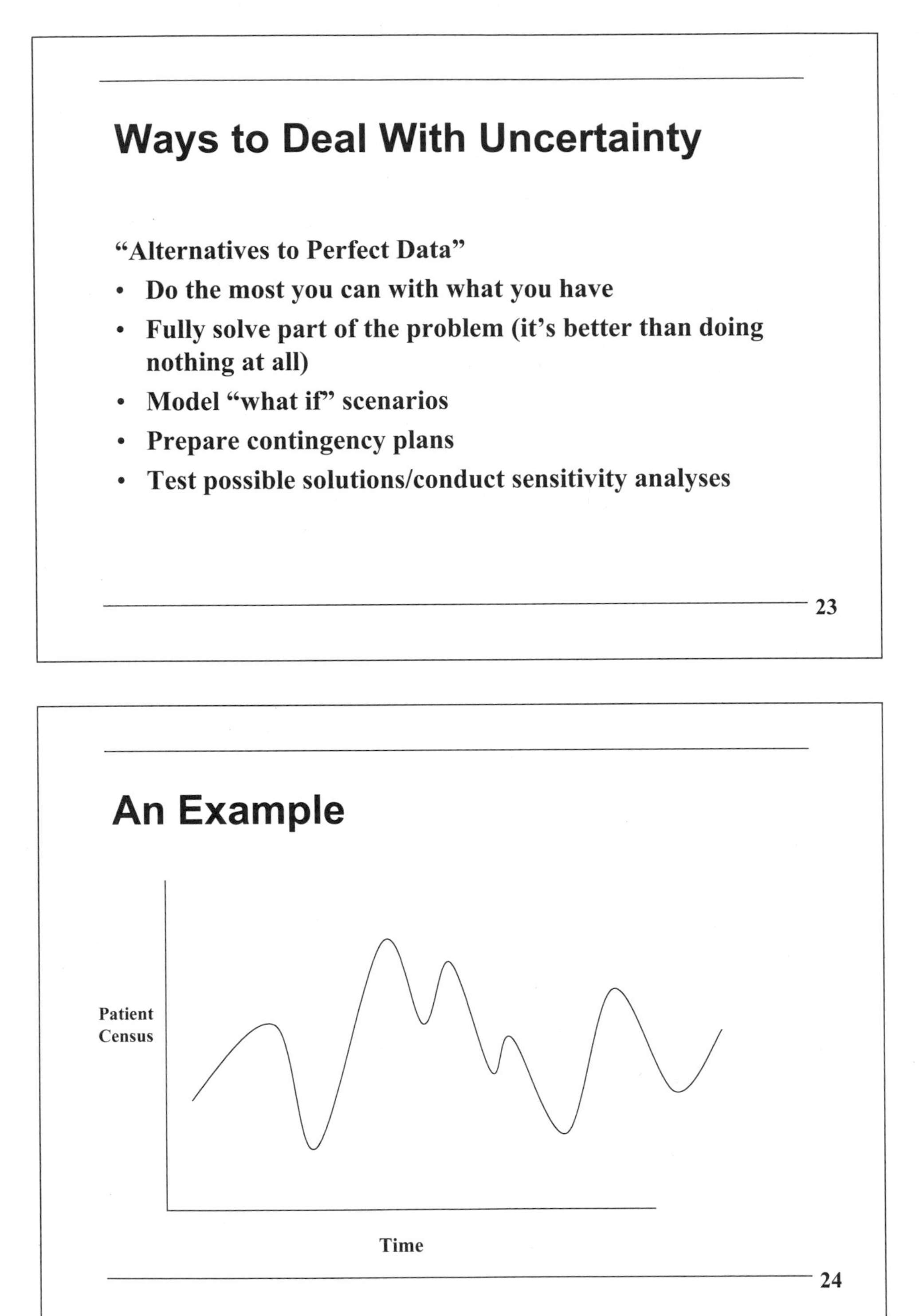
Ways to Deal With Uncertainty
"Alternatives to Perfect Data"
• Do the most you can with what you have
• Fully solve part of the problem (it's better than doing nothing at all)
• Model "what if" scenarios
• Prepare contingency plans
• Test possible solutions/conduct sensitivity analyses
23
An Example
Patient Census
Time
24

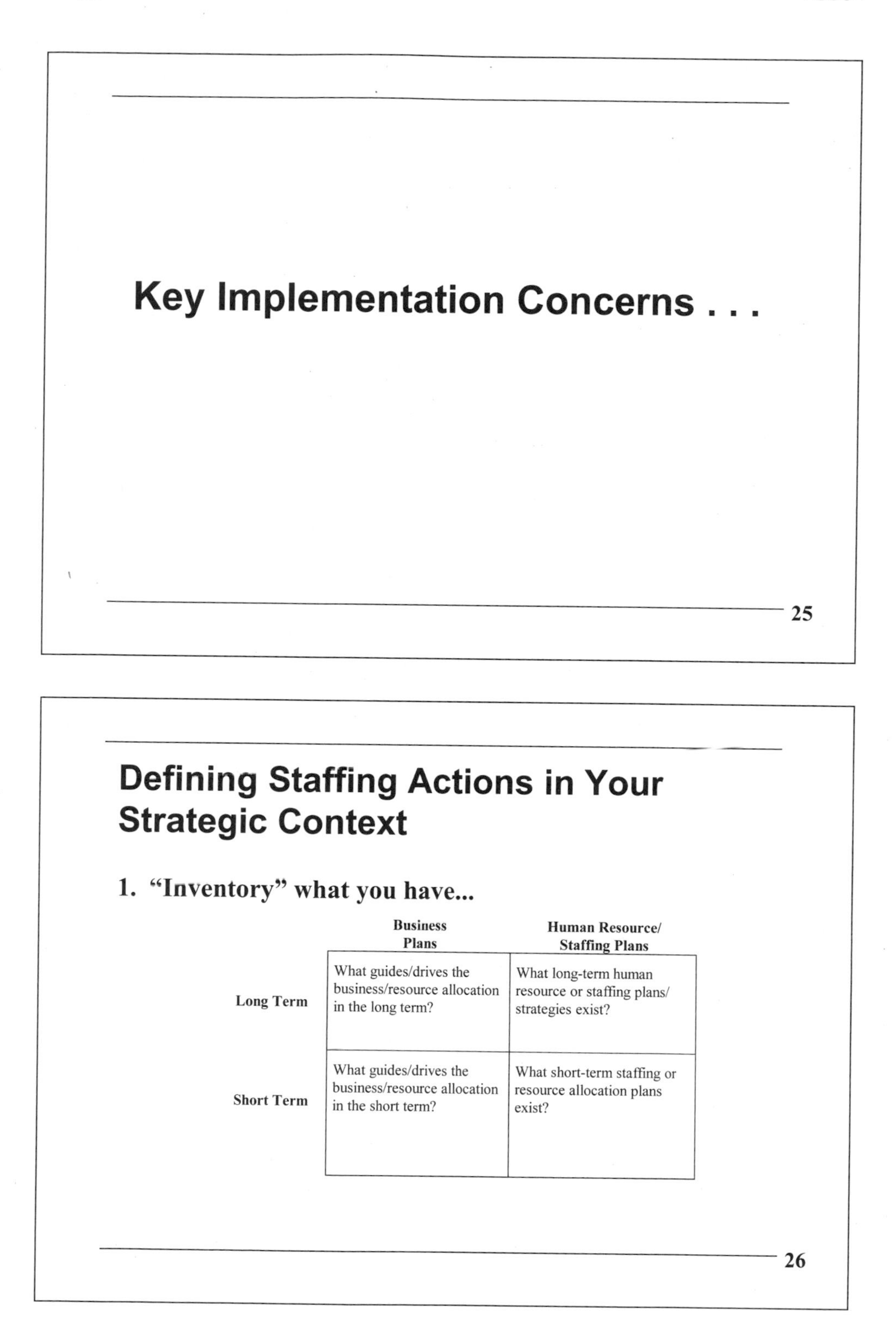
Key Implementation Concerns . . .
25
Defining Staffing Actions in Your Strategic Context
1. "Inventory" what you have...
Business Plans
Human Resource/ Staffing Plans
Long Term
What guides/drives the business/resource allocation in the long term?
What long-term human resource or staffing plans/ strategies exist?
Short Term
What guides/drives the business/resource allocation in the short term?
What short-term staffing or resource allocation plans exist?
26

2. Now answer these questions:

Are any pieces missing?

How consistent are the initiatives in each cell?

Are they well integrated?
Do they flow?
Do they build on each other?

How do the cells relate?

How do the cells link?
In what direction does information flow?
Are any links missing?
Might some need to be strengthened?

27

Defining Staffing Actions in Your Strategic Context

	Business Plans	Human Resource/ Staffing Plans
Long Term	Mission Vision Objectives Strategies	HR strategies Staffing strategies
Short Term	Operating plans/ budgets	Recruiting Movement Career planning Succession planning Development Training

28

Roles and Responsibilities

The development and implementation of staffing strategies requires a line/staff partnership

Line managers are ultimately responsible for managing people and thus should be involved in defining staffing requirements and strategies

Human resource staff support the development of staffing strategies

- Act in partnership with line management to identify staffing issues and develop required strategies
- Act as internal consultants to help managers participate in the process
- Create/integrate the plans and actions needed to implement strategies
- Implement changes in management practices as needed to implement strategies

29

Potential Obstacles

Organizations may have to overcome significant obstacles to develop and implement staffing strategies

Managers:

- Typically have a short-term/results orientation that is not consistent with planning or the development of people
- Are sometimes unaware/unconvinced of the benefits of staffing strategies because it is difficult to measure the benefits

HR Staff:

- Do not take a sufficient long-term, business perspective
- Think (and sometimes act) within functional "silos"

30

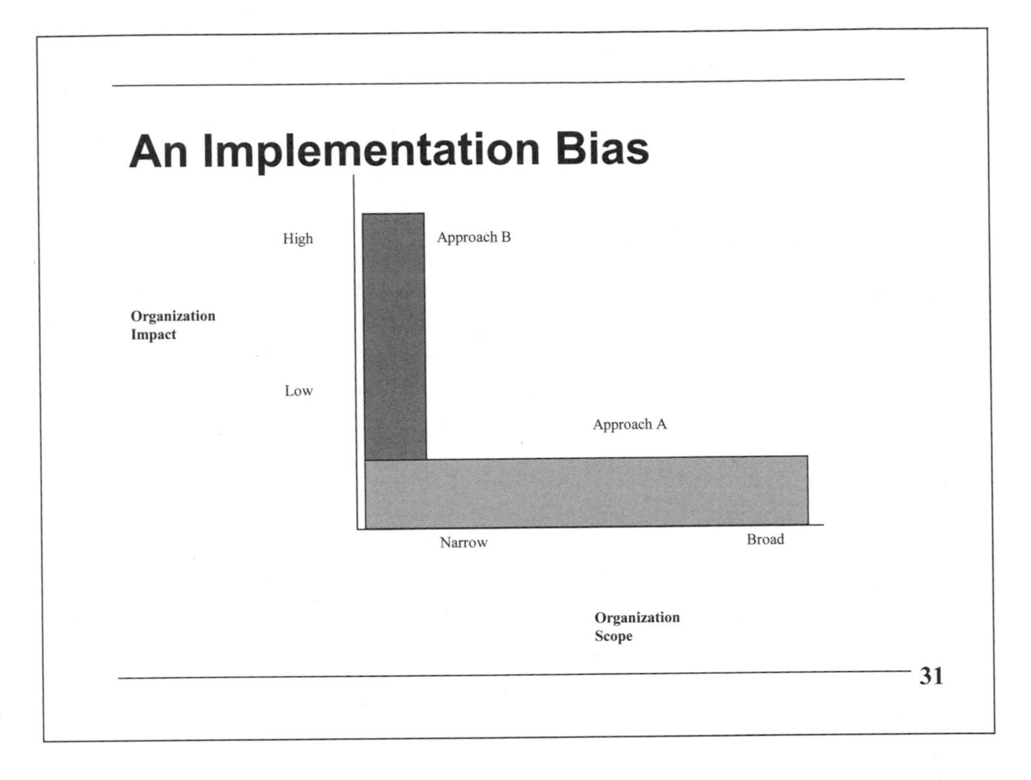
An Implementation Bias
High
Approach B
Organization
Impact
Low
Approach A
Narrow
Broad
Organization
Scope
31

Presentation 2:
Detailed Description

Strategic Staffing:

Tools for Developing Staffing Strategies and Plans

Prepared for
ABC Company
Date

Your Name
Title
Telephone Number
E-mail Address

1

Session Objectives

Developing Staffing Plans

- **Detailed Process Definition**
- **Staffing Models, Tools, and Techniques**
- **Example**
- **Automation**
- **Next Steps for ABC**

2

Some Reminders

3

Our Definitions

An *issue* is a gap between where you are and where you need to be in order to achieve business objectives or implement business strategies

A *strategy* is a long-term directional plan of action that describes how objectives will be met

Staffing includes all managed movement into, around, and out of an organization (e.g., recruiting, hiring, promotion, transfer, redeployment, attrition, retention)

. . . and what's the difference between *data* and *information*?

4

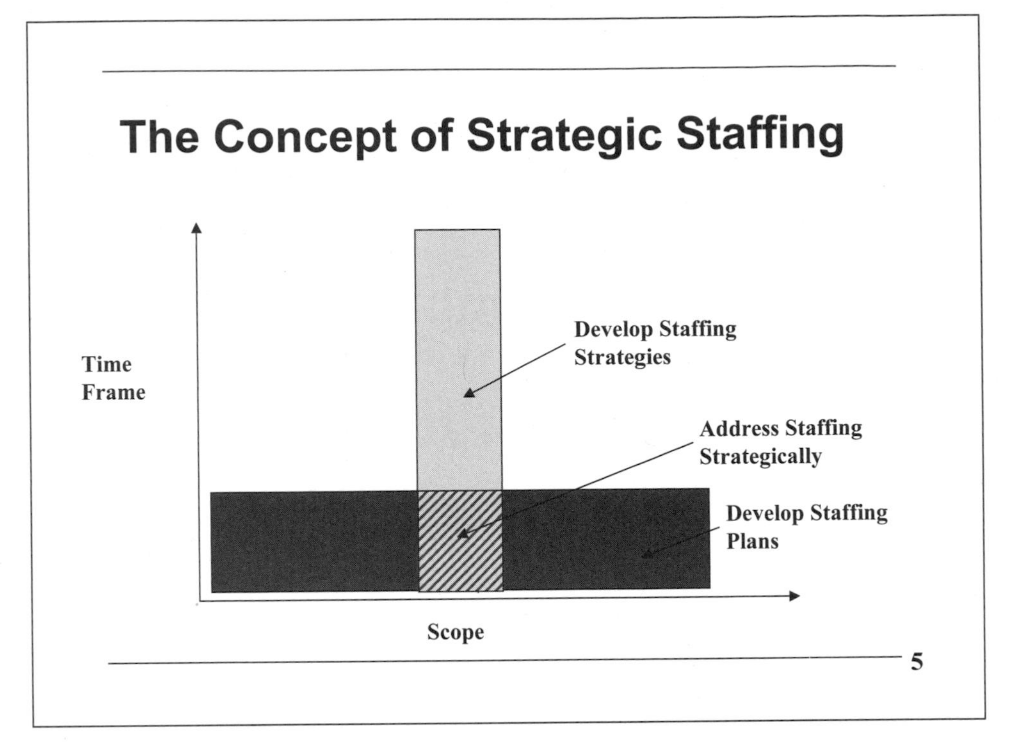
The Concept of Strategic Staffing
Time Frame
Develop Staffing Strategies
Address Staffing Strategically
Develop Staffing Plans
Scope
5

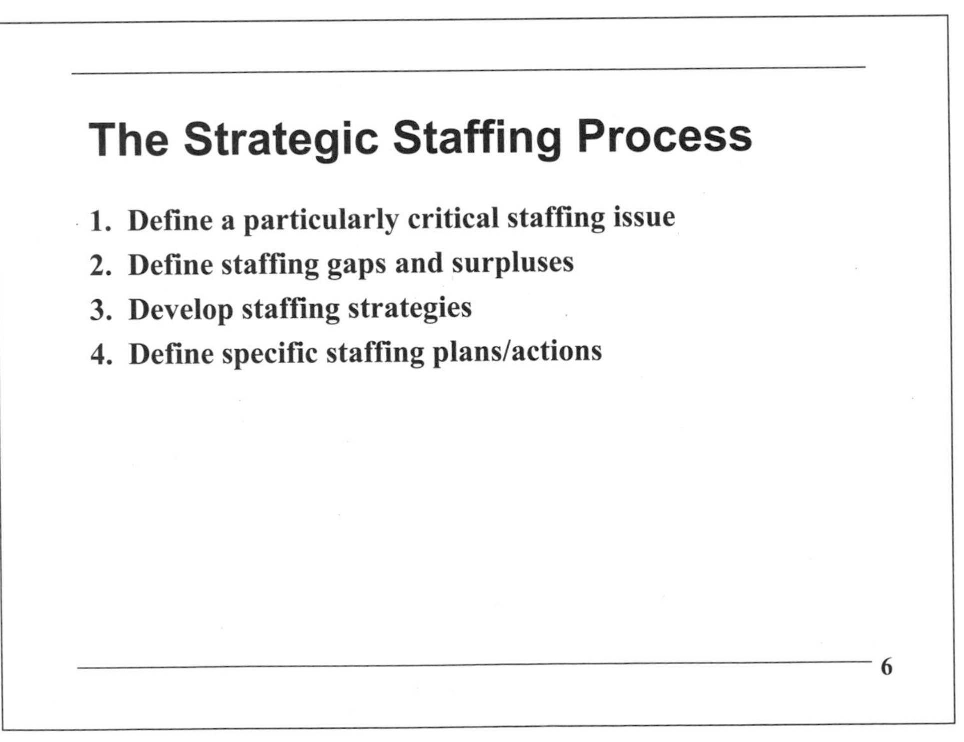
The Strategic Staffing Process
1. Define a particularly critical staffing issue
2. Define staffing gaps and surpluses
3. Develop staffing strategies
4. Define specific staffing plans/actions
6

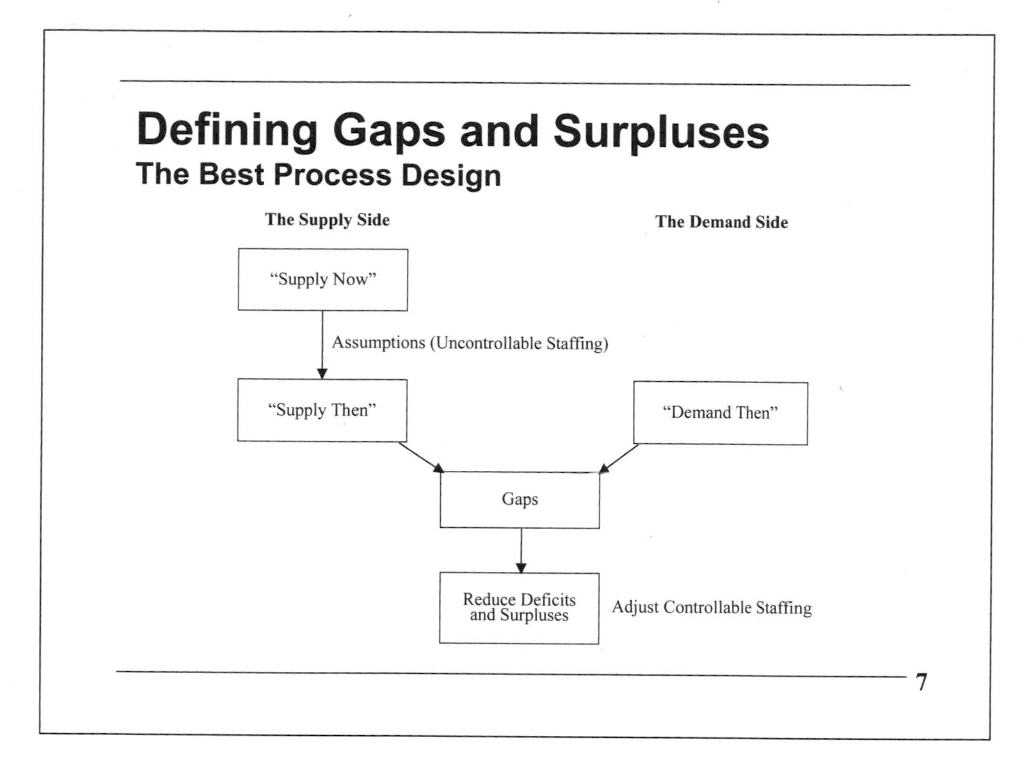
Defining Gaps and Surpluses
The Best Process Design
The Supply Side
The Demand Side
"Supply Now"
Assumptions (Uncontrollable Staffing)
"Supply Then"
"Demand Then"
Gaps
Reduce Deficits and Surpluses
Adjust Controllable Staffing
7

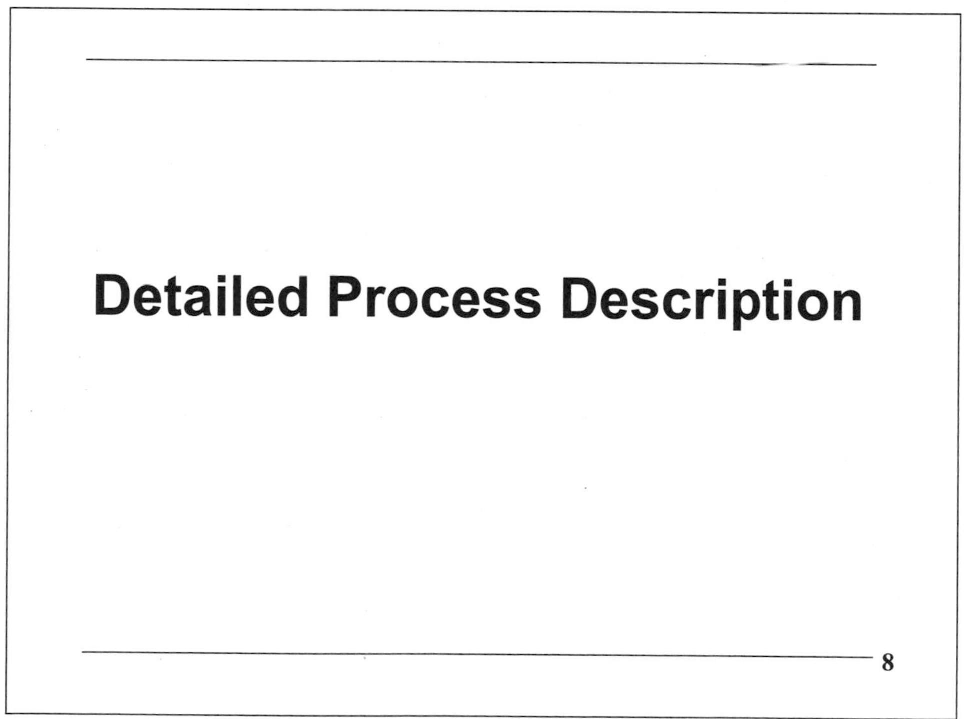
Detailed Process Description
8

The Strategic Staffing Process

1. **Define a particularly critical staffing issue**
2. **Define staffing gaps and surpluses**
   - Define staffing requirements
   - Forecast staffing availability
   - Compare supply to demand
3. **Develop staffing strategies**
4. **Define specific staffing plans/actions**

9

1. Define a Staffing Issue

Understand the long-term business context

Identify the issue(s) to be addressed

10

Example:
1. Define a critical staffing issue

Understand the long-term business context

- Significant business growth
- Implementation of a new IT platform

Identify the issues to be addressed

- Software engineering, because these skills are needed to
  - Support the transition to the new platform initially
  - Build new applications in the new environment
- Object-oriented programming, because
  - These skills are scarce
  - We have not looked for people with these skills before (and don't know where to look)

11

2. Define Staffing Gaps and Surpluses

Define model parameters for addressing the issue

- Population to be included (e.g., the positions and individuals)
  - The target population
  - Likely sources of needed talent
  - Possible users of surplus talent
- Planning horizon (e.g., each of the next three years)
  - How long
  - How often
- Model/matrix structure (e.g., row and column headings)
  - Columns often denote capability areas, organization units, functions, or geographic locations
  - Rows usually denote capability level

12

Example:

2. Define staffing gaps and surpluses

Define model parameters

- Population: Focus on
  - The two key job families
  - Across the IT organization
- Planning horizon:
  - One year
  - Updated quarterly
- Structure:
  - Columns: Function/area of expertise
  - Rows: Levels of expertise ("roles")

13

Example:

Model Structure	Software Engineers	Object-Oriented Programmers
Project Manager		
Lead		
Individual Contributor		
Entry Level		

14

2. Define Staffing Gaps and Surpluses (cont.)

Define staffing requirements (see staffing exercises)

- Define both
  - Critical skills
  - Staffing levels
- Define overall staffing requirements, not increments/changes
- Break a big problem with no solution into little ones that can be addressed (e.g., "mix and match" techniques)

15

2. Define Staffing Gaps and Surpluses (cont.)

Define staffing requirements: capabilities

- Focus on competencies that will be needed in the future
- Identify a small number of critical competencies for each job category (perhaps only 5 or 10)
  - Those "make or break" for performance
  - Those absolutely needed to implement strategy/achieve objectives
  - Those needed to win, not just play the game
  - Those that differentiate rows and columns

16

2. Define Staffing Gaps and Surpluses (cont.)

Define staffing requirements: staffing levels

- Using the staffing framework created above, estimate the *number* of positions (either whole positions or full-time equivalents) required in each cell
  - Statistical techniques (e.g. regression)
  - Staffing ratios
  - Staffing by project
  - Delphi techniques or structured interviews
  - Staffing profiles

17

2. Define Staffing Gaps and Surpluses (cont.)

Define staffing requirements: staffing levels

- Regression
  - Relate staffing drivers to headcount
  - Consider one or more independent variables
  - Could be linear or curvilinear
  - Assess degree of fit (“r squared”)
  - Use to predict future staffing levels or analyze current levels
  - Best used when past is prologue or when comparing similar locations

18

2. Define Staffing Gaps and Surpluses (cont.)

Define staffing requirements: staffing levels

- Staffing Ratios
  - Relate staffing levels to some other known variable (e.g., the number of new sales dollars to be generated per salesperson, number of calls per customer service rep, span of control)
  - Relationships could be direct (e.g., directly related to work/outputs) or indirect (e.g., proportional to another job category)
  - Could reflect actual data or targets (e.g., desired relationships)
  - Best used when staffing is driven by volume

19

2. Define Staffing Gaps and Surpluses (cont.)

Define staffing requirements: staffing levels

- Project-Based Staffing
  - Desired output: overall staffing levels
  - Available input: staffing estimates for individual projects
  - Usually zero-based
  - Aggregate estimates at particular points in time
  - Especially helpful in a project environment

20

2. Define Staffing Gaps and Surpluses (cont.)

Define staffing requirements: staffing levels

- Delphi Techniques or Structured Interviews (Incremental)
  - Define staffing needs for individual units
  - Define incremental changes, not overall levels/capabilities
  - Follow a structured interview
    - Discuss business objectives/changes
    - Discuss current staffing levels and capabilities
    - Define how staffing should change (incrementally) to support business plans/objectives
  - Especially appropriate where specific "demand" data are not available

21

2. Define Staffing Gaps and Surpluses (cont.)

Define staffing requirements: staffing levels

- Staffing Profiles
  - Define the staffing required to support one "unit" (e.g., location, facility, or project)
  - Define the number of units that are planned
  - Multiply profile requirements by number of planned units to define required staffing levels
  - Could have multiple profiles addressing several staffing drivers
  - Most applicable where there are multiple units that recur

22

Example:

2. Define staffing gaps and surpluses

Define staffing requirements: capability levels

- Project Manager: Project management skills, "bottom-line" accountability
- Lead: In-depth technical skills in a particular platform or technology
- Individual Contributor: A sufficient understanding of *your* technology and platforms to perform tasks on your own
- Entry Level: Basic skills and aptitude, but no particular understanding of your technology or platforms

Define required staffing levels (e.g., 15% increase)

23

Example:

"Demand Then"	Software Engineers	Object-Oriented Programmers
Project Manager	12	9
Lead	25	21
Individual Contributor	62	52
Entry Level	83	77

24

2. Define Staffing Gaps and Surpluses (cont.)

Forecast staffing availability

- Define the current population in each cell
- Subtract voluntary turnover (e.g., rate times starting population for each cell)
- Subtract retirements (if any)
  - Based on average age
  - Based on a window of eligibility
- Subtract other "planned losses"
- Add in hiring in progress that will be completed during the period

25

Example:

2. Define staffing gaps and surpluses

Forecast staffing availability

- Assume a voluntary turnover rate of 15%
- Subtract retirements (if any)
- No other staffing actions are anticipated

26

Example:

"Supply Now"	Software Engineers	Object-Oriented Programmers
Project Manager	10	8
Lead	22	18
Individual Contributor	53	44
Entry Level	71	65

27

Example:

"Supply Then"	Software Engineers	Object Oriented Programmers
Project Manager	10 - 0.15(10) (voluntary) - 1 (retirement) = 7	5
Lead	22 - 0.15(22) (voluntary) - 1 (retirement) = 18	16
Individual Contributor	46	40
Entry Level	61	60

28

2. Define Staffing Gaps and Surpluses (cont.)

Compare supply to demand

- Compare "demand then" to "supply now" for each cell
- Consider both capabilities and staffing levels
- To show deficits/gaps as negative numbers, subtract demand from supply

Repeat for subsequent periods

29

Example:

Gaps and Surpluses ("Supply Now" – "Demand Then")	**Software Engineers**	**Object-Oriented Programmers**
Project Manager	**7 – 12 = -5**	**5 – 9 = -4**
Lead	**18 – 25 = -7**	**6 – 21 = -6**
Individual Contributor	**46 – 62 = -16**	**40 – 52 = -12**
Entry Level	**61 – 83 = -22**	**60 – 77 = -17**

30

3. Develop Staffing Strategies

Review needs across periods

Define overall approaches for reducing gaps and surpluses

31

Example:

3. Develop staffing strategies

Staffing Strategies (assuming a multiple-period view)

- At project manager and lead levels, promote from within where possible
- At the individual contributor level, promote where feasible and supplement with new hires
- At the entry level, rely solely on new hires

32

4. Develop Specific Staffing Plans

Define the specific staffing actions for each period that best eliminate gaps and surpluses (consistent with staffing strategies)

Define each type of action

- The kind of move (e.g., recruiting, transfer, promotion)
- From what job/to what job
- How many such moves are needed
- The date by which the move should happen
- The individuals responsible

Make sure plans are realistic (e.g., that the assumed number really are promotable)

33

Example:

Staffing Plans		Software Engineers	Object-Oriented Programmers
Project Manager		-5 (↑ 5 from Lead)	-4
Lead		-7 (↑ 12 from Individual Contributor)	-6
Individual Contributor	12 →	-16 (↑ 16 from Entry Level)	-12
Entry Level	38 →	-22	-17

34

Example:

Staffing Plan for Quarter 1 (Software Engineering)

- **Promotions:**
  - 5 from Software Engineers/Lead to Software Engineers/Project Manager
  - 12 from Software Engineers/Individual Contributor to Software Engineers/Lead
  - 16 from Software Engineers/Entry Level to Software Engineers/Individual Contributor (with training)
- **Hiring:**
  - 12 into Software Engineers/Individual Contributor
  - 38 into Software Engineers/Entry Level

35

Automation Supports Modeling

- An effective, well-designed model/system should:
  - Support, not define, your process
  - Be easy to learn, use, and maintain
  - Maximize the use of data already available
  - Allow for ad hoc and defined reporting
  - Be flexible and allow for future changes/enhancements
  - Link to other systems
  - Be supported by a responsive, experienced vendor (whether internal or external)
- Choices, choices, choices . . .
  - Build your own or buy someone else's?
  - Purpose built or based on readily available software/packages?

36

Let's Get Started!

- Identify the issue(s) to be addressed
- Define model parameters
  - Population
  - Planning horizon
  - Rows and columns
- Define data requirements and potential sources
- Define specific "next steps" and accountabilities

37

Glossary

This glossary defines some of the key terms as they are used throughout this book.

Demand: The number and type (i.e., defined in terms of capabilities) of staff that are required in each job category at a particular point in time in order to implement business plans and strategies.

"Demand then": The number and type (i.e., in terms of capabilities) of staff that are required in each job category at the end of a particular planning period for which a staffing model has been built.

Human resource strategy: An overall strategy for managing people within the context of business plans and strategies. It is not a strategy for managing the human resource function itself.

Net needs: The difference between "supply then" and "demand then" for a particular period of a staffing model (also referred to as *gaps and surpluses*).

Planning horizon: The overall time frame between the start of the first period of a planning model and the end of the last period of that model (e.g., a five-year plan). A planning horizon consists of multiple planning periods.

Planning period: One component of the overall planning horizon (e.g., the first year of a five-year plan).

Population: The individuals and/or job categories to be included in a given staffing model.

Staffing: Any action or movement in an organization that relates to getting people into, around, or out of an organization in a planned way. This includes (but is not limited to) hiring, retention, promotions, lateral moves, redeployment, transfers, retirement, turnover, and terminations.

Staffing actions: Specific lists of the names of the individuals to be moved, hired, or terminated in a given planning period.

Staffing assumptions: An organization's best guess as to what staffing actions will be implemented in a given planning period (e.g., between now and then). These assumptions can be divided into two categories: uncontrollable (i.e., those staffing actions that will probably occur no matter what management does) and controllable (i.e., those that will happen because management makes them happen).

Staffing issue: A significant difference (a gap or surplus) between the staff that will be available and the staff that will be needed at a particular point in time. The gap can be defined in terms of staffing levels, required capabilities, or both. Staffing issues are also referred to as *staffing implications*.

Staffing model: A quantitative analysis (usually spreadsheet-based) that defines staffing requirements ("demand then"), defines the staffing available currently ("supply now"), forecasts future staffing availability ("supply then"), and compares "demand then" to "supply then" to calculate staffing gaps and surpluses for a given set of job categories.

Staffing plans: Short-term, tactical plans that describe what an organization will do in the near term to address immediate staffing gaps and surpluses. Staffing plans are created within the longer-term context of staffing strategies. In most cases, staffing plans describe the numbers and types of staffing moves that are required (e.g., the number of people to be moved, hired, or terminated from or to each job category), but they do not identify the specific individuals to be moved.

Staffing strategy: A long-term, directional plan of action that describes what an organization is going to do over the course of its planning horizon to ensure that its supply of staff matches its demand for staff as effectively as possible.

Strategic staffing: The process of identifying and addressing the staffing implications of business strategies and plans. It may also be defined as the process of identifying and addressing the staffing implications of significant change.

Strategy: A long-term, directional plan of action that describes in broad terms what an organization plans to do to achieve its long-term objectives.

Supply: The number and type of staff (i.e., defined in terms of capabilities) that are available in each job category at a particular point in time.

"Supply now": The number and type (i.e., defined in terms of capabilities) of staff that are available at the beginning of a planning period for which a staffing model has been built.

"Supply then": The number and type (i.e., defined in terms of capabilities) of staff that are available at the end of a planning period for which a staffing model has been built.

Template: A generic staffing model spreadsheet that can be copied to develop multiple specific staffing models.

Index

About the Author

Tom Bechet, Principal of Bechet Consulting LLC, has consulted in the areas of strategic staffing, workforce planning, and human resource strategy development for more than twenty years. He has provided consulting services to a variety of organizations, including large corporations, mid- and small-sized companies, and the public sector. He is known for being practical; his hands-on perspective and creative approaches have proved to be a welcome alternative to more theoretical, process-laden methods.

Tom has worked with companies (both globally and domestically) to create human resource plans (including the identification of human resource issues and the development of human resource strategies) and develop human resource planning processes. He has developed, run, and applied the results of staffing strategies and workforce plans for companies in such industries as aerospace, health care, petroleum, pharmaceuticals, electric utilities, insurance, engineering/construction, and telecommunications. He has also assisted many companies in designing, developing, and implementing PC- and network-based systems to support forecasting, workforce planning, executive development, and human resource information management.

Prior to starting Bechet Consulting LLC in 2000, Tom was a partner with the Walker Group (1986–1999). He also spent eight years with Towers, Perrin and its general management consulting division, Cresap. Tom consulted on a wide variety of human resource planning topics. Tom also worked for five years with two consulting engineering firms.

Tom received his MBA from Columbia University in 1979, specializing in management and finance. He received his Bachelors of Engineering (Civil) from Manhattan College in 1974.

Always active in professional circles, Tom has served as Chairman of the Professional Development Committee of the Human Resource Planning Society (HRPS) and as a member of the society's board of directors. He also lectures in human resource strategies, strategic staffing, management succession, and development as part of the University of Michigan's Executive Education Programs. Tom is a member of Human Resource Planning Society (HRPS) and the Society for Human Resource Management (SHRM).

In addition to being the author of *Strategic Staffing: A Practical Tool Kit for Workforce Planning,* he is a co-editor of the book *Human Resource Forecasting and Modeling* (one of the volumes in the HRPS Best Practice Series). Tom is a frequent speaker on human resource planning, forecasting, and executive development.

If you have questions, visit Tom's Web site:

www.bechetconsulting.com

Or call him at (630) 443-4170.

STRATEGIC STAFFING
A Practical Tool Kit for Workforce Planning
Using Your Bonus Computer Files

Included in the purchase of this book is a set of computer files that include examples, the strategic staffing templates, and suggested overheads.

As stated in the text, these files (and any files derived from them) may be loaded onto a single PC or server. If multiple copies of the files are needed, simply purchase additional copies of this book.